# Mission and Development

ALSO AVAILABLE FROM CONTINUUM

*Mission and Evangelisation*, Michael A. Hayes
*Religion and Politics in International Relations*, Timothy Fitzgerald
*Understanding Christian-Muslim Relations*, Clinton Bennett

# Mission and Development

## God's Work or Good Works?

*Edited by Matthew Clarke*

continuum

**Continuum International Publishing Group**

The Tower Building
11 York Road
London
SE1 7NX

80 Maiden Lane
Suite 704
New York
NY 10038

**www.continuumbooks.com**



**British Library Cataloguing-in-Publication Data**
A catalogue record for this book is available from the British Library.

ISBN: HB: 978-1-4411-8263-0
PB: 978-1-4411-0811-1

**Library of Congress Cataloging-in-Publication Data**
Mission and development : God's work or good works?/edited by Matthew Clarke.
p. cm.
Includes bibliographical references and index.
ISBN 978-1-4411-0811-1 (pbk.)
ISBN 978-1-4411-8263-0 (hardcover)
1. Missions. 2. Missions–Developing countries. 3. Economic assistance. I. Clarke, Matthew.
BV2063.M557 2011
266–dc23
2011024640

Typeset by Deanta Global Publishing Services, Chennai, India
Printed and bound in India

# CONTENTS

## Part Three: Case Studies: Mission Organizations and Development

# NOTES ON CONTRIBUTORS

Steve Bradbury is the director of the Micah 6.8 Center at Tabor Victoria and Chair of Micah Challenge International. He served as the national director of TEAR Australia for 25 years and was the founding Chair of the Micah Network, a global community of over 300 Christian organizations committed to integral mission.

Matthew Clarke is Professor and Head of the School of Humanities and Socila Sciences, Deakin University, Australia. His research interests include religion and development, faith-based organizations, HIV and AIDS and the Millennium Development Goals. Matthew regularly undertakes evaluations of community development projects within Asia and the Pacific for NGOs and donors.

Kirstie Close is a PhD candidate in history at Deakin University, Australia. Her thesis examines the processes by which the Methodist Mission of Fiji became an independent church in 1964. Her interests include missions and their involvement in matters surrounding land and labor in Australia and the Pacific.

Kerry Enright is the national director of UnitingWorld, the Uniting Church's Assembly agency for international partnerships, including Relief and Development, Experience, Peacemaking and Church Solidarity. Kerry's experience was mainly with Pacific churches and communities and more recently he has visited partners in Asia and Africa. He is particularly keen to enable the Uniting Church to renew its heritage of international connection as a core part of its identity.

Philip Fountain completed his PhD in anthropology at The Australian National University in 2011. He is currently a postdoctoral fellow at the Asia Research Institute at the National University of Singapore. His research focuses on the ethnography of Christian NGOs. He has carried out fieldwork in Indonesia, Papua New Guinea, the US and Canada.

Gerhard Hoffstaedter is a research fellow at the Institute for Human Security, La Trobe University. He conducts research in development studies, refugee and immigration policy and spiritual and existential security as well as religion and the state. His first book entitled Modern Muslim Identities: Negotiating Religion and Ethnicity in Malaysia is published by NIAS Press.

Jacob Kavunkal SVD is lecturer of Mission Theology at the Yarra Theological Union/Melbourne College of Divinity, Australia. He has published extensively on missiological topics and his latest book is *Anthropophany: Mission As Making A New Humanity* (ISPCK: Delhi, 2008).

Roger O'Halloran is the executive director of Palms Australia with a hands-on role in program management and volunteer recruitment and preparation. The first 15 years of Roger's working life was as a teacher of politics and economics after which he spent 18 years in international development volunteering by training teachers in Samoa. A masters in Educational Leadership energized him to develop a network model of organization, which sees Palms facilitate global cross- cultural volunteering that builds sustainable, interdependent development from a small hub in Sydney.

Jonathan Ryan is part of the missional community, Servants to Asia's Urban Poor, in which he currently serves as New Zealand coordinator. He is also a minister at Highgate Presbyterian Church, Dunedin. As a graduate of Regent College (Vancouver), his ongoing academic work has explored the vocation of the church in the contexts of poverty and marginality.

Vicki-Ann Ware is a research associate of the School of International and Political Studies, Deakin University, Australia. Her research interests are faith-based organizations in development, the role and benefits of the arts in development and community building, and cultural heritage preservation in contexts of rapid culture change. She has worked in faith-based organizations in Southeast Asia for many years, and is co-director of one such new faith-based development agency.

Brad Watson is a senior lecturer at Avondale College and is undertaking his PhD at Deakin University, Australia. Brad's research interests child sponsorship, maternal health in Nepal, and the impacts of short-term missions on participants. Each year, Brad leads student trips to developing countries within the Asia-Pacific region.

# 1

# Introduction: Good and God—Development and Mission

Matthew Clarke

## Introduction

Approximately one billion people live in extreme poverty, with another two billion people surviving on around US$2 per day. Life for those living in poverty is characterized by ill health, limited access to clean water and hygienic sanitation, poor quality housing, hunger, illiteracy and premature death. Such material deprivation in developing countries has been the impetus for international efforts to eradicate poverty throughout the second half of the last century. More recently, the global community has responded by committing to the achievement of the Millennium Development Goals (MDGs). Emanating from a number of international conferences during the last decade of the last century, the MDGs are a set of eight internationally agreed goals to improve the well-being of the poor in developing countries. They are designed to address many of the multidimensional aspects of poverty and include: (1) eradicating extreme poverty and hunger; (2) achieving universal primary education; (3) promoting gender equality; (4) reducing child mortality; (5) improving maternal health; (6) combating HIV/AIDS, malaria and other diseases; (7) ensuring environmental sustainability; and (8) developing a global partnership for development. Both developing and developed nations pledged to meet these goals by 2015.

However, improving the lives of the poor is a complex undertaking with often little agreement as to how can this be best achieved.[1] The intrinsic goal of development is to advance human dignity, freedom, social equity and self-determination. Good development outcomes are best achieved when communities have the ownership of the goals and processes of development and where there areparticipatory representation, transparency and accountability mechanisms. Good development outcomes must also explicitly consider gender and diversity. Development involves processes that require an appreciation of existing endogenous strengths and (often) exogenous interventions. Successful development requires critical analysis, mutual learning and acceptance of its paradoxes and dilemmas. Those working to improve the material lives of the poor (including the poor themselves as well as those external to the community) rightly view the interventions implemented as good works.

This book considers how the good work (or development) described above intersects with God's work undertaken by religious organizations, specifically missionary organizations. In this sense, mission—as understood in mainstream Christian teaching[2]—is a continuation of Jesus' mission of service rooted in 'love', which itself was entrusted to his disciples whom He had sent out to share His Good News. While the root desire of mission therefore dates back to Jesus sending out his disciples, the practice of mission has differed sharply since then with the focus ranging from religious conversion to Christian belief through preaching to serving the poor and the marginalized without being vocal in faith (Nemer, 2001). It is not the purpose of this book to seek a consensus on the appropriate approach to mission; rather, it is to consider how mission activity intersects with development interventions as currently being implemented.

Therefore, the mission approach that emphasizes action over words is most similar to modern development practice. Moreover, this history of active engagement with material well-being, long pre-dates secular interests in improving the lives of the poor. For example, the fourth-century missionaries encouraged literacy through the development of alphabets in Europe, the twelfth-century missionaries enhanced agricultural production techniques in Europe, the seventeenth-century missionaries in the New World promoted the legal rights of local indigenous people, while the nineteenth-century missionaries supported gender equity through creation of educational facilities for girls in Asia and provided medical care in Asia and Africa (Pierson, 2007). These endeavours—education, food security, human rights, gender and health care—dating back several centuries are all fundamental to current development initiatives and are central to the achievement of the MDGs.

## Development Best Practice and Religion

President Truman's 1949 inauguration speech is often cited as the beginning of the international community's recognition of the need to improve the lives of the poor in developing countries. While development occurs at all levels of society, non-government organizations (NGOs) have been the primary agents of secular developmental activities at the local community level over the past six decades. Promoters of NGOs suggest that they are cost-effective in service delivery, have an ability to target the poor and vulnerable sections of the population, are able to develop community-based institutions and are able to promote community participation to ensure the likelihood of sustained impact. In addition, NGOs are considered to have intrinsic characteristics 'such as strong grassroots links; field based development expertise; the ability to innovate and adapt; [a] process oriented approach to development; participatory methodologies and tools; long term commitment and emphasis on sustainability; [and] cost-effectiveness' (World Bank, 1995, p. 15).

NGOs can be effective across a range of development issues. NGO activities may include both service provision and advocacy. Work with communities, or *grassroots* programmes, account for a significant proportion of NGO activities. This includes activities such as the provision of education services, care and support for those with HIV or malaria, feeding programmes to improve child nutrition, agricultural extension programmes or microfinance schemes. Depending on the nature of the activity, NGOs include men and women, local leaders, youth representatives, religious leaders and local government officials in decision-making.

The importance of NGOs in improving the lives of the poor is evidenced by the increasing resources provided to them from official development assistance budgets. Funds flowing to and through these organizations have grown rapidly in recent years. NGOs also receive funding directly from private donations, with this support for NGOs also increasing in recent years (Agg, 2006). Indeed, the public does respond very generously to appeals launched by NGOs for humanitarian emergencies (Feeny and Clarke, 2007) and those events, such as the 2004 Indian Ocean Tsunami, generate significant financial resources for NGOs (Clarke, 2008).

Success in improving the lives of the poor by NGOs has improved in recent years as these agencies have better understood community dynamics and the importance of supporting community empowerment (Ife, 1995). The structure of power and domination is overturned when community activities are strengthened and people themselves are allowed to run and take control of these development interventions. Their sense of self-worth is restored when they are able to sustain these interventions through their own efforts (Kirk, 2000). They are more encouraged as they see themselves partaking and contributing as members owning their projects. However, empowering communities do not happen immediately and it takes a great deal of struggle, time and effort among people who are committed to genuine community development. Further, cooperation in the community, as well as participation, inclusiveness and consensus, are among the different facets of community development that also need to be taken into consideration.

Without active (as compared to passive acceptance) involvement in all stages of community development, including needs analysis, project identification and design, implementation, monitoring and evaluation, it is unlikely that any impact of the particular intervention will be sustained (Uphoff et al., 1998; Dale, 2004). Sustaining the impact of a community development intervention is therefore more likely to be achieved if the beneficiaries, local community and other key stakeholders have actively participated in and 'own' the intervention. There are a number of reasons for this. First, inclusion of those directly affected group in the planning stages will more likely ensure that the rights development needs and their causes are identified. Secondly, the responses planned will take into account local resources and strengths of the local communities in a better manner, which will ensure that there is less reliance on external inputs. Finally, community participation will also aid in the ongoing management of the project as the decision-making processes would have been developed in the initial stages to include the relevant local beneficiaries and key stakeholders, which will continue once the external funding has ceased.

In recent years, international financial institutions, multilateral agencies, national governments and NGOs have, by and large, incorporated the term 'empowerment' into their development jargon (see Stiglitz, 1999; Craig and Porter, 1997; Sihlongonyane, 2003). If the rhetoric is transformed into practice, this means that community members are actively encouraged to identify their own needs, design the response, implement the project activities and also monitor it and evaluate its progress. Community empowerment requires participation from all sectors of the community—not just entrenched community leaders or those with interests to protect and enhance. Community participation requires the voices of women, the young, old, landless, disabled and other marginalized groups, just as it requires from traditional leaders, religious leaders and landowners. Community empowerment within development interventions has now become widely accepted as the minimum requirement for successful and sustained development outcomes (see Chambers, 2005). At this point, it is clear that religious organizations, including missionary organizations, can play a very important role in achieving effective and sustained community development outcomes.

As discussed above, a concern with the material deprivation of the poor has been felt and acted upon for many hundreds of years by religious organizations undertaking successful 'development' interventions within their missionary work (Luzbetak, 1988). Organized religions have long played an important role in enhancing the welfare of the local communities. While religious teaching is primarily concerned with providing spiritual leadership, an interest in the physical welfare of their communities has also been a core aspect of their existence. This concern with physical welfare is often expressed and delivered through affiliated faith-based organizations, such as missionary organizations, which operationalize this outreach. Yet, religion and religious organizations have long been invisible in the discussions of development

(Marshall and Van Saanen, 2007). This apparent invisibility though should not be mistaken as non-existence. More correctly, their invisibility reflects a blindness of the development sector itself in failing to recognize the importance of religion within the development sector. This may be partly explained by religious organizations—including missionary organizations—being embedded within communities and being less external agents and more 'organic' to the community. It can also be explained by organized religions choosing to position themselves outside the development sector when working to improve the material lives of their congregation (Clarke, 2008).

The invisibility of religion and religious organizations in development work, however, has recently begun to diminish. There has been recognition both within the development sector and by religious organizations themselves, that there is importance and synergy to be gained by being aware of one another and incorporating an understanding of religion more purposely into the development domain (Harb, 2008). As participatory community-focused models of development have become increasingly dominant in recent years, religious organizations have become increasingly 'attractive' as agents or key stakeholders in the development process due to their strong links to local communities. Moreover, religious bodies themselves have also begun to initiate contact with aid donors to seek increased involvement (and funding) in community development interventions (Clarke and Jennings, 2008). Over the past decade, a number of international forums have been developed, which have brought together religious leaders and large international donors to explore how to leverage the experience and expertise that both groups can bring to improving the lives of the poor (see reports emanating from these events, such as Marshall and Keogh, 2004).

Religious and missionary organizations are uniquely placed within communities to operate outside the mainstream local, the national and the international structures that constrain activities and networking of other civil society groups. Unlike secular non-government organizations, they have a natural constituency at the local level but also have organizational networks both nationally and internationally. Utilizing the networks that exist at these different levels supports their ability to undertake effective community development. Feeny and Clarke (2009) describe the different roles that non-government organizations can play at the micro, messo, macro and supra-macro levels in both advocacy and programming. Religious and missionary organizations are also able to operate in these levels by piggybacking on the pre-existing structures their associated religious organizations have in place. This therefore aids their efficiency and provides advantages over secular aid agencies.

## Contents of This Book

This book considers the implications, consequences, opportunities and constraints faced when mission and development endeavours coincide. This is explored from various perspectives, including that of history, theology and professional practice of those involved in mission work and missionary organizations. This book is broken into three parts. Part I introduces the concept of Christian mission and how it relates to the secular notion of development. Part II considers three historical case studies of mission and development interconnecting, before Part III delivers a number of case studies on a number contemporary faith-based organizations grappling with the mission/development nexus. In this sense, Part I lays the groundwork for the analysis that follows—both historical and contemporary.

As Ryan points out in Chapter 2, the concept of mission differs widely within Christianity. Ryan argues that various biblical stories are used to provide authority for a range of engagement approaches. Mission though should, according to Ryan, set itself apart from simply focusing on imparting God's word, but consider the full purpose of God's plan for human life. In this sense, mission closely mirrors that of development objectives in terms of seeking a flourishing of human well-being. Ryan distinguishes the secular development practitioner from missionary though by pointing to the biblical concept of servanthood—specifically, servanthood modelled by Jesus when he washed the feet of his Disciples during the Last Supper. This model inverts traditional concepts of power and redefines the relationship between those who are often the 'object' of development. This great challenge of mission, therefore, sets a paradigm in which partnerships and mutuality are preferred over authority and expertise. As Ryan finally notes though, such a view of mission is a challenge that is compounded when mission and development objectives conflated.

Kavunkal's Chapter 3 examines the biblical basis of human development as well as the Catholic teaching on it in the context of the church's missionary service. Kavunkal argues that at the heart of the whole theology of involvement in development is the Christian faith in the truth that humans are created in the image of God. Analysing the Exodus event and the Jubilee Institution, this chapter sets out to show how Jesus' own ministry was a proclamation of the Jubilee as good news to the poor and its spin off for the church's mission in today's context of dehumanization and exclusion. Finally, Kavunkal argues how mission today has to be a manifestation of the human person, all women and men enjoying the rights befitting human dignity, for humans fully alive is Divine glory.

In the first of the three chapters considering the historical role of missionaries in Part II of this book, Close examines the rhetoric and action of Methodist missionaries in Fiji in the lead up to the church's independence. Focusing on the 1930s, Close looks at important junctures that affected the Fijian, Indian and European branches of the mission and how these periods affected schools and hospitals established by Methodist missionaries. The missionaries aimed to produce 'productive citizens' through religious education, teaching literacy and numeracy, and encouraging agricultural enterprise. In fact, being a successful farmer was considered by some missionaries as equivalent to being a successful citizen. From its establishment in Fiji in 1835, the Mission began constructing schools, hospitals and orphanages throughout the islands. Close's Chapter 4 builds on histories written by Harold Wood and John Garrett, focusing more on the services the Mission delivered to the community rather than personalities within the Mission. The Mission emerged from the 1920s from a heavy argument over the degree to which the colonial administration would interfere with their schools. The 1930s was heralded by the financial strain of the Great Depression, which compelled the Mission Board to decide which projects were the most valuable and most productive. Missionaries in the field as well as at the Davuilevu base and the Mission Board of Australasia in Sydney all weighed in on these deliberations. Though their attitudes varied, all those involved agreed on the importance of the Mission's delivery of both education and health care to the community. Another important juncture was the 1935 centenary of the Mission's establishment in Fiji. The way in which achievements in education and health care were celebrated was equally telling. This chapter thus highlights the goals of the Methodist Mission in Fiji, which were so heavily focused on the creation of useful citizens and the entrenchment of modernity through infrastructure. It will also incorporate the concept of the industrial mission and examine the development of this philosophy in the community.

In Chapter 5, Clarke looks at the role of the churches in Melanesia's Independence. Following decolonization in the 1970s, it was clear that welding multiple languages and diverse cultures into unified nations would be difficult within Melanesia. Indeed, nation-building still remains a key challenge across Melanesian societies, including Solomon Islands, Papua New Guinea (PNG), Vanuatu and the more recently independent state of Timor-Leste. Yet, despite these challenges, some success has been achieved, much of it as the result of the role that the Church plays in these countries. The role of the various Christian churches has been pivotal in the development and sustenance of the Pacific nations prior to and since their independence. These churches include Anglican, Catholic, Pentecostal and Evangelical denominations. Missionaries and later local church leaders were involved directly in independence movements and shaped the legal and social infrastructure of these new nations. Their involvement and influence have continued to the present. Clarke's chapter considers the role the Church has played in the development of the 'nation' in this region in two parts. First, the chapter presents case study analysis of both the historical and contemporary role the Church has played in the development of Solomon Islands and Vanuatu. This review considers the impact of key individual Church leaders who played central roles in nation-building as well as in the emergence of a 'theology of independence' that evolved during this period within the Pacific. Secondly, the chapter draws on new findings of approximately 1,000 surveys of tertiary students within this region to more clearly understand the contemporary role of the Church and religion in nation-building and national identity. This new survey and focus group data on the attitudes towards national identity among tertiary students covers four states, including the Solomon Islands, Vanuatu, Papua New Guinea and Timor-Leste. This data casts new light on the attitudes of potential future elites towards regional, ethnic, intergenerational and linguistic fault lines in the region, and the challenges of building a cohesive sense of political community and national identity and the role of the Church in this process.

The third historical case study is that of the Seventh Day Adventist (SDA) missionaries working in Papua New Guinea. Watson notes in Chapter 6 that the SDA church has had a significant impact on the people of Papua New Guinea since the arrival of three pioneering missionaries in 1908. In the first decade of 2010, church affiliation had reached 10 per cent of the population and 21,000 students were being educated in a school system that spanned primary schools and a university. As a service provider, the church also operates clinics and aid posts. Further, SDA politicians have contributed significantly to the PNG parliament in the past decade. Accordingly, the SDA church has influenced service provision, national identity as a Christian country, and the nation-building process itself. This chapter explores the emergence of early SDA church work and pioneering provision of health care and education. It then explores the reflections of a medical missionary, Pastor Lester Hawkes, and argues that such men and women were the forerunners of later Pacific NGO workers who represented the Seventh Day Adventist Welfare Service (established 1956) and eventually the Adventist Development and Relief Agency.

In considering more contemporary case studies in Part III, Bradbury focuses on Evangelical Christian faith-based development organizations and mission organizations, which he argues in Chapter 7 are noteworthy contributors to the delivery of humanitarian relief and development programmes around the world. In recent decades, this contribution and the commitment behind it have provoked some controversy both among evangelical Christians and within the broader development community. Bradbury's chapter then briefly explores the theological debate regarding the Church's mission mandate, and the place of relief, development and advocacy for the oppressed and/or marginalized within it. In the last decade, the Micah Network, a loose global alliance of over 330 Christian relief, development and justice organizations, has deliberately and significantly contributed to this debate, in pursuit of one of its three core aims. In so doing, the Micah Network and its members continue to wrestle with a host of vitally relevant faith/development issues, including faith as motivator and sustainer in the demanding work of relief, development and advocacy; the practical and programmatic implications of the Bible's teaching on justice and mercy, including its radical focus on the marginalized and excluded; the role and ethics of evangelism in integral mission; the character of faith-informed collegiality and its relevance to partnership practice and protocols; and the role of the local church in relief and development.

Chapter 8 by O'Halloran draws on the cross-cultural communication experiences of Palms Australia, a volunteer-sending organization. International development volunteers face a significant barrier to achieving goals if they are unable to develop cross-cultural relationships in sufficient depth. A recent literature search on international development volunteering indicated that very little academic research exists on what influences the achievement of a volunteer's goals. In a qualitative study, Georgeou considers such influences on a small cohort of volunteers and also considers the relationship between programme design, underlying ethos and the realization of programme goals in order to examine the impact of pre-departure preparation on a volunteer's philosophy and how the preparation by their sending agency, Palms Australia, appeared to influence placement outcomes. Palms emphasizes cross-cultural preparation, believing that building relationships with those of a culture different from one's own is the primary objective and key to achieving any other goal that might be the basis of international volunteering. This chapter, based on the experience of Palms in international development volunteering, suggests that more effective preparation of international development volunteers and more realistic placement goal setting can be achieved. It also supports the view that an effective relationship between the volunteer and their host community allows them to determine how the knowledge and skills of the volunteer can be best applied and utilized to achieve the goals of a placement.

A popular view among those who work for and donate to the Mennonite Central Committee (MCC), a North American Christian NGO in the Anabaptist-Mennonite tradition, is that it is a 'church organisation that does not plant churches'. However, this should not be taken to mean that MCC does not engage in Christian mission. Fountain's chapter draws on ethnographic research on MCC in Indonesia, the US and Canada, and explores the blurred and fluid boundaries between 'missionary' and 'development' work. This chapter focuses on three particular instances where MCC has actively engaged in the making of Mennonites. In the first case, the work of MCC evangelists who in the 1970s were sent to an 'animist' Dayak community in Kalimantan for agricultural development and to tell them about Jesus is examined. It is suggested this was a dual evangelism in that in the context of early New Order Indonesia, conversion to Christianity, as one of the five officially recognized religions, was also a conversion to being proper citizens of the Indonesian nation. Secondly, this chapter examines MCC's vital role as a conduit connecting Indonesian and North American Mennonites. This connection has had considerable impact on Indonesian Mennonite churches, for without MCC's intervention it is likely that they would have been incorporated into other larger structures that were forming in the heady days of post-Independence ecumenical ferment. By brokering this transnational denominational connection, MCC was influential in spurring Indonesian Mennonites to remain Mennonite. However, being Mennonite for the Indonesian churches was more of an associative claim than a theological one; the substance of faith remained oriented around local epistemologies and practices. In contradistinction to the first two examples, this chapter then argues that MCC's *primary* missionary work has not been carried in 'the field'. Instead, MCC has been most active in making these Mennonites as one among the constituent communities in North America. MCC has been a central actor since the Second World War in re-forging what it means to be an American or Canadian Mennonite. This includes reworking and inculcating particular values such as peace and justice, service, global consciousness and generosity. Some MCC members have seen themselves as 'peace evangelists' to North American Mennonites. MCC has also been crucial in counteracting the powerful forces of fragmentation and division that mark North American Mennonite communities. In addressing MCC's mission to Mennonites in North America, this Fountain draws attention to implicit imaginative cartographies that assume that transgressive boundary crossing between 'mission' and 'development' necessarily relates only to that which is 'over there' rather than the work of NGOs, religious and otherwise, in re-creating identities among supporters 'at home'.

Enright and Ware argue in Chapter 10 that, both theologically and practically, development is a form of mission and therefore dividing 'mission' and 'development' is artificial. A theological understanding of mission clearly incorporates upholding rights especially of people most excluded and vulnerable, the core task of development. One church agency involved in both development and supporting the partners in communicating the gospel is UnitingWorld—the national agency of the Uniting Church in Australia, responsible for international partnerships including development. The Uniting Church was formed in 1977 from the merging of three denominations, all of which had a long history of overseas engagement—for example, with Fiji since 1844 and Korea since 1889. Such partnerships have endured and spread to the point where the Uniting Church now has 36 formal partners, mainly in the Pacific and Asia. Over the past 20 years, a range of social trends, such as decolonization, climate change and increased global commitment to justice, as well as changes in missiological thinking, have influenced collaboration with indigenous churches as well as organizations that are not explicitly Christian. Recolonizing approaches by international inter-government bodies and by the Australian government through promoting predominantly Western neo-liberal economic values to neighbours invites the church to collaborate in valuing partner cultures, spiritualities, values and world views. For UnitingWorld, this is most evident in its Pacific engagement, especially with programmes arising from the Pacific Conference of Churches. These factors have further relativized the tensions between what was seen as 'mission' and what was seen as 'development'. Evangelism as communication of good news exhibits a different hue—now coming out of the natural conversations between partners and speaking of God's life-giving alternatives to destructive social and economic models. While development is inherent in mission, the major challenge faced by

UnitingWorld is with the Protestant partners strongly influenced by an era of church teaching that emphasized personal commitment tied to distinctive religious expressions. In this chapter, Enright and Ware use case studies from the Pacific to show how UnitingWorld is partnering with a range of churches and other organizations to support people in exercising their rights and re-engaging the Australian church communities in this task.

Hoffstaedter and Clarke conclude the book in Chapter 11 by considering mission work through the development lens. This perspective reverses that taken throughout the book in which development was largely discussed in the context of mission. By concluding the book with this short discussion, Hoffstaedter and Clarke remind the reader that despite the evidence to the contrary presented throughout this book, development remains dominated by a secular world view and religion and mission remains a periphery issue. In issuing this reminder though, Hoffstaedter and Clarke do issue a challenge to the wider development field that engagement with religion and the religious is of fundamental importance to achieving lasting and effective improvements in the lives of the poor.

## Conclusion

This book purposely takes an appreciative view of the role played by mission organizations and missionaries in development. That said, it is important to acknowledge that mission organizations and missionaries also have a past replete with inappropriate actions. The impact of missionaries on local cultures and living standards is not consistent, with a great deal of activities failing the modern standards. For example, the Catholic Church entered the New World soon after Columbus and with the support of the Crown, set out to match the secular colonialization with its own religious kind. It viewed the 'natives' as non-human and readily had them killed by the Crown if they did not accept conversion (Gibillini, 1987). These critiques should not be ignored. Indeed, persuasive arguments can be made that mission activity exacerbated poverty through their actions. However, while not denying these problematic issues, this book holds the view that missionary work must also be considered as an important constitutive force that requires proper consideration. For example, even during the period of New World colonization, there were notable examples such as Father Jose de Acosta who challenged the structures of violence and spoke against their superiors on behalf of the oppressed.

These notable examples provide the impetus for what follows in the following chapters. A narrative that places mission work and missionary organizations side by side with the process of development will be constructed in which the interconnection between the spiritual and material is explored. While an appreciative view is taken, the chapters within this book do realistically highlight the challenges faced, mistakes made and incorrect courses sometimes taken. However, they also highlight the strengths mission organizations and missionaries bring to improving the lives of the poor and point to a very real conflation between good works and God's work.

## Notes

1 See, for instance, Sachs (2005), Stiglitz (2007) and Easterly (2002) for divergent overviews of past failures and future approaches to development.
2 The focus of this book is Christian mission, though work on how mission activities of other faiths intersect with development warrants further study.

## References

Agg, C. (2006), 'Trends in support for NGOs', *Civil Society and Social Movements Programme Paper No. 23*, Geneva: UNRISD.
Chambers, R. (2005), *Ideas for Development*, London: Earthscan.
Clarke, G. and Jennings, M. (2008), *Development, Civil Society and Faith-based Organizations*, London: Palgrave-MacMillan.
Clarke, M. (2008), 'Raising the funds – spending the funds: a case study of the effectiveness of BOTH roles of NGOs', in Renzao, A. (ed.), *Measuring Development Effectiveness*, New York: Nova.
Craig, D. and Porter, D. (1997), 'Framing participation: development projects, professionals, and organizations', *Development in Practice*, 7(3), 229–36.
Dale, R. (2004), *Development Planning*, London: Zed Books.
Easterly, W. (2002), *The Elusive Quest for Growth*, Cambridge: MIT Press.
Feeny, S. and Clarke, M. (2007), 'What determines Australia's responses to emergencies and natural disasters', *Australian Economic Review*, 40(1), 24–36.
—. (2009), *The Millennium Development Goals and Beyond: International Assistance to the Asia-Pacific*, London: Palgrave-MacMillan.
Gibillini, R. (1987), *The Liberation Theology Debate*, London: SCM Press.
Harb, M. (2008), 'Faith-based organizations as effective development partners? Hezbollah and post-war reconstruction in Lebanon', in Clarke, G. and Jennings, M. (eds), *Development, Civil Society and Faith-based Organizations*, London: Palgrave-MacMillan.
Ife, J. (1995), 'Principles of community development', *Creating Community Alternatives – Vision, Analysis and Practice*, South Melbourne: Longman.
Kirk, A. (2000), *What is Mission? Theological Explorations*, London: Fortress Press.
Luzbetak, L. (1988), *The Church and Culture*, Maryknoll: Orbis Books.
Marshall, K. and Keogh, L. (2004), *Mind, Heart and Soul in the Fight Against Poverty*, Washington, DC: World Bank.
Marshall, K. and Van Saanen, M. (2007), *Development and Faith*, Washington, DC: World Bank.
Nemer, L. (2001), 'Formation for SVD mission: present and future', *Verbum SVD*, 42(3), 331–42.

Pierson, P. (2007), 'Development', in Bonk, J. (ed.), *Encyclopedia of Missions and Missionaries*, New York: Routledge.
Sachs, J. (2005), *The End of Poverty*, London: Penguin.
Sihlongonyane, M. (2003), 'The rhetoric of the community in project management: the case of Mohlakeng township', *Development in Practice*, 11(1), 34–44.
Stiglitz, J. E. (1999), 'The role of participation in development', *Development Outreach*, Summer, Washington, DC: World Bank, 1–4.
Stiglitz, J. (2007), *Making Globalization Work*, New York: Norton.
Uphoff, N., Esman, M. and Krishna, A. (1998), *Reasons for Success: Learning from Instructive Experiences in Rural Development*, West Hardtford: Kumarian Press.
World Bank (1995), *Working with NGOs*, Washington, DC: World Bank.

# PART ONE

# History and Setting

# 2

# Washing Our Dirty Feet: Christ and Development

Jonathan Ryan

## Introduction

To speak of the 'dirty feet' of development is simply to acknowledge this unfortunate truth: that the project of development has been a rather messy business and that those arriving from the outside have generally had the muddiest footwear. The post-World War Two programme for development announced a new era of international relations, in which outside involvement would be cleansed of the imperialistic motivations of the preceding colonial age. However, as Ivan Illich (1973, p. 131) observed in 1970, 'the plough of the rich can do as much harm as their swords'. It was a characteristically prescient observation for, as we are now well aware, six decades of development has not diminished global inequality, but has in many cases exacerbated it.

In wrestling with the disappointments of development, contemporary critique has tended to focus on questions of power, a question that, as we shall see, Christian scripture has much to say on. The persistence of colonial power dynamics has been traced through virtually every dimension of the development paradigm. Certainly, they have been observed in the behaviour and attitude of development practitioners, who 'believed that their knowledge was superior and that the knowledge of farmers and other local people was inferior . . . . Treated as incapable, poor people behaved as incapable, reflecting the beliefs of the powerful, and hiding their capabilities even from themselves' (Chambers, 1994, p. 963).

This critique has also been sustained at the level of regional projects and initiatives, where it is argued that development has been conceived, not as an organic process of local cultures but as a 'a top-down, ethnocentric and technocratic approach, which treated people and cultures as abstract concepts' (Escobar, 1997, p. 91).

However, the more pressing critique has been of the development paradigm itself. The inevitable consequence of the Enlightenment ideal of 'progress' and capitalism's obsession with economic measures has led the development ideology to view the world's eclectic cultures on a linear plane, a hierarchy ranked from developed to underdeveloped. Of the birth of this paradigm in the late 1940s, Mexican writer Gustavo Esteva (1992, pp. 6–7) notes that:

> On that day, two billion people became underdeveloped. In a real sense, from that time on, they ceased being what they were, in all their diversity, and were transmogrified into an inverted mirror of others' reality: a mirror that belittles them and tends them off to the end of the queue . . . .

And, while this paradigm seems to promise the possibility of economic mobility, where regions might rise above their place in the queue, as Michael Hardt and Antonio Negri (2000) observe, this is in fact a mirage. Though particular regions might have improved by some measures over time, their place in the hierarchy, by and large, still persists, for they 'remain subordinate in the global system' in which 'the dominant regions will continue to develop and the subordinate will continue to underdevelop as mutually supporting poles in the global power structure' (Hardt and Negri, 2000, p. 283). For the majority of the world's population, then, development—for all its commendable hopes and aspirations—remains 'a reminder of *what they are not* . . . ' (Esteva, 1992, p. 10).

It should be noted that the church has been no stranger to development's troubling history, but rather an active contributor. While some within Christian churches, like Illich (1970), have questioned the assumptions of the development paradigm, it has nonetheless been embraced by Christian churches, particularly in their global missionary activity. Of course, the Enlightenment spirit of 'progress', so central to the notion of development, had already exerted a significant influence on the churches' understanding of 'mission' in preceding eras:

> Sometimes it manifested itself as the belief that the entire world would still be converted to the Christian faith; at other times Christianity was regarded as an irresistible power in the process of reforming the world, eradicating poverty, and restoring justice for all . . . . The spread of 'Christian knowledge' would suffice in achieving these aims (Bosch, 1991, p. 271).

Although by the twentieth century many Christians were becoming uncomfortable with this 'civilising' language of their colonial forebears, the underlying world view nurtured by the ideal of progress remained. This is plainly reflected, for example, in the opening line of the 1967 papal encyclical, *Populorum Progressio*: 'The progressive development of peoples is an object of deep interest and concern to the Church' (Populorum Progressio, 1967). Furthermore, this 'progressive development' became increasingly measured in terms of inputs and outputs, yields and dividends—an indication, Bosch (1979, p. 31) argues, that Christian mission had become 'indissolubly fused with the ethic of capitalism'.

So it was that, in the post-World War Two era, the concept of development held great appeal to the church, and by the 1960s, had been adopted by virtually all Christian denominations as the defining paradigm for mission. Regrettably, the church's embrace of development has typically been an uncritical one. Rather than calling into question development's implicit hierarchy of 'developed' and 'underdeveloped', and the problems of power this inevitably produces, Christian mission has often accepted development as a given, simply supplementing its 'material' measures with a 'spiritual' dimension. The fundamental flaw with this approach is illustrated clearly by Bryant Myers (1999, p. 66):

> To make their understanding of poverty holistic, Christians add knowledge of the gospel to the list of other things the poor do not have. Thus proclamation of the gospel is added to the development programme . . . . Our view of them, which quickly becomes their view of themselves, is that they are defective and inadequate. We do not treat them as human beings made in the image of God. We act as if God's gifts were given to us and none to the poor. This attitude increases their poverty and tempts us to play god in the lives of the poor.

In wrestling with the failings of development, Christians might be tempted to point to contemporary mission as a redeemed alternative, cleansed of the colonizing sins of their forebears. However, as Jonathan Bonk (2007, p. 344) frankly states, the supposed differences between these generations of missionary activity are 'largely cosmetic, a façade fashioned from sheer forgetfulness, selective memory, and self-delusion'. Christian missionaries are not immune to the temptations of power, and along with other development practitioners, must strive to resist 'the siren allure of human systems so fatally addicted to selfinterest' (Bonk, 2007, p. 345).

## Jesus and Servanthood

Though sobering and severe, such critiques have become commonplace among post-development discourse. That being the case, however, these claims should not lead us to an ethical apathy. For do not those with bread still, in some sense, bear responsibility towards those who hunger? And if so, is it possible for those of 'colonial' origins to serve others without simultaneously imposing neo-colonial agendas?

Undoubtedly, a Christian engagement with these questions would want to respond with an emphatic 'Yes'. But what should the nature of this 'Yes' be? In a compelling 2009 speech, Rowan Williams (2009) argues that within the discourse of development, the role of faith is not to simply endorse the pre-established goals of 'some independent universal authority', but rather 'to provide a critical perspective on how some of those goals can be pursued unthinkingly, and in ways that will do further damage in the long run'. For the Christian community, such a critique would need to reframe the narrow terms of development discourse to consider the broader meaning and purpose of human flourishing (as modelled, for example, by the more recent papal encyclical, *Caritas in Veritate*, 2009).

However, within such an engagement, faith must still wrestle with the problem of power within the work of development. Williams (2009) commends to development practitioners—whether or not they belong to a faith community—the importance of identifying the 'elements in a particular religious culture . . . most fruitful in terms of the struggle against poverty'. The purpose of this chapter, therefore, is to draw attention to the 'element' of servanthood within the Christian tradition, and to illustrate its pertinence to these challenges of development. To identify such an image is not to champion a particular method or technique, but rather to locate an important reference point for those seeking to resist the pervasive pull of power in an age of neocolonialism.

Each of the synoptic gospels relates a story in which, against the backdrop of imperial Rome, the disciples dispute about which of them would be regarded as the greatest. In a stern rebuke of this thinking, Jesus responds by saying:

> You know that the rulers of the Gentiles lord it over them, and their great ones are tyrants over them. It will not be so among you; but whoever wishes to be great among you must be your servant, and whoever wishes to be first among you must be your slave; just as the Son of Man came not to be served but to serve, and to give his life as a ransom for many (Matt 20.25–27).[1]

It should be noted that in Luke's rendering of this account, the word 'tyrant' (katexousia¿zousin) is replaced with 'benefactor' (eujerge÷tai), thus reading 'those who exercise authority over [the Gentiles] call themselves Benefactors' (Lk. 22.25). In Roman antiquity, charitable support would result in relationships of patronage, which essentially became another form of tyranny over the recipient. But whether through political authority or through benefaction, there is no place for such relationships of domination among the disciples of Jesus, 'it will not be so among you'.

For the visual learners among them, this point is forced upon the disciples most plainly when Jesus himself takes on the role of a servant, as depicted in Jn 13:

> [Jesus] got up from the table, took off his outer robe, and tied a towel around himself. Then he poured water into a basin and began to wash the disciples' feet and to wipe them with the towel that was tied around him (Jn 13.4-5).

Of all the regular tasks of a servant, Jesus had chosen the basest:

> So menial a task was it that in a household with a hierarchy of slaves and servants, it would be the duty of the slaves, not of the servants who performed less demeaning tasks such as waiting at table. It was, in fact, the quintessentially servile task, the one thing that no one else would do (Bauckham, 2007, p. 192).

For the disciples, this is deeply problematic. We gain sense of this in the protest of the disciple Peter, who refuses to allow his Lord to play this role (v. 8). This is not a response of ignorance, but rather, as Lesslie Newbigin (1982, p. 168) suggests, 'the protest of normal human nature':

> All normal management procedures require chains of authority. All of us except those at the very bottom have a vested interest in keeping it so, for as long as we duly submit to those above us we are free to bear down on those below us. The action of Jesus subverts this order and threatens to destabilize all society.

Notably, however, Jesus has not denounced authority itself: 'You call me Teacher and Lord', he comments, 'and you are right, for that is what I am'. What has been reconfigured is the way those in authority relate to others; his action calls for 'the abolition of relationships based on status.' (Bauckham, 2007, p. 195). 'So if I, your Lord and Teacher, have washed your feet, you also ought to wash one another's feet' (v. 14).

At the conclusion of this task, Jesus explains his actions, saying 'I have set you an example, that you also should do as I have done to you' (v. 15). In a context where conceptions of power and authority were deeply shaped by Roman colonialism, the radical implications of this example would be clear. 'It takes very little reflection', says Tom Thatcher (2009, p. 138), 'to see that Jesus turned Caesar's world upside down when he washed his disciples' feet'.

## Mission and Servanthood

Of course, no biblical image is immune to distortion, and this is certainly true for the image of servanthood. As Marion Grau (2005, p. 168) puts it, 'a text has the potential to interrogate structures of dominance, but can at the same time function as the reinscription of the *status quo*'. If the motif of servanthood is to avoid colluding with colonial aspirations, we must first address two concerns.

First, feminist critics have suggested that, while the call to servanthood may be a fitting corrective to the typically 'masculinist' errors of pride and power, for many females—only too-well acquainted with the call to self-denial and subordination—servanthood is an inappropriate and potentially abusive emphasis. This is an important question for the present discussion, which challenges us to further consider whether servanthood is a valuable motif for all partners in development, or ultimately only a privileged hobby for the elite, those who have power and resources to divest themselves of in the first place.

Secondly, we must consider the capacity for both wilful deception and self-deception, driven by an ideal or ideology of servanthood. As Stephen Sykes (2006, p. 115) observes:

> The invocation of service refers to the intention which lies behind the action. It does not describe the action itself, which might be illegal or monstrously unjust. Nor does it bear upon how the action will be experienced or interpreted by those affected by it. The agent, moreover, could lack insight into his own motivations, with the result that what is spoken of as service in the interest of others is, in fact, self-serving . . . . The mere invocation of service precludes none of these possibilities.

Such deception can occur in a myriad of ways. For example, Sykes (2006, p. 115) draws our attention to Maurice Duverger's notion of 'camouflage', in which power holders dress themselves in whatever popular opinion regards as 'respectable motives for wanting to be powerful'. That is to say, in certain contexts—Christian mission, perhaps—we might deem it advantageous to clothe our development agendas in the language of servanthood. Or perhaps this could take place unconsciously. Marianne Gronemeyer (1992) argues that, within development, 'helping' has become a self-deceptive expression of the 'elegant exercise of power'. 'Power is truly elegant' she suggests, 'when, captivated by the delusion of freedom, those subject to it stubbornly deny its existence . . . ' (1992, p. 53).

These are critiques that cannot—and should not—be readily dismissed, and in spite of the response that follows, any discussion of servanthood must acknowledge these voices. As Sykes (2006, pp. 131–2) correctly identifies, the nature of the power expressed in servanthood and self-sacrifice is not one 'free of ambiguity', and therefore, will always wrestle with these challenges.

However, the fundamental problem revealed in both critiques of Christ's example of servanthood is one of definition. As Karl Barth (1957, p. 524) cautions in his discussion of divine power, 'the forgetfulness which would lead us to define the subject by the predicate instead of the predicate by the subject would lead us to disastrous consequences'. The sweatshop labour of our own time should remind us that there is nothing particularly pleasant about oppressive slavery, and any attempt to valourize demeaning servility demands rigorous critique. A Christian account of power and servanthood must be wary against such 'forgetfulness', instead allowing these predicates to be defined by the subject; that is, to allow the God revealed in Jesus Christ to define our understanding of servanthood, and not vice versa.

Obviously, appeal to an omnipotent God can further exacerbate one's 'god-complex', not least in the work of development or mission. As Newbigin (1982, p. 170) observes, 'the natural [human] makes gods in [their] own image, and the supreme God will be the one who stands at the summit of the chain of command'. But how, he asks,

> can the natural [human] recognise the supreme God in the stooping figure of a slave, clad only in a loincloth? . . . If this slave who stoops to wash his disciples' feet is indeed master, then we must frankly declare ourselves atheists with reference to the normal use of the word 'God'.

So it is, then, that redefinitions are required. The 'point' of the foot-washing episode is neither that the disciples should be subjugated to the domination of others (like a slave of the Roman empire), nor that they should adopt the pose of a servant in order to manipulatively dominate others. Rather, the servant action of Jesus demands a transformation of this 'will to power', so that for his disciples, power is no longer defined by those who stand 'at the summit of the chain of command', but rather by those who kneel at another's feet. Unlike the power of the tyrants or benefactors, the power of God is a power 'perfected in weakness' (2 Cor. 12.9), and is revealed in the acts of self-giving love. This transformation of power is most fully revealed in the act prefigured by this foot-washing, in which the power of God is nailed to an imperial cross. Power so defined makes little sense to tyrants and benefactors; it is both foolish and scandalous to those in authority (1 Cor 1.18,23). But for a Christian response to development, the redefinition of power that takes place on the cross is of decisive importance, as Jürgen Moltmann (1991, p. 3) insists:

> Whether or not Christianity, in an alienated, divided and oppressive society, itself becomes alienated, divided and an accomplice of oppression, is ultimately decided only by whether the crucified Christ is a stranger to it or the Lord who determines the form of its existence.

The disciple Peter is himself scandalized by this redefining act (John 13.8). However, Jesus responds, 'Unless I wash you, you have no share with me', and here lies the crux of his challenge. To accept the foot-washing action of Jesus demands first that our conceptions of power and entitlement be radically transformed, lest we too be scandalized. But to refuse the transformation of our regnant definitions of power—to refuse the washing of our own dirty feet—is to refuse the example of servanthood Jesus models. Serving simply remains, as Gronemeyer (1992, p. 53) puts it, a more 'elegant exercise of power'.

Furthermore, the earlier caution of feminist scholars reminds us that this transformation must also take place among the powerless, as well as among the powerful. As Rosemary Radford Ruether (1981, p. 54) notes:

> neither existing lords nor existing servants can serve as a model for this servanthood, but only the Christ . . . who represents a new kind of humanity. The essence of servanthood is that it is possible only for liberated persons, not people in servitude.

That power be redefined in this way is just as important for the colonized as for the colonizers, lest they simply aspire towards the repressive power they have suffered from. Iranian academic Majid Rahnema (1992) draws our attention to the many instances in which the power modelled in development has prompted local regimes to exert 'new forms of domination and exclusions they had never previously known'. Sarah Coakley (2002, p. 32) makes a similar observation in her own incisive engagement with this feminist critique, asking how women, in their quest to gain power, are to avoid aping the 'masculinism' they criticize. This is a crucial question, not only for women, but also for those in development who perceive themselves as powerless. For as Coakley (2002, p. 33) warns,

> there is another, and longer-term, danger . . . in the *repression* of all forms of 'vulnerability', and in a concomitant failure to confront issues of fragility, suffering or 'self-emptying' except in terms of victimology. And that is ultimately the failure to embrace . . . the power of the cross and resurrection.[2]

## Conclusion

It should be clear, then, that to speak of servanthood within the sphere of development is not only to take on the role of a servant, but in doing so, to call into question other conceptions of power, not least the linear hierarchy so often presupposed by development. In the instruction, 'You ought to wash one another's feet', Jesus directs us towards relationships of mutuality. There can be no pretence of one group being more advanced or of higher worth than another, for here, each is subject to the other and seeks the good of the other. Rather than developed and underdeveloped, or donor and recipient, or missions expert and local; there is just servant and servant. This does not spell an end to expressions of responsibility and compassion, but it does demand a rethinking of the top-down, patron-client relationship that often accompanies them. Williams (2009) unpacks well the implications for development:

> We are not trying to solve someone else's problem but to liberate ourselves from a toxic and unjust situation in which we, the prosperous, are less than human. The way forward is not simply the shedding of surplus wealth on to grateful recipients but an understanding that we are trying to take forward the process by which the other becomes as fully a 'giver' as I seek to be, so that the transaction by which I seek to bring about change in the direction of justice for another is one in which I come to be as much in the other's debt as they are in mine.
>
> This is not, in other words, simply about the prosperous giving something to the poor, but about a gift that contributes to the liberation of both poor and prosperous and transforms both.

Such a transformed perspective is demanded also in the professional practice of development. For many decades, servant-like 'techniques' and 'methods' have been employed to address the challenge of power in development. From the late 1950s onwards, the development toolbox was expanded by grassroots activists to include more participatory methods of decision-making and intervention in the hope of countering top-down approaches to development (for example, Participatory Action Research and Participatory Rural Appraisal). However, ironically, these methods for bottom-up development have also been used to perpetuate a top-down ideology. Due to their political attractiveness and fundraising appeal, 'participatory' methodologies have been co-opted by the largest and most powerful groups, including repressive governments seeking development aid. Even in grassroots practice, and in contexts of mission, 'participatory' methods have been used uncritically to assert power over others. Rahnema (1992, p. 123) formulates the problem as follows:

> When A considers it essential for B to be empowered, A assumes not only that B has no power—or does not have the right kind of power—but also that A has the secret formula of a power to which B has to be initiated.

'Methods' or 'techniques' of servanthood are of little value if the underlying interests and motivations of those employing them have not first been transformed. Chambers (1994, p. 963), though one of the most outspoken advocates of participatory methodologies, concludes that, ultimately, 'in facilitating PRA the behaviour and attitudes of outsiders matter more than the methods and their correct performance'.

For development practitioners, then, the challenge of servanthood is one that needs to be outworked personally. One cannot simply adopt the 'persona' of a servant, without being prepared to accept the diminished status and mundane tasks of a servant. However, as Chambers (1983) has comprehensively identified, the geographical and professional dynamics of development practice tend to draw practitioners *away* from the lives of the least.[3] He argues that practitioners have been slow to acknowledge that 'the fine words "participation", "ownership" and "empowerment", by and for the poor, demand institutional change by us' (Chambers, 1995, p. 197). Bosch (1979, pp. 65–6) poses a similar challenge to practitioners working in the context of Christian mission, noting that though we may use the language of servanthood, 'we want to be servants in our own way'. He continues:

> All missionaries, says Joinet [a French Roman Catholic missionary], like to say, with John the Baptist, "He must increase, but I must decrease" (John 3:30), and it is easy to say that during a retreat. But in actual practice, who wants to decrease? This is especially difficult if we are absolutely convinced that we know better . . . (Bosch, 1979, pp. 65–6).

For this reason, the foot-washing of Jesus remains an essential image for the type of servanthood that Jesus advocates. Washing the dirty feet of another is not an attractive task, nor one that successful professionals would naturally gravitate towards, but it reminds us that to be a servant is necessarily to not be a master, to not be in control, to instead be guided by and subject to others.

This helps us recover, in Rahnema's (1997, p. 393) poetic phrasing, a 'respect for the 'right size' of everything . . . ' Rather than seeking a godlike omnipresence, controlling and covering vast areas, it may demand of us a more local commitment. Rather than affecting a divine omniscience, it may challenge us to become learners as well as experts. And rather than assuming a colonizing omnipotence, we have the task before us of allowing power to be redefined through servanthood, allowing our own dirty feet to be washed, in order that we in turn might recover a true sense of our place in humanity in the faces of the ones we serve.

## Notes

1 All biblical references are taken from the NRSV translation.

2 Coakley (2002, pp. 36–7) also qualifies this critique with a number of 'fine, but important, distinctions': 'between this 'right' vulnerability and mere invitation to abuse; between this contemplative 'self-effacement' and self-destruction or self-repression; between the productive suffering of self-disclosure and the decentring torture of pain for pain's sake'.

3 See, for example, the opening chapter of Chambers, R. (1983), *Rural Development: Putting the Last First.* London: Longman.

## References

Barth, K. (1957), *Church Dogmatics II: The Doctrine of God,* (Part One), Bromiley, G. W. and Torrance, T. F. (eds), (Trans. T. H. L. Parker et al.), Edinburgh: T&T Clark.

Bauckham, R. (2007), *The Testimony of the Beloved Disciple: Narrative, History, and Theology in the Gospel of John*, Grand Rapids: Baker Academic.

Benedict XVI, (2009), *Caritas In Veritate: Encyclical Letter of the Supreme Pontiff Benedict XVI on Integral Human Development in Charity and Truth*, retrieved 9 August 2010, <www.vatican.va/holy_father/benedict_xvi/encyclicals/documents/hf_ben-xvi_enc_20090629_caritas-in-veritate_en.html>.

Bonk, J. (2007), 'Following Jesus in contexts of power and violence', *Evangelical Review of Theology*, 31(4).

Bosch, D. (1979), *A Spirituality of the Road*, Scottdale: Herald Press.

—. (1991), *Transforming Mission: Paradigm Shifts in Theology of Mission*, Maryknoll, NY: Orbis Books.

Chambers, R. (1983), *Rural Development: Putting the Last First*, London: Longman.

—. (1994), 'The origins and practice of participatory rural appraisal', *World Development*, 22(7).

—. (1995), 'Poverty and livelihoods: whose reality counts?' *Environment and Urbanization*, 7(1).

Coakley, S. (2002), *Powers and Submissions: Spirituality, Philosophy, and Gender*, Oxford: Blackwell Publishers.

Escobar, A. (1997), 'The Making and Unmaking of the Third World through Development', in Rahnema, M. (ed.), *The Post-Development Reader*, London: Zed Books.

Esteva, G. (1992), 'Development', in Sachs, W. (ed.), *The Development Dictionary: A Guide to Knowledge as Power*, London: Zed Books.

Grau, M. (2005), 'Divine commerce: a postcolonial Christology for times of neocolonial empire', in Keller, C. et al. (eds.), *Postcolonial Theologies: Divinity and Empire* (2nd edn), St. Louis: Chalice Press.

Gronemeyer, M. (1992), 'Helping', in Sachs, W. (ed.), *The Development Dictionary: A Guide to Knowledge as Power*, London: Zed Books.

Hardt, M. and Negri, A. (2000), *Empire*, Cambridge: Harvard University Press.

Illich, I. (1973), 'Planned poverty: the end result of technical assistance', in *Celebration of Awareness: a Call for Institutional Revolution*, Harmondsworth: Penguin Education.

Moltmann, J. (1991), *The Crucified God: The Cross of Christ as the Foundation and Criticism of Christian Theology* (1st edn), San Francisco: HarperSanFrancisco.

Myers, B. (1999), *Walking with the Poor: Principles and Practices of Transformational Development*, Maryknoll: Orbis Books.

Newbigin, L. (1982), *The Light Has Come: an Exposition of the Fourth Gospel*, Grand Rapids: Eerdmans.

Paul VI, *Populorum Progressio: Encyclical of Pope Paul VI on the Development of Peoples*, retrieved 9 August 2010, <www.vatican.va/holy_father/paul_vi/encyclicals/documents/hf_p-vi_enc_26031967_populorum_en.html>.

Radford Ruether, R. (1981), 'Christology and feminism: can a male saviour save women?', in *To Change the World: Christology and Cultural Criticism*, New York: Crossroad.

Rahnema, M. (1992), 'Participation', in Sachs, W. (ed.), *The Development Dictionary: A Guide to Knowledge as Power*, London: Zed Books.

—. (1997), 'Towards post-development: searching for signposts, a new language and new paradigms', in Rahnema, M. (ed.), *The Post-Development Reader*, London: Zed Books.

Sykes, S. (2006), *Power and Christian Theology*, London: Continuum.

Thatcher, T. (2009), *Greater than Caesar: Christology and Empire in the Fourth Gospel*, Minneapolis: Fortress Press.

Williams, R. (2009), *Relating Intelligently to Religion*, retrieved on 4 August 2010, <www.guardian.co.uk/commentisfree/belief/2009/nov/12/faith-development-rowan-williams>.

# 3

# Christian Mission at the Crossroads of Development: Biblical and Magisterial Perspectives

Jacob Kavunkal SVD

## Introduction

As the community of the disciples of Lord Jesus committed to continue his mission, we find that every new day is a challenge for 40 per cent of our sisters and brothers of the world population, with inadequate food and shelter; with no health care systems; not knowing how to read and write; not having an employment to earn a living; and with little prospects of improving their harrowing situations of dehumanization, humiliation and shame. This is aggravated by a process of awareness building that has filtered down through to the bottom of most societies due to various technological developments and communication, and this in turn makes the existing conditions doubly unbearable, frequently leading to frustration and acts of violence like the Maoist movement in India.

The relation between development and mission has been a moot point of discussion in missiological circles since the second half of the twentieth century, even though works of charity have always been considered integral to Christian practice. The Christian social tradition is a tradition of thinking and acting, as the manifestation of the ethical intuition and commitment to the Gospel. Understanding of the Christian mystery that inspires social commitment has attracted deeper reverence from the majority of Christians since the end of the nineteenth century. According to the North American theologian Frederick Herzog (1988, p. 46), this expresses God's closeness to history.

Our age is experiencing the need to build up a just and fraternal world, and it is looking for a better understanding of the complex problems of development and social justice and the way the world is functioning. The community of the disciples of Lord Jesus needs biblically based theological principles to guide the link between development and social justice.

What this chapter tries to present is a firm scripturally based framework for development without the spiritual/physical wedge that normally bedevils theologizing. We will show how the Bible, both the Old and New Testaments, does advocate a transformational development.[1] Eventually, this chapter argues that the Christian mission is a manifestation of the transformational development with its relational emphasis accruing from the Kingdom ministry of Jesus Christ, as the manifestation of the transforming power of God. Though this chapter presumes a wider readership, it is written from a Catholic experience and relying on the Catholic social teachings.

Development is concerned with human beings and social systems so that they can organize their activities to satisfy their basic needs and non-material wants like education, knowledge, spiritual fulfilment and others in keeping with the basic human dignity, leading to the reduction of poverty, unemployment and inequality (Todaro and Smith, 2009, p. 12). Obviously, it is a question not only of income generation, but also of the quality of life as human persons with the freedom of choice to determine the course of one's life, with self-respect, triggering happiness.[2]

*Transformational development* is different from the Developmentalism that was in vogue in the post-World War Two days. The success of the United States (US) economy created a euphoria, leading to the presumption that economic growth was the key to the solution of poverty. US model economic development was recommended to all the poor countries across the world, with the presumption that if the third world countries abandoned their agricultural societies and industrialized, their expanded gross national product and the subsequent improved status in international trade would relieve them of their national poverty. However, this whole developmental theory did not take into account how the US and other major powers through the Marshall Plan gained access to trade relations with Africa and South America, who held colonial ties with major European countries in exchange for aid to Europe for post-war reconstruction. This in turn moved the natural resources from the poorer nations to the richer nations. 'The "new economy" of development theory developed "centres" or richer economies and "periphery" or dependent economies', observes Judith Merkle (2004, p. 113). The resources, balance of trade and brain power were monopolized in a dependent relationship with the first world, ending development, with increased poverty. This, along with the conviction that some nations are poor, not because they failed to develop, but because they have been prevented by others from doing so, and the conviction that how large segments of populations are excluded from active participation in shaping the social, economic, and political structures, has popularized the terminology of liberation over development, more so under the impact of liberation theology, which seeks to bring the Gospel to the concrete struggle for human liberation and social transformation. Poverty is not just a question of underdevelopment or the fruit of laziness; rather, it is the result of a well-laid out social system, though unjust, with its vice-like grip.

Today all would agree that no civilized people can feel satisfied when a section of their fellow humans exist in conditions of such absolute human misery, and this is reflected in the emphasis every religion places on the importance of working for the alleviation of poverty and inequality.

## Biblical Perspectives

### Old Testament

The biblical revelation begins with God's self-manifestation in relation to the dehumanized situation of some people (Exod. 3:6-7). Later, due to their unfaithfulness, Israel suffers exile from which they are restored to their land under the Persian emperor Cyrus. When we examine the prophetic literature, we see how the all-important theme is that of justice towards the poor (Isa. 58:6-7; Jer. 9:24; Hos. 2: 19; Amos 4:1; 5:24; Mic. 6:8). The God of the Bible is a God of justice, bringing peace through justice insofar as it is distributive justice that seeks all to have enough to live. God is just because God stood against the Egyptian Empire to save some doomed slaves. God prefers justice to injustice, righteousness to unrighteousness, and therefore God is liberator. This ancient Jewish tradition was destined to clash with the Roman commercialization, urbanization and monetization in the first-century Jewish homeland (Crossan, 1999, p. 182).

For ancient Near Eastern peoples, land played a key role in their lives.

> We can see a tension within the attitudes towards land tenure in the ancient Near East. On the one hand, there was the recognition that land was a unique resource that must receive special regulation in order to prevent the ruin of the people. On the other hand, there was a movement toward greater individual freedom in the use and disposal of the land, allowing for the possibility of latifundism (agribusiness) and the pauperization of masses of people. It appears that the ancient Near East was pulled in the latter direction, and it was in such a context in which Israel came into being. (Fager, 1987, p. 27 cited in Crossan, 1999, p. 182).

This could have been the background of the Jubilee legislation enshrined in Lev. 25. The logic behind divine justice is human equality, radical egalitarianism that manifests in specific laws. Inequality among God's people is insistently shown to be against the justice of God. God is against indebtedness, control, enslavement and dispossession. Equality and egalitarianism are constitutive of biblical thinking. The core message of the Old Testament is that, 'Israel's God is the one true God of all the earth and all nations because this God alone is a God of justice and righteousness for those systematically vulnerable, for the weak, the orphan, the lonely, the destitute and the needy' (Crossan, 1999, p. 208).

Though Israel was restored to its own land from exile in Babylonia, it continued to experience suffering under foreign overlords, a suffering interpreted as punishment for Israel's sins. Hence, the promise of forgiveness, spoken by the exilic prophets like Isaiah, Jeremiah and Ezekiel, continued to ignite the mind of Israel, making the post-exilic prophets speak of the liberation still to be completed (Wright, 1996, p. xvii). They described this liberation by employing the language of the return from exile: the new exodus. It is against this background that Jesus announced that God's reign is at hand (Mk 1:14)—the very centre of his mission.

## Jesus' Ministry

The coming of the Kingdom of God was not a matter of abstract ideas or timeless truths or a sort of new religion, a doctrine or a soteriology, but was the pinnacle of Israel's story and its climax, its decisive moment (Wright, 1999a, p. 35). However, at the same time, Jesus was gripped by a strong sense of vocation from God whom he experienced as 'Abba', implying a specific role as the Son. In this sense, his mission was manifesting the Father (Jn 12:45; 14:9). Through all that he did and said, Jesus not only manifested God but also showed how God's reign was breaking in and through him, through his ministry.

At the time of a tense and unstable political situation in Palestine under the Roman rule and in the context of Galilee becoming more urban and cosmopolitan, there was a crisis of culture and uncertainty. The Roman rule made life for the Jews the antithesis of everything they believed about themselves and their relationship with God. The imperial Roman theology claimed the emperor as God and Roman culture as the unifying element of the empire. At this time of change and crisis, hopes about God's reign and God's messiah were high. The Jesus movement was in sharp contrast to the Roman urbanization that dislocated the common rural folk, pushing them from poverty to destitution. Jesus' primary focus was on the peasants dispossessed by Roman commercialization and Herodian urbanization in the late twenties in lower Galilee (Crossan, 1999, p. 325).

The coming of the Messiah as presented by the gospels was radically different from the way people had understood God and God's ways. God does not come in clouds of glory, but in a way unimportant and unrecognized.

Even Jesus' own family does not understand what is happening (Mk 3:21). At about 30 years of age, he left his work and his family and inspired a group of people that was willing to leave everything and journey with him. He wandered the countryside for about 1 to 3 years preaching, teaching and healing. The central point was that God's reign has broken into history through him and in him. This he manifested in the most unconventional ways: he touched the untouchables and he stood against systemic injustice, particularly that of the religious institutions; he showed that God is not pleased by the blind following of laws of rituals and ritual purity, but by entering into the lives of the victims of these laws, whom he characterized as the little ones: the blind, the lame, the leprosy-affected, the elderly, those with bodily oozing, those who knew nothing of the law, the poor, those who mourn, hunger, the persecuted, widows, . . . the list goes on. Through all these he showed how the divine reign, foretold and passionately hoped for by the prophets, was manifesting itself. It is a time when the oppressed go free, when those who are bound are set at liberty and when the blind receive sight. He showed through his ministry how the Kingdom would look and how his followers could associate themselves with him in this work by reversing the situations of those who mourn, who hunger and so on.

The Matthean beatitudes have been traditionally spiritualized to encourage the poor and those suffering to continue in their dehumanized situation, but promising a spiritual reward! Warren Carter (2000), however, has convincingly argued that the Matthean gospel is a counter-narrative, standing over against the status quo of the domineering imperial power and synagogue control. In this vision, the first part of the beatitudes (Mt. 5: 3-6) refers to righteousness and the oppressive situations of distress, which God's reign will reverse as shown in the second part (vs. 7–10). The first part critiques the political, economic, social, religious and personal distress that results from the powerful elite, who enrich their own position at the expense of the poor who mourn and hunger for righteousness, who are meek because they are helpless. The remaining four beatitudes are concerned with human actions to reverse the situation of the poor. Through the human actions of compassion, mercy, justice, and disinterested service, God manifests God's reign; they enact God's purposes for just societal relations. Thus the poor will experience the coming of the Kingdom (Carter, 2000, pp. 136–9).

## The Lucan Manifesto

The Lucan inaugural proclamation of Jesus (4:18-19) is considered to be a sort of manifesto of Jesus. It is linked with the great Jubilee year that is described in Lev. 25:10-17 insofar as the text Jesus quoted, Isa. 61:1-2, was the synagogue reading for the celebration of the Jubilee. By quoting this very passage Jesus is claiming how the Jubilee, the acceptable year of the Lord, has come in him. The Jubilee was good news to the poor insofar as the main ingredients of Jubilee were the return of the land as well as freeing the slaves and giving them sufficient means of livelihood. The poor benefited by the arrival of Jubilee. It was a divine revolution to retrieve the original equality and fraternity, which the Israelites enjoyed when all had their own fig trees and vineyard (1Kgs 4:25), a symbolic expression of social and economic well-being. Due to human weakness, this ideal situation could be destroyed. However, Yahweh did not want such an unnatural situation to continue endlessly and hence, we have the Jubilee prescription.

At the time of Jesus, the poor, the blind, the lame and the bonded were eking out a dehumanizing existence insofar as they had to beg for their livelihood—they were not considered to be fully human. Jesus not only quoted Isaiah but also systematically carried out his claim of ushering in the year of the Lord, through his healings and other symbolic gestures like the oft-repeated all-inclusive table fellowship, thereby manifesting that the poor of any sort are restored to their human dignity and reinstated into the society. The many table-fellowships of Jesus described in the gospels, in the words of G. S. Key (1983, p. 85) 'are not only a well-known, historically certain feature of his ministry, but a highly significant feature as well'. Crossan (1994), one of the best of the *Historical Jesus* scholars, upholds open commensality as a leading aspect of Jesus' ministry. Crossan (1994, p. 71) writes: 'Open commensality is the symbol and embodiment of radical egalitarianism, of an absolute equality of people that denies the validity of any discrimination between them and negates the necessity of any hierarchy among them'. Joachim Jeremias (1971) too writes about the significance of the frequently held Table Fellowships of the Lord:

> They are an expression of the mission and message of Jesus (Mk 2:17), eschatological meals, anticipatory celebrations of the feast in the end time (Mt. 8:11 par.), in which the community of saints is already being represented (Mk 2:19). The inclusion of sinners in the community of salvation, achieved in the table fellowship, is the most meaningful expression of the message of the redeeming love of God (Jeremias, 1971, pp. 115–16).

Even the Johannine gospel, the object of frequent spiritualization by commentators, has to be understood from this perspective of justice and righteousness to the poor. The key text used for the spiritual understanding of John is 3:16: 'God so loved the world . . . whoever believes in him should not perish but have eternal life'. However, this verse is to be read along with the following verses, more so vs. 20:

> For all who do evil hate the light, and do not come to the light, lest their deeds should be exposed. But those who do what is true come to the light, that it may be clearly seen that their deeds have been wrought in God.

It is an engagement with the world choosing the deeds of light over those of evil. It is a question of how one responds to people and structures that are dark, evil and bring death to the world.

Jesus not only cures the leprosy-affected person but also makes sure that he is reinstated into the society (Mk 1:44). He does not allow human relationships to be derailed due to sickness or bodily situations. His ministry was the definitive divine revolution of recapturing the original equality and acceptance, a society without discrimination and hierarchization.

## Human Centred Ministry

From what has been said so far, it is already clear how the ministry of Jesus was centred on human beings. In fact the very Incarnation, the single most important aspect of Christianity, was the affirmation of the human person, for as the Second Vatican Council document *Gaudium et Spes* insisted, through his Incarnation, Jesus united himself with every human being (GS 22), with whom, I would suggest, he was united already at the moment of creation. Hence, the Incarnation is the affirmation of the glory and dignity of the human person. Donal Dorr (2007) argues how the title 'Son of Man' has actually to be translated as 'the Human One' (ho huios tou antropou), which in turn is the affirmation of the humanity that Jesus shared with every single individual. Dorr (2007, p. 24) goes on to say: 'The title may even hint that Jesus is "THE human" – one who is the epitome of humanity'. Thus, Jesus is the representative and fulfilment of humanity's aspirations. Not only what Jesus was, but also all that he did, point to how humans are to live a full human life with all its glory and dignity.

Jesus' oft-repeated breaking of the Sabbath laws is in fact a relativizing of the Divine in terms of the human person. For the Jews, the Sabbath rules could not be broken since they were given by God, the Absolute. But Jesus' standard attitude is, the Sabbath is made for human beings, that is, for their well-being (Mk 2:27).

Similarly, the purity pollution laws too are to be seen in the context of the significance of the human person. Jesus touched women (Mk 1:21), touched leprosy-affected people (Mk 1:41), called the polluted and polluting woman who touched him, 'My daughter', (Mk 5:34), defended the woman caught in adultery (Jn 8:3-11), accepted the hospitality of a tax collector (Lk. 19:1f.) and so on.

Jesus showed how the way to God is through the neighbour (Mt 25:31-46). In fact, as far as the final judgment is concerned, the way we treat the neighbour is the only thing that counts. The Christian specificity is this concern for the human person, the neighbour, anyone who is wounded in any way (Lk. 25:30-37). Restoring the dignity of the human person was his mission manifesto as we saw; it is his very identity as the Messiah (Lk. 7:22-23).

Daniel Groody (2007, p. 49) draws attention to how Jesus, by becoming a Galilean, identifies himself with a rejected group so that he can reveal the lie of the world that degrades human beings. Jesus showed how the reign of God is the radical inclusion of all, by welcoming all, especially those whom the world of his time rejected (Lk. 14:13-14). A sector that he showed special concern for was that of the women in the society. The typical outlook on women at the time of Jesus is manifested in the thanksgiving by Jewish men that God had not made them women! (Megilla, 2007, p. 122).

At the time of Jesus, the wife was considered to be her husband's property and in many ways disadvantaged (Gnilka, 1997, p. 64). Yet Jesus, contrary to the prevailing presumption, pronounces how a man can commit adultery against his wife, and this was revolutionary (Mt 19:9). We have already spoken of the compassionate way Jesus treated women.

Jesus was speaking in terms of the Jewish hopes of the times, viz., Israel's God is ushering in God's reign, which affects the entire world in its space and time (Wright, 1996, p. 203). Wright (1999, p. 38) elsewhere shows how, when the Jews looked forward to the coming of God's Kingdom, they did not think of the end of the space-time world, but rather that God is going to act dramatically within the space-time world, as he had done at the time of the Exodus. Jesus was showing how divine reality is breaking into their midst, doing what they have been longing for, through his very presence and ministry.

Further, the use of the Kingdom symbol did not always imply a resurrection or life after death insofar as Israel's basic world view did not imply them. Hence, the priority of making the salvation of souls as the aim of our mission cannot be fully justified. This does not mean a rejection of the latter; it only reminds us of how mission has to be integral as Jesus' mission was, culminating in his resurrection, manifested also in his promise to the thief at his right on the cross, 'Today you shall be with me in paradise' (Lk. 23:43), a salvation that Jesus describes elsewhere as having come already due to a changed life and social outlook (Lk. 19:9).

Jesus not only taught about the Kingdom, but enacted it in his own life and ministry through symbolic acts like the table-fellowships, dealings with women, healings, forgiving, feeding, casting demons and so on. Through these symbolic deeds and teachings, he was not only presenting a new vision of the Kingdom, but also, at the same time, challenging other visions of the Kingdom like those of the Pharisees and Essenes. In contrast to the traditional expectations of the Kingdom as a time of perfect adherence to the cultic rules (Sadducees), or the meticulous observance of the law (Pharisees), or the following of the monastic life of the Qumran community (Essenes), or a radical direct divine intervention (Apocalyptic hopes) or a violent revolution (Zealots), Jesus showed that the Kingdom is a matter of radical love and communion. When others saw God's forgiveness in terms of the temple and cult, for Jesus it was welcoming the sinner, dining with them and accepting the unacceptable and unconditional forgiveness like that of the prodigal Father. In Jesus, God celebrates all that God has been and is. As Diarmuid O'Murchu (2005, p. 5) has underlined, the divine involvement with humans that started 6 million years ago when the first humans appeared on the face of the earth and with that human salvation as well reaches its fulfilment in Jesus Christ.

## Kingdom and Salvation

Though we already had the occasion to see the Kingdom in the context of the Jewish expectations, we still need to speak about the traditional understanding of salvation associated with Jesus' ministry, and more so with his death and resurrection.

Redemption was the central concept of Israel's religion and life. Beginning with Exod. 6:6, there is an overwhelming understanding of the divine restoration, reflected in various biblical texts. The idea of redemption is reflected in no less than 150 verses of the Bible (Metzger, 1991, pp. 1040–1). This in turn makes the eschatological hope of YHWH's saving intervention or visitation the focus of Israel's faith, in the context of the lived experience of evil, represented by foreign rule. For Israel, what was important was their understanding of redemption as an existence of original equality and fraternity and as described in I Kgs 4: The prophecies made in the context of the deportations and exile, to console the people, lead to the hope of a future Messiah—redeemer. He need not have been a divine person; in fact, Cyrus is described as a redeemer in Isa. 45.1.

The three central aspects of the traditional hopes were the return from exile, the defeat of evil represented by foreign rule and the return of YHWH to Zion. These Jesus applied to himself through his prophetic Kingdom announcement (Wright, 1999b, p. 80). The long night of exile, the present evil age would give way to the dawn of renewal and restoration, the age to come. This hope was associated with the royal settings, the king who would come would be the agent through whom YHWH would accomplish this great renewal (Zech. 1:8). This royal connotation had links also with the Temple as the central theme as exemplified by David, Solomon, Hezekiah and Josiah. Judas Maccabaeus gave rise to a priestly and royal dynasty by cleansing the Temple. 'Temple and kingship went hand in hand', points out Wright (1996, p. 483). Jesus' triumphal entry into Jerusalem, riding on a donkey, and his actions in the temple, constituted the messianic praxis. John Meier (1979, p. 99) writes: 'Jesus' entry into Jerusalem and the cleansing of the temple constituted a messianic demonstration, a messianic critique, a messianic fulfilment event, and a sign of the messianic restoration of Israel'. This in turn alarmed the chief priests who ruled the Temple and thus the Jewish religion and nation indirectly. Jesus' symbolic action spoke unmistakably to the priests who were well versed in texts like Zech. 9.9f. The first-century mainstream Jewish leaders, the self-styled guardians of the Jewish faith, decided to eliminate him and they did it with the help of the Roman administration. The ministry of the Lord culminates on the cross. However, the God who affirmed him to be God's Son and thus affirmed his ministry at the time of the baptism at Jordan (Mk 1:11) and at the time of the transfiguration on a high mountain (Mk 9:7), now intervenes and raises him up and thus definitively affirming him and his ministry (Acts 2:22-24).

The disciples who had abandoned him at the crucifixion regroup themselves in the light of their Easter experience. Easter is the key to the recognition of Jesus as the Messiah. However, this recognition raises the question of how the Messiah could die on the cross, a curse according to Deuteronomy (21:22). Hence, we come across the explanation why Jesus died for our sins; he became a curse for us (1 Cor. 15:3; Gal. 3:13) to fulfil the scriptures.

Though according to the gospels, the Incarnation took place as part of the divine plan, rooted in God's love and Jesus' being put to death, in Neil Ormerod's (2007, p. 90) words, it 'was the result of a fairly grubby story of power and politics, of enemies and rivalries, of people who very early in the ministry of Jesus set out to destroy him, discrediting his teaching and his mission (Mark 3:6)', Scripture scholars interpreted Pauline writings as an act of atonement (Rom. 3:25), a justifying act (Rom. 5:9). This has been further buttressed by the 'cup of blood . . . sign of forgiveness' (Mt. 26:28). However, as Dominic Crossan and Jonathan L. Reed (2004, p. 381) have shown, for Paul, divine righteousness refers to distribution and not retribution. God's justice is God's righteousness. God does what is just by doing what is right. God *is* justice, that is, righteousness, it is the very character of God. Crossan and Reed (2004, p. 382) argue that the modern confusion regarding justification arises due to a wrong interpretation of justice, that is, rather than seeing it as distributive, it is seen as retributive, based on the modern law courts. In the Hebrew Scriptures, the primary and basic meaning of God's justice is distributive. When justice is done by humans by distribution, retribution follows.

Similarly, the cup of forgiveness is to be understood in the context of forgiveness in the gospels. As Wright (1999, p. 273) has stressed, forgiveness is the sign of the return of YHWH, the eschatological times. Through the cup Jesus asserts it is already now. The gospels attribute Jesus' conflict with the authorities to his human-centred interpretation of the law, his forgiving sins and his attack on the Temple and the authorities, and these in turn precipitate his arrest and execution. The subsequent theological reflection to a large extent focused on the images contained in the Pauline writings. Tertullian (1977, pp. 299–300) (ca. 160) developed the notion of ransom. Gregory of Nazianzus questioned this motive of ransom, but Gregory of Nyssa justified it by saying that it was a sort of deceiving the devil! Origin made it a sacrifice, prompting God to grant propitiation and pardon for sins (Ormerod, 2007, pp. 94–5). Today, as Wright (1999, p. 105) has shown, by and large, scripture scholars like Meier, Sanders, Chilton, Crossan and others would link Jesus' death with the Kingdom proclamation and his action in the Temple. If at all we want to talk about the salvation from sin that Jesus brought about, it is that of the overcoming of selfishness. It is a transition from self- centredness to other centredness. Selfishness is the root of all sin that we come across everywhere, including among Christians.

## Social Teaching of the Catholic Church

The modern social teachings of the Catholic Church were occasioned by the deplorable conditions of the poor in the wake of the industrial revolution and the emergence of capitalism that forced the Church to search for justice as a fresh expression of its own mission and service to the world. The enormous human suffering resulting from the unresolved issues of industrialization and the rise of socialism and communism challenged the Church to play a proactive role, leading to Pope Leo XIII's encyclical, *Rerum Novarum* (RN) (New Order of Things) of 1891. The encyclical led the way to the new concept of 'social justice', where justice is applied to structural questions such as the relationship between capital and labour; the family; the state; equality and inequality; and ownership (Merkle, 2004, p. 93). The encyclical deplored the conditions of the working class where 'a very few rich and exceedingly rich men have laid a yoke almost of slavery on the unnumbered masses of non-owning workers' (RN 6) and argued for the workers' right for a living wage for a family rather than a wage determined by the law of supply and demand and pleaded for healthy working conditions.

*Rerum Novarum* became a trailblazer for a series of teachings on the social mission of the Church from the Catholic Magisterium. On the fortieth anniversary of RN, Pope Pius XI came out with another equally powerful encyclical, *Quadragesimo anno* (QA) (Fortieth Year), occasioned by the Great Depression, the consolidation of the Russian Revolution and the emergence of fascist dictatorships in Italy and Germany. The Pope emphasized the centrality of human dignity as the basis of all human rights. Pius XI argued that all must receive their due share in the distribution of created goods according to the demands of common good and social justice (QA n 58).

Both RN and QA were concerned with the conditions of the workers and the poor in the *first* world. This was rectified by Pope John XXIII (1961) in his encyclical *Mater et Magistra* (Mother and Teacher). The Pope extended the notion of welfare for the poor beyond the capitalist system, and internationalized the Catholic social teaching saying: 'Perhaps the most pressing question of our day concerns the relationship between economically advanced commonwealths and those that are in process of development. The former enjoy the conveniences of life; the latter experience dire poverty' (MM n 157). John XXIII's *Pacem in Terris* (Peace on Earth) (1963) outlined new avenues of social justice in light of major changes across the globe. The Pope recognized freedom and human rights as the foundation of the social order.

John XXIII's approach is continued in the Ecumenical Council, Vatican II that he convoked. Of all the decrees and declarations of the Council, *Gaudium et Spes* (GS) (Pastoral Constitution on Church) deserves special mention as it captures the Council's approach to the poor and the marginalized of the world. The very opening words speak volumes: 'The joys and hopes, the griefs and anxieties of the people of this age, especially those who are poor or in any way afflicted, those too are the joys and hopes, the griefs and anxieties of the followers of Christ'. GS warmly welcomes modern human longing for dignity, brotherhood, participation, freedom and equality. It encourages the social movements that embody those legitimate aspirations (n 41). God intended the earth and all that it contains for the use of every human being and people. 'If a person is in extreme necessity, that person has the right to take from the riches of others what that person needs', and exhorts all individuals and governments to 'Feed the people dying of hunger, because if you have not fed them you have killed them' (n 69). There cannot be true peace without a just economic world order. The distinctive contribution of Vatican II was the way in which it brought the whole social ministry to the centre of the Catholic Church's mission through the Pastoral Constitution, GS.

*Populorum Progressio* (On the Development of Peoples) (1967), Pope Paul VI's social encyclical, refers to the 'political pressure and economic domination, aimed at maintaining or acquiring control of a few' (n 57). Integral human development, a development of the whole person and of all persons and peoples is a guide towards social action. The importance of basic education and literacy is the key that enables people to assume responsibility for themselves, their lives and their world. Paul VI constituted the social wing of the Catholic Church, the Pontifical Commission of Justice and Peace. The Synod of Bishops 1971, declared how action on behalf of justice and participation in the transformation of the world is constitutive of the Church's mission. In the encyclical *Octogesmo Adveniens* (OA) (A Call to Action) (1971), Paul VI recognized clearly the significance of political activity for solving economic and social problems (OA n 50).

John Paul II (1981) in the encyclical *Laborem Exercens* (On Human Work) affirmed the priority of labour over capital and called for respect for human subjectivity and the dignity of the human person in the organization of labour and production. In *Sollicitudo Rei Socialis* (On Social Concern), John Paul (1987) called for solidarity as a remedy for the growing isolation of people from ties that would generate concern for the neighbour. Community formed through solidarity is related to sustainable development. Good society is not only a growing domestic product but it also includes a better quality of family life and friendship, satisfaction with work, more leisure and a sense of spiritual richness. John Paul II called for a moral understanding of development that includes the trajectory of human growth towards otherness and depth that is inherent in the Catholic social tradition (SRS 28). The Pope reiterated his call for a change of life style, of models of production and consumption and of the established structures of power that govern societies, in his encyclical *Centesimus Annus* (Hundredth Year) (1991).

The social teaching of the Church is not just a listing of principles for social action, not strategies to solve problems of poverty, welfare, environment, globalization and others and not even the social action itself. It is much more complex. It could be described as the Church's effort to provide a systematic normative theory relating to the social vision of the faith to the concrete conditions in which faith is lived. 'It is an act of the church in context', comments Merkle (2004, p. 12).

## The Social Mission of the Church

In continuation with the Jewish apocalyptic vision, the primitive community saw the resurrection of Christ as ushering in the 'new age', the celestial world completely ruled by God, already now, as opposed to 'this age', which is sin-dominated. The full manifestation of the new age would take place at the second coming of Christ, and it was expected to be imminent. However, with the transition from the primitive community to the early community, we see the Hellenistic world view gradually mingling with the apocalyptic vision. The Hellenistic world view contained another dualism: that of the world of the senses and that of true understanding, the intelligible world, the spiritual world and the world of the senses. Through his ascension to the spiritual world, Jesus Christ becomes the mediator between the spiritual and the sensible worlds. The whole theology of victory over death is developed in the context of the Hellenistic dualism, of the world of the senses and the spiritual, the world of matter as opposed to the transcendent world. Whereas, Jesus brought a salvation connected with life on earth, now it is transferred to the other world! Hence, we can speak of the need to retrieve the prophetic ministry of the Lord that was affirmed by his resurrection.

The prophetic service of the Church is the logical sequence to its call and mandate to follow its Lord, who identified himself as a prophet (Mk 6:4, Mt. 13:57; Lk. 4.24). The Church has to judge itself by the content of its ministry rather than the content of its doctrinal claims. It is not primarily the cult and the institution that make the Church what it is, but its continuation of the ministry of its Lord. It has to draw inspiration from the life and ministry of the Jesus as in history and has to identify itself with the cause for which he was killed and was raised again. We have seen how he had neither time nor interest in moving among the religious leaders of the time whose only concern was their own belly and their image. In fact, his strongest woes are pronounced against them (Mt. 23:13ff). He was, by contrast, in constant fellowship with the little ones and the 'no-people', weighed down by the burdens imposed upon them by the religious rulers.

At the heart of the whole theology of involvement in development is the Christian faith in the truth that humans are created in the image of God and God has entered into a covenant relationship with all human beings. This human dignity calls for certain rights and freedoms that enable humans to live as humans. In other words, the mystery of humans cannot be understood without the mystery of God.

The Church exists above all to be at the service of the poor and the victims of society, so that they can experience the fruits of the arrival of the acceptable year of the Lord (Lk. 4:19). Wherever and whenever artificial dependency is created in the socio-economic or even in religious fields for the benefit of the powerful, it generates dehumanization. This is compounded by laws of ritual pollution or laws that segregate sectors of humanity as permanently impure. This has no logical basis, but it is a sheer figment of the mind. Though God created them in God's own image (Gen. 1:26), this image is irrecognizably disfigured in them due to the inhuman treatments that they have to endure. The urgent need of any 'God-talk' today is the recovery of human dignity for these people.

Commenting on Jesus' association with the outcasts, Roger Haight (1999, pp. 106–7) argues: 'It seems fairly certain that Jesus directed his attention to people who stood outside the margins of society, and that this was a disturbing factor in his ministry and message for the religiously upright'. We saw how Jesus, through his association with sinners and tax collectors, became the externalization of the divine in rapport with the human. God's action in history is primarily manifested through his involvement with those on the margins and the dehumanized.

If Jesus' main concern was saving people from alienation, marginalization and negation and to restore them to wholeness, the Church's route should not be any different. Jesus needs followers for the mediation of God's compassionate love to all those who suffer, all those who are oppressed and all those who are forced to the margins. It is the project that he has bequeathed to the community of his disciples in the world, God's plan for history.

Jesus' mission is to be read in the context in which we live, in which human suffering and marginalization are crystallized into forms of oppression imposed by human beings on other innocent human beings. Human suffering has to become the focus of Church's service today. This, as Haight (1999, p. 26) rightly emphasizes, is 'not because Christology will bear messianic solution to these problems, but because Jesus cannot be the Christ and salvation cannot be real without having some bearing on this situation'. The God manifested in his ministry is not a God who is inviolable, but the God ready to go through violation for the sake of the least and the lost. *Antodaya* (the rise of the least) is God's concern. We saw how this concern prompted Jesus to bypass laws regarding the Sabbath and purity-pollution. Moving in the same spirit, mission today has to be moulded in the experience of people.

What are to be dismantled today are not so much of religious differences as it was thought in the past, but the disgusting structures of dehumanization. These structures made Antony Raj (1988, p. 51), an Indian Dalit theologian write: 'I feel that it is better for us Dalits to die on our feet than live on our knees before insolent men'. Jesus, through his ministry of identification with the poor and challenge of the structures that keep them dehumanized, sets into motion the resistive forces that seek to challenge the social, cultural, economic and religious structures today.

'What do you want me to do for you?' (Mt. 20:32), Jesus asked the blind man. The dehumanized and marginalized poor of today are asking the Church: that we may see, so that we can live as human beings, accepted and respected as such; that we may have equal opportunities. It is the blindness of the powerful of the society that condemns these to lead lives bereft of human dignity. The Church's mission today, above all, is in this sphere of human existence. The poor want a share in decision-making so that they can benefit from the fruit of their labour and the product of their creativity.

If mission today does not take up the cry of the poor for the recovery of their lost human dignity and restore justice to them, it is empty of the Christian content that Jesus in his ministry had so much insisted upon. He is not concerned with the mediocre solutions of following the letter of the law but appeals to the generous depth of the human spirit, as we see in the case of the rehabilitation of the woman caught in adultery (Jn 8:3-11).

Our mission must be ruled by the methodological orientations of Jesus Christ, whose tireless concern for individuals left him with little time to eat or sleep (Jn 4:7ff). He spares no words over the arrogance of the official religious powers that had little regard for individuals (Mt. 23:13ff). The Church, collectively and as individuals, must renounce making use of power for crippling others, or for instrumentalizing and dehumanizing others. This could mean, for instance, religious and ecclesiastical authorities would not use power for subjugating the members of their congregation, but only to serve them (Mk 9:35). The Gospel should never become a power for domination and marginalization.

The prophetic hermeneutic of the Gospel in our times cannot tolerate any exploitative, divisive or oppressive force. The poor of our time must feel that the God of the Bible is with them and has heard their cry and seen their affliction (Exod. 3:7ff), through the creation of an egalitarian and participative society. Informed by the vision of Jesus in the Gospels, the community of his disciples must come to the aid of people who need to be helped. The basic objective of mission is not the future of Christianity or the Church, but the future of humankind as a whole plus that of planet Earth, which has come to be victimized as merely a resource to be plundered as much as possible to satisfy the greed and pleasure of the relatively few who can afford it. The earth, of which we are an integral part, also shares a lot of the disfigured and exploited poor, crying for recognition and restoration.

The social fabric of modern humanity is interwoven with two realms of existence: politics and religions. We must collaborate with both. A real concern and genuine care for the weak, the poor and the oppressed cannot be achieved fully without associating ourselves with political life; the empowerment of the weak and the dispossessed cannot be attained without political collaboration. Today we need a sort of political spirituality as exemplified by Mahatma Gandhi. In his first letter, Peter instructs Christians to always give an account of the hope that is in them (3:15-16). We have to ask ourselves how we can bring hope to the people. In the light of the praxis of Jesus, we cannot push that hope entirely to an eschatological level, something that happens 'when we die'. Christianity is not an alternative to this world; it is a guide to live well in this world so that this world itself can be transformed into the pre-figuration of the world to come. We have to insist on the salvific character of history and life in history. Our involvement in history must make God's presence effective. It is a question of the relation between salvation and liberation.

Mission today must change the perspective from the past crusade against other religions, including its aggressive proclamation with claims of exclusivism, to an effective solidarity with the suffering. It is a participation in the brokenness of people, in their hopes, disappointments and anxieties. Instead of an imposing and dominating attitude, we should have the spirit of fellow-pilgrims. As we stand in common origin and common destiny with the rest of people (*Nostra Aetate* 1), we are pilgrims along with them. In this pilgrimage of solidarity, we become people manifesting the God-experience in Jesus Christ. This in turn becomes an attraction, an invitation, a sharing in the form of storytelling, leaving the decision to the listener. That is the type of proclamation to which the modern world is ready to listen.

Jesus was interested in people and their problems. He backed up his preaching with the deeds of compassion and acceptance; he promoted the Jubilee spirit of equality, sharing, participation and reconciliation. Similarly, we are invited to shift our emphasis from an attitude of uniqueness to the God-experience and the living of the same experience. True, there is a danger that the God-experience can tend to remain on the vertical level and it is precisely here that Christianity can make its contribution: the true path to God is through the neighbour. Thus, mission becomes a process of mutual complementarity and harmony as Pope John Paul II (1999, n 6, p. 15) has taught.

Religions take pride in themselves and in their cultural values, but they are often open to mutual enrichment in the midst of the plurality of religions. This requires a greater awareness of the dignity of the individual. Modern massification tends to anonymity, leaving little room for the individual. As opposed to mass movements and mega media projects, Christians must remind themselves how Jesus' approach was personal, directed to the individual. Our society at every level and in every place requires this concern for the individual.

Today, like the prophets of the Old Testament, the Church must be able to read and interpret the signs of the times from God's viewpoint. This involves conflict and risk insofar as the message may go against the vested interests of the privileged and the powerful, the monopolizers of the riches of the world whose selfishness and callous blindness deprive many of their right to have the basic requirements for leading a life consonant with human dignity.

Prophetic service is two-sided, involving God and God's perspective as well as that of humans and human equality, which has been derailed by the greed and selfishness of the powerful. Hence, prophetic ministry is different from sheer social reform. Prophets provoke people to their true religious commitment where one cannot detach the divine from the human. Jesus' mission was certainly focused on God, whom he experienced as the intimate parent (*Abba*), but expressed in terms of his concern for the neighbour. It was a proclamation of the nature of humanity, derived from the nature of God. In other words, human beings and their life context is the field in which the Church has to exercise and manifest its mission. As Gustavo Guttierrez (2000, p. 184) has pointed out, mission is not only a question of geographic space but also a matter of human space as well. The 'human landscape' is the true locale of mission.

God is not a monster whose sole concern is self-glory, but the one who is honoured when a neighbour is accepted and respected. This is the greatest need today. One may say that we do not need new religions as much as living the existing religions according to the will of God, leading to the divine reign, the divine 'Household', God's future. The Christian role is not that of denying the validity of other religions, but of affirming the humanity of human beings. A Christian must be engaged with humanity and all that is related to it, because the God whom the Christian has experienced in Jesus Christ follows the same path. There is no Christian service divorced from human life in history.

The Christian preoccupation should not be over the 'right' religion that leads to God, but the right channels through which God reaches humans today. The latter becomes the test of the former. In the midst of injustices and oppression condemning millions to a dehumanized existence, God, as we have experienced in Jesus Christ, is not thinking of the embellishments of the liturgy or the niceties of the doctrinal formulations, but the elimination of the inhuman conditions in which the poor are embedded. Theology must express itself in a 'humanology' grappling with the human problems that we face today.

Most Scripture scholars would emphasize the apocalyptic character of the kingdom movement where the socially, politically and economically marginalized people experience the divine vindication. Following Jesus is not primarily a matter of believing Jesus' words, rather it is a matter of accepting Jesus' lifestyle, following his programme of ushering in the divine reign for the poor of our times, here and now. Albert Schweitzer (1970), Scripture scholar, realizing the true spirit of the mission of Jesus, gave up a teaching career in Europe and preaching religion, to become a medical doctor and serve the people of Africa, at the age of 35, for Schweitzer was convinced that eschatology in Jesus is apocalypsis, that is the end time in God's manifestation today, here and now. A similar picture emerges from the vision of Jan Jaworski, chief surgeon, Kundiawa Hospital, PNG, qualified in general surgery, orthopaedics and traumatology, vascular surgery and other medical fields, becoming a Catholic priest at the age of 44 to bring the blessings of the Kingdom to the people of PNG combining priesthood and medical profession.

When we are confronted with the spectre of starvation deaths, violence, the commoditization of human persons, international conflicts not infrequently ignited by the powerful nations of the world, global warming triggered by human consumerism, the diverting of food crops for the production of bio fuels and the spread of HIV/AIDS, we are reminded of God's concern: 'I have seen their affliction, I have heard their cry. . . . I am sending you to lead my people out of Egypt' (Exod. 3:7-10).

Struggling for the creation of a new humanity in the midst of suffering and dehumanizing forces is a key aspect of mission today. It is a struggle to win historical selfhood and subject-hood for the non-people of our times. The emerging new humanity can only be understood in the context of alienation, exploitation and marginalization. This makes the search for community inseparable from the search for new humanity. In the existing situation of the poor crushed by fears, fear of not having anything to eat, fear of eviction, fear of extortion and fear of violence, we cannot be in a genuine community. In the eyes of the powerful, the poor are the problem people. This is a gross misdesignation. The misdescribed and the dehumanized must be restored to their right to name the reality they experience. Naming the reality is the biblical symbol of empowerment (Gen. 2:19-20).

## Conclusion

This chapter is basically an attempt to integrate and apply Christian ministry in the light of the Bible and the teachings of the Catholic Church, challenging any dualism that bedevils normal Christian thinking, limiting God's transforming work to spiritual realities and assigning earthly matters to secular specialists. A truly holistic approach to Christian ministry rooted in biblical truth is essential to the Church's mission today. The God of justice and righteousness for all the earth, a God who stood on the side of the oppressed and the exploited, and opposed every form of systemic evil, is the God whom we encounter in the Bible. The same perspective is continued in the Kingdom ministry of Jesus, which was a distancing from any form of injustice and discrimination. People could experience what it might mean to be if God were ruling. In this perspective, engagement in development is proclaiming the gospel always, not in word but in deed. This aspect of the Christian mission is reflected in the teachings of the Catholic Magisterium, which can be summarized as: Between mission and development/liberation, there are three-fold links: anthropological, theological and evangelical. It is making the Gospel a good news to the people.

## Notes

1 I am influenced by Bryant L. Myers for the phrase transformational development.

2 In September 2000, the United Nations (UN) adopted eight Millennium Development Goals to be achieved by 2015: (1) eradicate poverty and hunger; (2) universal primary education; (3) equality of gender and empowerment of women; (4) reduce child mortality; (5) improved maternal health; (6) combat HIV/AIDS, malaria and other diseases; (7) sustainable environment and (8) global partnership (Todaro and Smith, 2009, p. 24).

## References

Carter, W. (2000), *Mathew and the Margins: A Sociopolitical and Religious Reading*, New York: Orbis Books.

Crossan, D. (1994), *Jesus: A Revolutionary Biography*, San Francisco: Harper.

—. (1999), *The Birth of Christianity: Discovering What Happened in the Years Immediately after the Execution of Jesus*, New York: Harper One.

Crossan, D. and Reed, J. L. (2004), *In Search of Paul. How Jesus's Apostle Opposed Rome's Empire with God's Kingdom: A New Vision of Paul's Words and World*, New York: Harper Collins.

Dorr, D. (2007), 'Christian mission and the millennium development goals', *Sedos Bulletin*, 39(1/2), 24.

Fager, J. A. (1987), 'Land tenure and the biblical jubilee', JSOT Series 155: Sheffield, 27, cited in Crossan, D. (1987) *The Birth of Christianity*.

Gnilka, J. (1997), *Jesus of Nazareth: Message and History*, Massachusetts: Hendrickson.

Groody, D. (2007), *Globalization, Spirituality and Justice*, New York: Orbis Books.

Guttierrez, G. (2000), 'Mission et I'signes des Temps', *Spiritus*.

Haight, R. (1999), *Jesus Symbol of God*, New York: Orbis Books.

Herzog, F. (1988), *God-Walk: Liberation Shaping Dogmatics*, Maryknoll, NY: Orbis Books.

Jeremias, J. (1971), *New Testament Theology: The Proclamation of Jesus*, London: SCM.

John Paul II, (1999), *Ecclesia in Asia*, Vatican: Libreria Editrice Vaticana.

Key, G. S. (1983), 'The table fellowship of Jesus: its significance for Dalit Christians in India today', *Jeevadhara* XIII.

Megilla, T. (2007), '4.11', in Burridge, R. (ed.), *Imitating Jesus: An Inclusive Approach to New Testament Ethics*, Grand Rapids: Eerdmans.

Meier, J. (1979), *The Aims of Jesus*, London: SCM.

Merkle, J. A. (2004), *From the Heart of the Church: The Catholic Social Tradition*, Collegeville, MI: Liturgical Press.

Metzger, B. M. (ed.) (1991), *New Revised Standard Version Exhaustive Concordance*, Nashville: Thomas Nelson.

O'Murchu, D. (2005), *Catching up with Jesus: A Gospel Story for our Time*, New York: Crossroad.

Ormerod, N. (2007), *Creation, Grace, and Redemption*, New York: Orbis Books.

Raj, A. (1988), 'Disobedience: a legitimate act for Dalit liberation', in A. Nirmal (ed.), *Towards a Common Dalit Theology*, Delhi: ISPCK.

Schweitzer, A. (1970), *On the Edge of the Primeval Forest*, London: Collins Fontana Books.

Tertullian, (1977), 'Disciplinary, moral and ascetical works', in H. Dressler (ed.), *Fathers of the Church*, 40, Washington, DC: University of America Press.

Todaro, M. P. and Smith, S. C. (2009), *Economic Development*, London: Addison-Wesley.

Wright, N. T. (1996), *Jesus and the Victory of God*, Minneapolis: Fortress Press.

—. (1999a), 'The mission and message of Jesus', in M. J. Borg and N. R. Wright (eds), *The Meaning of Jesus*. San Francisco: Harper.

—. (1999b), *The Challenge of Jesus: Rediscovering Who Jesus Was and Is*, Downers Grove: Intervarsity Press.

# PART TWO

# Theology of Mission and Development

# 4

# Fiji's Methodist Mission and Its Role in Development Through Education, Agriculture and Self-Governance in the Early Twentieth Century

Kirstie Close

## Introduction

This chapter identifies the ways in which the Methodist Mission in Fiji, particularly during the 1920s and 1930s, contributed to what may now be seen as the country's 'development'. This chapter will examine the role of the Mission in education, health care and industry. Often the Methodists, as the largest Christian denomination in Fiji, worked in liaison with the chiefs and the colonial administration to action development programmes. Historian Norman Etherington has suggested that missions were, in some cases, the 'pioneers of modern welfare states and international philanthropy' (Etherington, 2005, p. 261). As the largest Christian denomination in Fiji, the Mission assumed a key role in providing support to the growing infrastructure alongside the secular colonial administration. The missionaries fluctuated between a position of protectionism (often crossing the line to paternalism) and a push for modernity and 'civilisation'. Despite some tensions, ultimately the Mission and administration worked towards similar goals, but with different motives. This chapter looks at the Methodist Mission and how it collaborated with the colonial administration to 'develop' Fiji through the establishment of key infrastructure, mainly education, agriculture and health. The missionaries did not write about *developing* the islands, but instead spoke of civilization, and as the twentieth century loomed, the Mission's position generally reflected a push towards Western ideals of modernity. Despite differences in discourse, there were some similarities between Missionaries of the earlier centuries and modern development workers.

This chapter, though largely historical, engages with issues emerging in development studies focused on the Pacific. Ben Burt and Christian Clerk's (1997) edited text has been a useful launching point to link the Mission's work with modern concepts of development in the Pacific. The imposition of external ideas is an undercurrent throughout this chapter. Burt and Clerk suggested that Marxist and capitalist ideologies acted as a platform for many international development agencies entering the islands. The Methodist Mission was very similar, despite having different goals as compared to many modern non-government organizations (NGOs). Burt and Clerk (1997, p. 7) outlined the tenets of the Pacific Way as rural-focused, promoting self-reliance and local culture. While they suggest that this emerged in force in the 1970s, it is clear that some of these concepts underpinned the Mission's policies. Further, Suliana Siwatibau (1997, p. 35) discussed the strategy of modern NGOs working at a community level, promoting 'small scale entrepreneurial development and sustainable utilisation of resources'. While it can hardly be said that agricultural practices pushed by the missionaries in the early twentieth century were environmentally suitable and sustainable, there were certainly instances of small-scale entrepreneurial development in Fiji. These were generally considered a mode of empowering Fijians and Indo-Fijians economically, and therefore socially and politically. In this chapter, I attempt to draw out some of the Mission's policies on what we now would term as 'development' and how the Mission colluded with the colonial administration to convert these ideas into action. This chapter outlines the projection of capitalist, individualistic idealism onto the Fijian community as it morphed into a polarized society, with Indo-Fijians in equal number to Indigenous Fijians by the middle of the twentieth century yet remaining distinct from the Indigenous community. The missionaries navigated the local culture to try and gain the highest number of converts, and though claiming to (like the colonial administration) maintain traditional social organization, they ultimately advocated for change in areas that are now the focus of NGOs (health care, economic welfare and so on).

## The Mission and the Establishment of the Colonial Administration

Though focused on the conversion of Fijians to Methodism, missionaries played a crucial role in paving the way for the British colonial government, which was established some 40 years after the first European missionaries established a base in the islands. Unwittingly, Methodist missionaries were heavily involved in constructing the framework for infrastructure, which was furthered by the colonial administration, though they became savvier about this as Cession became a likelihood. One example of this was the way in which the Missionaries, and then the colonial administration, interacted with the chiefs. This is explored further on in this chapter. Both the Mission and the colonial administrators attempted to work (to an extent) within the traditional power structures to obtain influence. This was arguably one of the reasons why Methodism was popular, with its popularity reflected in high rates of conversion. By 1865, 15,000 Fijians professed the Methodist faith (Thornley, 2005, p. 136).

Fiji was a highly stratified society with several layers in the community hierarchy. The Missionaries' knowledge of the community system thus became a great benefit to the colonial establishment. For example, the *I tokatoka* organized operations of the *vanua* (people of the land) at the local village level. Above the *I tokatoka* were the *matanitu*, or the chiefs of the confederacies, who oversaw allied *vanuas*. (Routledge, 1985, p. 28). On arrival in Fiji in 1835, European missionaries established a system of operation whereby they liaised with the chief of a village. Once the chiefs' support was attained, it was much easier to convert the rest of the community—or so their theory went. Considering that the chiefs from the east of Fiji were particularly more powerful compared to those in the west, the missionaries sought their support and conversion. Traditionally, Fijian priests (*bete*) had been the only people to challenge the chiefs' authority, and as the Mission supplanted the priests through creating a literate religious authority, the Mission too challenged the chiefs (Mangubhai, 1987, p. 126). Fijian men were trained as ministers as early as the 1860s; however, their power was limited in the broader Mission structure (Thornley, 2005, p. 132). However, Fijian chiefs sometimes contributed to this change by inviting missionaries to establish schools in their village to ensure education for young men so that they could be employed with the colonial administration or the Mission (Thornley, 2002, p. 322). The status of the chiefs, therefore, was in a state of flux during these decades as the Mission sought to solidify its position in Fiji.

Officially, Methodist missionaries to Fiji had always hoped to see an independent Fijian church established, as it was one of the main tenets of Methodist Mission (Burton, 1923, p. 2). However, by the turn of the century and on into the twentieth century, authority within the church was firmly entrenched among the white missionaries. By doing so, the missionaries further solidified the chiefs' power (France, 1969, pp. 24, 30). The missionaries therefore originally supported and attempted to sustain the existing social standing of the chiefs.

Once the chief's support was attained, the missionaries set about spreading the word of the Lord to Fijian converts. The founder of the Wesleyan church John Wesley had advocated that the missionaries preach, teach and provide pastoral care, so this is exactly what William Cross and David Cargill aimed to do. At this early stage, there was little thought as to the ongoing development of an educational system in Fiji, though the Methodist Mission was to become instrumental in this area. The first school commenced at Lakeba in 1835, within a fortnight of David Cargill and William Cross' arrival—the first Wesleyan European missionaries to establish the Methodist Mission post in the Fijian Islands (Wood, 1978a, p. 35). There were classes for men and women, with the women's classes focusing on handicrafts such as sewing taught by Mrs Cargill. The missionaries employed the Glasgow teaching method when teaching men, which included 'instruction in scripture knowledge, reading, spelling, writing, arithmetic, geography, natural history and singing' (Thornley and Vulaono, 2002, p. 62). Schools were first established in order to teach Fijian converts to read the Bible, with the overarching goal of 'providing moral and spiritual nurture for the people' (Wood, 1978a, p. 28). Education was a means of evangelizing the community (Wood, 1978b, p. 46). Despite teaching geography, arithmetic and literacy, the missionaries' main focus was conversion rather than preparing the students for occupations beyond their school years (Wood, 1978a, p. 28). Schools were popular, with the numbers of students rising from 7,000 in 1855 to 27,000 in 1860 (Thornley and Vulaono, 2002, p. 191). Etherington (2005, p. 266) suggests that the main requirement in these schools was that the students learn how to read the Bible, especially in Protestant missions where individual interpretation of the Bible was deemed crucial.

From the 1840s until the 1860s, Fijian ministers were trained and ordained, with the first Fijian minister ordained in 1851 (Thornley, 2002, p. 132). However, the missionaries lost momentum in training the Fijians for ordination, due to lack of manpower but also reservations about the Fijians' potential for leadership (Thornley and Vulaono, 2002, p. 224). Historian Thornley (2002, p. 150) has argued that the 1860s saw a decrease in efforts made by the Mission Board to promote Indigenous leadership and governance. Fijian ministers held separate district meetings starting from 1866 (Thornley, 2002, p. 137) and then a Fijian division was created, separating the Fijian from the European branches in 1873 (Thornley, 2002, p. 140). Wage rates demonstrated Fijian ministers' limited status in the Mission, as while their European counterparts earned £160 per year, they received only £5 (Thornley, 2002, p. 137). During the 1930s, theological training went from being taught in both Fijian and English, to English only (Green, 1976, p. 156).

Both the colonial administration and the Mission were fixated on the island of Bau, an island off the south-east coast of Viti Levu. Historians have attributed Cakobau's eventual acceptance of Christianity with the Cession of Fiji to the British in 1874. Historian J. D. Legge (1958, p. 40) suggested that the Methodist Mission straddled allegiances between Cakobau and the Tongan chief Ma'afu, as the Mission relied heavily on support from Tongan missionaries, particularly in the Mission schools. Bau became the 'headquarters' of the Mission until 1902, when it moved to Suva. The Bible was translated into the Bauan language, standardizing the language and spreading its influence throughout the new Fijian Methodist communities (Mangubhai, 1987, p. 125). When Synod considering changes to the Mission's constitution in 1944, missionary Stan Cowled suggested that the continued presence of European missionaries on Bau would be 'good politics', but that when the 'old school' at Bau passed away he thought there would be big changes, and the political dynamics of Fiji would change. The Mission recognized Bau as a point of power from which they could draw influence.

The colonial administration, followed suite, making use of the Missions established connections, as well as tactics, from throughout the empire. Under Sir Arthur Gordon, the administration adopted 'indirect rule' to formulate its structure, inspired by its considered success in African colonies (France, 1969, p. xiii). Signing the Deed of Cession with Cakobau immediately placed Bau at the forefront of colonial politics. The establishment of the Council of Chiefs in 1876 as a consultative forum for the colonial administrators aimed to maintain ongoing Fijian input into the affairs of the colony, which was expanded with the inclusion of Fijian representatives on the Legislative Council in 1904 (Norton, 2009). These were problematic, of course, in that it only gave certain chiefs a voice but not others, and even the voices that were heard were severely hampered by the colonial administration's interests and mindsets.

The Mission had little power to oversee or govern their village schools, leaving the quality of teaching difficult to monitor. The introduction of the colonial administration, and its interest in education, offered an opportunity for increased regulation of Mission schools. This was increased gradually overtime. To start with, the British administration was satisfied to watch over Mission schools. While Governor Arthur Gordon had been impressed with village schools in the 1870s, by 1911, Weir (2003, p. 216) suggested that only an estimated 50 per cent of the Fijian population was literate. Gradually, the administration assumed more responsibility over the system, leading to the establishment of government schools. These schools typically catered to the children of the chiefs and tended to produce the colonies' Indigenous government representatives. The Queen Victoria School, established in 1906 by im Thurn was one example, as was the Adi Cakobau School, which was established in 1948 (Gaunder, 1999, p. 34).

The Mission schools then assumed the role of catering more to non-chiefly children. The 'commoners', as the Missionaries called the non-chiefly people of Fiji, accounted for the majority of the population, but the education provided to them was limited, by Western standards. In the previous decades, the missionaries tried to maintain alliances with the chiefs in order to continue their work successfully, and so had a vested interest in maintaining chiefly power. Until the establishment of Queen Victoria School, the colonial administration and the Methodist Mission colluded to sustain continuity between the old regime (traditional chiefly control) and the new (the colonial authority). While in some instances the Mission still supported maintaining the traditional system as much as possible, there were some significant projects assumed by the Mission Board that challenged the chiefly system established during the first few decades of the colonial era.

This can be attributed in part to a series of enquiries by the colonial administration into the decline of Fijian births (Jolly, 1998, p. 179). It was concluded that this was due, in part, to women assuming the heavy jobs of men, as men were emasculated by a new, less rigorous lifestyle under the colonial rule. This was in addition to the impact of diseases such as tuberculosis and smallpox. A Commission into the dropped birth rate in 1896 concluded that the communal system must be subverted. One way in which this could be achieved, it was suggested, would be through enticing men into more robust activity and industry (Thomas, 1990, p. 156). The report was calling for the modernization and development of Fiji. The recommendation to subvert the communal system allowed the denigration of the traditional social structure. The missionaries interpreted this in a similar way to the colonial administration (MacNaught, 1974, pp. 3–4); as an opportunity to advocate the individualist, democratic principles on which the Methodist Church was based. Typically, the chiefs oversaw the villagers, all of whom contributed to the functionality of the village. They had set tasks and responsibilities. Each did their role to contribute to the community as a whole. The colonial administration under Sir Arthur Gordon had attempted to incorporate the communal system in the legislation, by building a communal framework for taxation and, under successive governors, applying additional taxes to those who left the villages (Ward and Kingdon, 1995, p. 213).

The missionaries' encouragement of increased individuality was reflected through the development of boarding schools, which separated the students from their villages. Though it was a part of life for British colonials, boarding school was an unfamiliar concept for Fijian students. One such boarding school was established in 1899 for girls at Nailaga. The school was called Matavelo. The school's goals included instruction in 'sewing, the care of the sick, the care of children, the English language, and sanitation' (*Missionary Review*, 1918, pp. 13–14). The education provided at Matavelo focused on delivering instruction on how to be good Western-styled mothers, rather than preparing young girls for roles in varied professions. The Colonial

Secretary closed by saying that the overall learning of the students was not as important as the 'decent habits and ideas that are instilled'.

Despite the sometimes-divergent paths of the Mission and colonial administration in education, the Mission sought the assistance of the colonial administration for its schools in a number of ways. There was a dialogue between the administration and the Mission about the construction of the educational system, such as teacher training. For example, in 1915, the Mission responded to a government report on its District schools. The Assistant Commissioner who authored the report echoed complaints made by the administration in earlier years, finding that over half of the 86 Mission schools to be 'carried on by incompetent teachers' who were in fact local preachers 'and others'. Noting an overall lack of potential teachers, the Mission sought assistance from the District and Assistant Commissioners in procuring more candidates for the Circuit Training Institution. To attract teaching staff, the Mission also requested that the candidates be exempt from at least some communal duties and taxation. More competent teachers could perhaps be exempted entirely from their duties so as to focus on their teaching and earn a better pay. This was one example of the Mission and colonial administration having similar aims and ideologies, as the requested exemption from taxation met with the colonial administration's concurrent attempts to promote individualism (MacNaught, 1974, p. 5).

However, there was resistance from the Methodists to the inculcation of other British values. The Methodists varied from other Missions with regard to whether or not to teach the curriculum in English or Fijian. English had been in other colonies such as India since the 1820s and 1830s, as government positions opened to those who could speak both English and the local language particularly in Madras (Etherington, 2005, p. 265). Learning the English language allowed easier navigation of the colonial community. With a longer experience in anti-colonialism, the Indo-Fijian was vocal in requesting English tutelage in schools (Mangubhai, 1987, p. 127). In many ways, learning English became a mode by which to subvert the colonial system and gain status within it and acquire positions within the colonial administration. The Mission was spurred by a belief that faith was best instructed in a person's 'mother tongue' (Gaunder, 1999, p. 8). The Methodist teachers were still primarily focused on conversion and believed that people learned better in their own language rather than one imposed from an external society (Mangubhai, 1987, p. 125). Some Fijian Methodists converted to Catholicism purely to obtain instruction in English at the Catholic Mission Schools (Wood, 1978a, p. 267). An education commission in 1926 concluded that English must become part of the colony's curriculum; however, the Methodist Mission ignored this suggestion and continued to teach in Fijian and Hindi (Gaunder, 1999, pp. 65–6). Despite efforts from the colonial administration to strengthen its education department, there was significant resistance from the Mission and its schools to maintain the status quo. The Methodist Mission eventually compromised, changing its policies in the 1930s to teach in the vernacular for the first 3 years of education, and then in English thereafter (Mangubhai, 1987, p. 126).

The Mission Board in Sydney were not so enthusiastic to have the colonial administration 'interfering' in their schools, preferring to remain a somewhat autonomous entity (Wood, 1978a, pp. 305–6). Missionaries in the field, on the other hand, were more willing to receive assistance. In addition to the British administration's influence on curriculum, by 1931, the Mission had entirely relinquished control of all but 30 schools—10 Indian schools and 20 Fijian. One missionary reported in the Mission publication, *The Spectator*, in 1933:

> If our Methodist Mission gives up control of the Village schools it cuts off its right arm, and renders itself proportionally ineffective as an evangelistic agency, for the teaching of the children has ever been a powerful agency for leading them to Christ.[1]

No matter what their theological position was, the Methodist Mission could no longer sustain educational enterprise alone, particularly with the Great Depression placing the Mission under financial strain.

Despite closer scrutiny, structure and assistance from the colonial administration, education remained non-compulsory into the 1930s, with approximately 10,000 children receiving no education at all. Most of these children were girls, with only four girls' schools in Fiji.[2] By 1928, Robert H. Green, an Australian missionary to Fiji, recorded over 200 girls at Matavelo school and over 50 at the *vuli vunan* (Davuilevu, near Nausori). Fijian women did not have the opportunity to attend Methodist secondary schools until 1942, when a secondary institution was constructed for them at Davuilevu.[3] Access to secondary schools had opened to Indigenous girls much earlier in India, with Madras being one of the more progressive colonial stations. There, women were enrolled in tertiary education in the 1870s (Etherington, 2005, p. 266). Only loosely organized secondary education had been provided at village schools until that time. For example, Matavelo incorporated a senior girls' component in 1941, with a continued focus on the 'domestic arts'.[4]

Therefore, the Methodist Mission had an instrumental role in the establishment of the educational system in Fiji, performing the job with or instead of the colonial administration over time. Both the Mission and the administration had a strong focus on the individual and egalitarianism, which led to their desire to change the Fijian society, instilling more Western-styled educational systems such as boarding schools. Even so, there were reasons for each to maintain the authority of the chiefs. The Mission and then the colonial administration had a complex relationship and status within Fijian society and with Indo-Fijians as it navigated through the best curriculum for students as the colony changed.

## Industrial Mission: The Mission and Economic Development Through Agriculture

During the 1930s, a time of great reflection on the style of education provided to Fijians and Indo-Fijians by the Mission and colonial administration alike saw an increased interest in industrial missions. The main aims of industrial Missions were to produce a 'peasant yeomanry' that could help develop the colonial economy and also assist the labourers in securing access and ownership of land.

The Methodist Mission had one official industrial mission post, in the form of an agricultural school. Navuso Agricultural College was established further inland up the Rewa River from Davuilevu, the headquarters of the Mission from 1902 onwards. Benjamin Meek was the principal in the 1920s. This style of evangelical work was highly contested by missionaries in the field. While some missionaries supported this approach, there were debates as to whether this type of training would, first, detract from efforts to convert Fijians and sustain this Christian community. Secondly, there was a concern that there would be confusion between the aim of self-support and what could become self-aggrandizement (Weir, 2003, p. 218). As has been highlighted, with Scripture as their continued focus, educationalists were sceptical about the power of industrial missions to convert and maintain a person in the Christian faith.

Conversely, working the land was seen as a means by which the Fijians retained control of their land as Indian indenture ceased and the farmers sought plots of their own. One missionary wrote to *The Spectator* in 1931: '[The Fijians] must be taught agricultural work to protect their national life and lands and their hands must be occupied'.[5] In the face of increasing demand for land from interested parties, both European and Indian, it became crucial that the Fijians demonstrated utilization of the land. Despite this, increased efforts to demonstrate productive use of the land were needed. In 1905, im Thurn disregarded Governor Gordon's earlier decree that 'unused' land was still to be considered Indigenous land. He enacted a proclamation that allowed for these lands to be sold, with profits going to both traditional landowners and the colonial administration (Blue et al., 2002, p. 239).

As missionary W. A. Heighway suggested in 1903, the Fijians knew more about farming than any European could teach them. Etherington (2005, p. 269) paints industrial missions in a negative light, referring to a commission in Rhodesia that suggested that education in labour practices should be part of the civilizing process for Indigenous Rhodesians. While conceptualizing industrial missions in this way may be useful, especially in light of the derogatory rhetoric about Indigenous peoples' intellectual capacity, which was expounded through the 1909 Education commission in Fiji, (Gaunder, 1999, p. 43) it is worth considering the perspective of individual Missionaries and the role of industrial missions in Fiji's 'development'. As Etherington (2005, p. 269) concedes, the concept was received with enthusiasm in many countries. In the broadest sense, especially under Chamberlain, there was significant interest in maximizing the potential of the Empire's natural resources, and thus this burgeoning interest in the development of labourers to meet this need in the pre-World War Two period (Hodge, 2007, p. 37). Again there seems to have been some support within the colonial administration for industrial missions (MacNaught, 1974, p. 14).

The Navuso Agricultural School catered mostly—but not exclusively—to Fijian students. In 1925, there were 35 Fijian and 3 Indo-Fijian students.[6] It seems that the government, if not the Mission, hoped that more Indian students would enrol. During a Vice Regal visit in 1925, the Governor Sir Eyre Hutson was disappointed 'to learn that Indo-Fijians were not offering more freely for instruction at the school. There can be few finer occupations [than farming] for men of any race'.[7] Similarly, a government official visited Navuso in 1925 and was disappointed that there were not greater numbers of Indian students enrolled. He, however, put the impetus for this on the students to enrol, rather than on the Methodist Mission to attract the students.[8]

In 1928, the students at Navuso were working 33 hours a week maintaining crops and livestock. They grew sugar cane, rice, maize and bananas and, in addition to this, learnt 'care of stock, botany, carpentry, drawing, farming, arithmetic, records, English, sanitation and hygiene, geography, and civics'.[9] The colonial government bought half a share of Navuso in 1926, to the sum of £2,500. This further demonstrates the practical support offered by the Mission to the administration, and vice versa, in the efforts to stimulate the workforce and therefore the Fijian economy.

John Wesley Coulter (1942), an American anthropologist who conducted fieldwork in Fiji for over 10 years later advocated agricultural education for both Fijians and Indo-Fijians. He claimed that no vocational training had been established for East Indians. He said; 'It is contended that East Indians are peasant farmers by heredity and, therefore, do not require the same measure of assistance as Fijians'. He argued that without vocational training, however, the skills and technical knowledge of Indian farmers would stagnate (Coulter, 1942, p. 131).

The 1930s were, as indicated with regard to academic education, a period of change within the colonial administration and the Mission, where both bodies promoted the idea of individualism more forcefully. In October 1929, Mr Young of the Colonial Sugar Refinery (CSR) wrote to the head of the school, Mr Thompson at Dilkusha, saying that CSR would gladly assist by 'placing on farms any who complete their course [at Navuso], if they desire to start out for themselves'.[10] This was hoped to be an added incentive for Fijian men to complete the course. It appears that the land offer to Navuso graduates for farming was taken up, with ten men taking up seven and eight acre blocks of land in May 1930 at Baulevu, north of Nausori.[11]

During the 1920s, Methodist missionary Arthur D Lelean (nephew of the better known Charles Lelean, after whom Lelean Memorial School is named) leased a 48 acre farm from the Colonial Sugar Refinery. On it, Fijian men tended to rice, maize and sugar cane crops. By 1931, there were two farming sites; one at Toko, where there were 75 farmers, and another at Varoka, where another 30 farmers laboured.[12] CSR allocated ten acre plots of land to each farmer, along with the 'plants, seed and supervision'. An article in *The Spectator* said:

> The men told Mr McDonald they would never return to the old conditions. However, they still recognised their obligation to their towns and the old people, but such a chance of making good as they now had [,] they would not miss for anything.[13]

Reverend Green, who was a missionary to Toko in the 1920s, recorded his first visit to the village. Until that, the village had never been visited by missionaries and had only seen two government officials. This was largely due to the steep terrain surrounding the village, which is now the site of Vatukoula mine. Green (1976, p. 75) said that at that stage there were about 25 people living there, with only 5 houses. Within the space of about 6 years, the population of this village had grown by 50 persons—a substantial 200 per cent—and its economic structure had drastically changed. *The Spectator* reported that Arthur Lelean had helped establish 600 families in cane growing by 1931.[14] This was in liaison with the Tui Tavua, the chief of the district, whose name was Ratu Nacanieli Rawaidranu.[15]

Fijians who left their villages to farm independently had to pay taxes to the colonial government. In principle, these industrial missions not only assisted Fijian assertion of land ownership, but also undermined the colonial administration's support for the traditional social system. The Mission did not financially support the initiative. The students received all of the profits—one sugar crop that was estimated to earn £200 was harvested in 1927.[16] In some ways, theories behind industrial missions align with those of development, when the aim is to convert subsistence economies into 'dynamic monetary' economies (Hooper, 2005).

## The Mission and Ideas of Self-Governance

The promotion of self-governance too can be considered part of the development policies in our modern era. It was a point of contention for missionaries, whose underlying goal was ever for the creation of a home-grown church. For example, one missionary said:

> . . . it is desirable that Fiji should ultimately become independent of outside guidance, and assistance, and should work towards self-determination and self-government in church and state. But how is it possible for the

> comparatively poor Fijian to do this? . . . One of the objectives of the Navuso Agricultural School is to create a Fijian yeomanry, which by the intelligent and industrious use of idle lands for the production of commercial crops, will obtain the means to satisfy the growing needs of the community. With increased resources, education will receive greater attention . . . with increasing prosperity they will be able to undertake the conduct of their country in its spiritual, social and commercial advancement.[17]

The industrial mission at Navuso and the resulting economic projects were therefore seen to pave the way to the independence of the Church, or at least greater autonomy. Other key schemes that I have outlined already, such as the training and ordination of Fijian ministers, demonstrated an interest among all involved in the Mission passing into an independent conference status, standing on its own outside the auspices of the overarching colonial Mission.

To contribute to this, the missionaries slowly loosened their grip on the Mission, a process hastened by global events. As a result of the Great Depression, the Mission Board in Sydney directed the redundancy of three European missionaries in Fiji. Fijian ministers acted in their place in most instances (though some remained vacant). Aseri Robarobalevu assumed the position of circuit superintendent in Bua in 1930. His duties included seeing to the congregation at Nabouwalu, including government officials and two boys' schools, and acting as hospital chaplain.[18] The hope was that if Robarobalevu went well, European missionaries could start to move out of Fiji and 'be set free for service in newer fields'.[19] Again, this change linked to the growing push towards individualism. The chairman at the time, Mr McDonald, was concerned about Robarobalevu's move away from a communal lifestyle, but hoped that, this, his taking on a leadership role in the field, would be the start of a move towards a self-governing church in Fiji.[20] A number of European missionaries felt threatened by this, or cited other reasons for not supporting the move towards self-support; however, in the midst of dire economic circumstances, and acknowledging the competence of the Fijian ministry at the time, the chairman was able to push forward towards this goal.

The Indian branch of the Mission also pushed for greater autonomy during this time. For this branch, it was more a push from within, rather than the external influences pointed to above. At the 1933 Synod, it was decided that Indian preachers had to be trained, and thus a 3-year course of training was suggested, to be followed by a year as circuit assistants. They could then be nominated for a 4-year period of probation.[21] Reverend Ramsey Deoki, who was the first Indian minister ordained in Fiji, was for many years paid a lower wage than his white counterparts. Norman Wright, who stayed on at Lautoka during Deoki's first years in the field, wrote repeatedly to the Chairman William Green on this point. In a letter written in 1940, he concluded that legally, as a worker for the Missionary Society, Deoki should have been receiving the same wage as European missionaries.[22] While Wood (1978b, p. 81) has said that Deoki did not 'seek the same salary as a

European missionary', it does actually seem to have been a point of tension. Burton wanted a special status and entrance standard for Indian ministers and argued that the Mission could not afford to pay Deoki on an equal wage. Burton compared Deoki's position with that of Indian Missionaries. In response to his requests in 1944, Deoki was severely chastised by Burton. Burton said that if the Mission was to pay Indian ministers at a rate equal to that for European ministers, an independent church would be unattainable. 'Your brethren in India are on exactly the same basis as yourself, but they are proud to be Ministers of their own Indian Church. Their salaries are very much lower than yours, for they live as do their fellow countrymen'.[23]

Synod had agreed that any wage should be paid from the Indian congregations' contributions; however, this left Deoki with dwindling funds and on the verge of debt.[24] Wright wondered whether some funds would be sent from the Suva circuit to support him, but this did not eventuate. Deoki threatened to resign from the Mission over this matter, and Wright wondered whether this was the intention of the Board, to test both Deoki and the support of his congregation.

While there were some positive steps taken by the Mission to encourage and foster autonomy in Fijian communities in particular, the conflict between Reverend Deoki and the Mission board in Sydney demonstrated plainly one way in which the Mission differed to what many advocates of 'development' would now admonish.

## Conclusion

While the establishment of Methodist institutions may be seen sometimes as working towards what we now call development goals, their motivation lay with the conversion of the people to Christianity and the development of the new Christian community, moving towards an independent Church for Fiji. Despite this motivation, they were often on par with the colonial administration and ready to assist with infrastructure and welfare programmes. While historians have tended to look at missionary involvement in education and health care, the role of the Mission in Fiji's economic development has been overlooked and underestimated. In all these spheres, the missionaries contended with questions of culture, environment and long-term projections of self-governance.

## Notes

1 18 October 1933, 837.

2 'Talented Fijian: Singer, Teacher and Footballer, *The Spectator*, 26 June 1935, 523.

3 Methodist Church in Fiji, Annual Synod Minutes and Journals, Synod Minutes 1942, PMB 1138.

4 Synod Minutes, 1941 PMB 1138.
5 'The Thin Red Line is Breaking: What we have we must hold', *The Spectator*, 9 December 1931, 981.
6 'Navuso, the Agricultural College, Fiji Vice Regal Visit', *The Missionary Review*, 4 June 1925, 9.
7 'Pacific Herald', quoted in 'Navuso, the Agricultural College, Fiji Vice Regal Visit', *The Missionary Review*, 4 June 1925, 10.
8 'Pacific Herald', *The Missionary Review*, 4 June 1925, 10.
9 *The Missionary Review*, 4 November 1928, 7–8.
10 Younger to Rev Thompson at Dilkusha, 8 October 1929, F/1/1930, NAF.
11 To Victor Clark, 14 May 1930, F/1/1930, NAF.
12 The land at Toko was said to be 'under Bill Mune' and 'all leased out to Fijian tenants'. Victor Clark to Richard, 7 June 1930, F/1/1930, NAF.
13 'Across Viti Levu: Rebuilding Towns: Successful Fijian Farmers', *The Spectator*, 30 September 1931.
14 'The Thin Red Line is Breaking: What we have we must hold', *The Spectator*, 9 December 1931, 981.
15 Talanoa at Yaladro and Toko, translated by Deaconess Una Matawalu, November and December 2010.
16 'The Great Ba Circuit', *The Spectator*, 20 April 1927.
17 5 March 1928, *The Missionary Review*, 14.
18 'Particulars of the First Native Minister Appointed to a Circuit in Fiji Formerly Worked by a European Missionary', F/1/1931, NAF.
19 'Particulars of the First Native Minister Appointed to a Circuit in Fiji Formerly Worked by a European Missionary', F/1/1931, NAF, 2.
20 McDonald to Mr Smith, 4 July 1930, F/1/1931, NAF, 2.
21 R. H. Green, 'Fiji Synod 1933', *The Spectator*, 11 April 1934, 301.
22 Wright to W Green, 24 December 1940, F/1/1940, NAF.
23 Draft letter, General Secretary of Methodist Mission John W. Burton to Rev Deoki, 30 November 1944, F/1/1944, NAF, 2.
24 N Wright to W Green, 6 December 1940, F/1/1940, NAF.

# References

Blue, G., Bunton M. P. and Crozier, R. C. (eds) (2002), *Colonialism and the Modern World*, Armonk, NY: M. E. Sharpe.

Burt, B. and Clerk, C. (1997), *Environment and Development in the Pacific Islands*, Canberra: National Centre for Development Studies Research School of Pacific and Asian Studies, The Australian National University.

Burton, J. W. (1923), *Commission Regarding Native Church: Information Collected for the Consideration of the Commission*, Melbourne: The Methodist Missionary Society of Australasia.

Coulter, J. W. (1942), *Fiji: Little India of the Pacific*, Chicago: University of Chicago Press.

Etherington, N. (2005), *Missions and Empire*, Oxford: Oxford University Press.

France, P. (1969), *The Charter of the Land: Custom and Colonisation in Fiji*, Melbourne: Oxford University Press.

Gaunder, P. (1999), *Education and Race Relations in Fiji, 1835–1998*, Lautoka: Universal Printing Press.

Green, R. (1976), *My Story: A Record of the Life and Work of Robert H Green*, Melbourne.

Hodge, J. M. (2007), *Triumph of the Expert: Agrarian Doctrines of Development and the Legacies of British Colonialism*, Athens: Ohio University Press.

Hooper, A. (2005), *Culture and Sustainable Development in the Pacific*, (second edition), ANU e-press and Asia Pacific Press, http://epress.anu.edu.au/culture_sustainable/mobile_devices/pr04.html.

Jolly, M. (1998), 'Other mothers: maternal 'insouciance' and the depopulation debate in Fiji and Vanuatu, 1890–1930', in Ram, K. and Jolly, M. (eds), *Maternities and Modernities: Colonial and Post-Colonial Experiences in Asia and the Pacific*, Cambridge: Cambridge University Press.

Legge, J. D. (1958), *Britain in Fiji 1858–1880*. London: MacMillan and Co Ltd.

MacNaught, T. (1974), 'Chiefly civil servants? ambiguity in district administration and the preservation of a Fijian way of life', *Journal of Pacific History*, 9.

Mangubhai, F. (1987), 'Literacy in Fiji: its origins and development', *Interchange*, 18(1/2).

Methodist Church in Fiji (1942), *Annual Synod Minutes and Journals*, Synod Minutes, PMB 1138.

National Archives of Fiji, files from the Methodist Mission collection including F/1/1930, F/1/1931, F/1/1940, F/1/1944.

Norton, R. (2009), 'The changing role of the great council of chiefs', in J. Fraenkel, et al. (eds), *The 2006 Military Coup: A Coup to End all Coups?* Canberra: ANU e-press, http://epress.anu.edu.au/coup_coup/html/frames.php.

Routledge, D. (1985), *Matanitu: A Struggle for Power in Early Fiji*. Suva: Institute of Pacific Studies, in association with the Fiji Centre Extension Services, University of South Pacific.

Siwatibau, S. (1997), 'Who controls development in the pacific?', in Burts, B. and Clerk, C. (eds), *Environment and Development in the Pacific Islands*. Canberra: National Centre for Development Studies Research School of Pacific and Asian Studies; The Australian National University.

Talanoa, translated by Deaconess Una Matawalu, Yaladro and Toko, November and December 2010.

*The Missionary Review*, held at the Uniting Church Archives, Elsternwick, Melbourne.

*The Spectator*, held at Queens College, University of Melbourne.

Thomas, N. (1990), 'Sanitation and seeing: the creation in state power in early colonial Fiji', *Comparative Studies in Society and History*, 32(1).

Thornely, A. (2002), *Exodus of the I Taukei*, Institute of Pacific Studies, Suva.

—. (2005), 'Through a glass darkly', in Herda, P. et. al. (eds), *Vision and Reality in Pacific Religion: Essays in Honour of Niel Gunson*. Canberra: Pandanus Books.

Thornely, A. and Vulaono, T. (2002), *Exodus of the I Taukei: The Wesleyan Church of Fiji, 1848–74*. Suva, Fiji: Institute of Pacific Studies, University of the South Pacific.

Ward, G. and Kingdon, E. (eds) (1995), *Land, Custom and Practice in the South Pacific*. Cambridge: Cambridge University Press.

Weir, C. (2003), *The Work of Mission: Race, Labour and Christian Humanitarianism in the South-West Pacific 1870–1930* (Ph.D. dissertation). Canberra: The Australian National University.

Wood, H. (1978a), *Overseas Missions of the Australian Methodist Church*, *Fiji*, 2. Melbourne: Aldersgate Press.

—. (1978b), *Overseas Missions of the Australian Methodist Church*, *Fiji-Indian and Rotuma*, 3. Melbourne: Aldersgate Press.

# 5

# God i givim ples ya long yumi (God Has Given Us This Land): The Role of the Church in Building Pacific Nations

Matthew Clarke

## Introduction

Building nations within the hundreds of islands that make up the Pacific island states is a difficult task. Multiple languages, diverse cultures, geographic dispersion and (often) difficult colonial histories have hampered the building of national identity within Melanesia. While independence was achieved throughout this region—including in Papua New Guinea, Solomon Islands and Vanuatu—over the past four decades, nation-building still remains a key challenge. A low level of 'national' development is exacerbated by relatively low levels of social and economic development. Despite often having substantial natural resources, countries within the Pacific are considered to have overall low levels of human development (Feeny and Clarke, 2009). Countries within Melanesia face a number of development obstacles, including: (1) remoteness, (2) susceptibility to natural disasters, (3) low institutional capacity, (4) limited diversification of economic activity, and (5) poor access to capital and investment (ADB, 2005).

Within this challenging environment of nation-building, the role of the churches has not been fully investigated or acknowledged. While development needs remain high, very important work has been undertaken by various churches to improve the material living standards throughout this region prior to and since their independence. These churches include Anglican, Catholic, Pentecostal and evangelical denominations.[1] Missionaries and later local church leaders were involved directly in providing social services, leading independence movements and actively participating in the civil sector of these new nations. Their involvement and influence have continued to the present. This chapter discusses the role that the Church has played in the development of the 'nation' in this region, in two parts. First, this chapter presents case study analysis of both the historical and contemporary role the Church has played in the development of Solomon Islands and Vanuatu. This review considers the impact of both key individual Church leaders who played central roles in nation-building as well as the emergence of a 'theology of independence' that evolved during this period within the Pacific. Secondly, this chapter draws on the new findings of approximately 1,000 surveys of tertiary students within this region to more clearly understand the contemporary role of the Church and religion in national identity. This new survey and focus group data on attitudes to national identity among tertiary students covers Solomon Islands, Vanuatu and Papua New Guinea.[2] This data casts new light on the attitudes of potential future elite towards regional, ethnic, intergenerational and linguistic faultlines in the region, and the challenges of building a cohesive sense of political community and national identity and the role of the Church in this process. The aim of this chapter is to directly assess the importance of religion to politics and governance in the Pacific.

This chapter is set out as follows: The second section looks at the historical role that various churches have played in building the nations of Vanuatu and Solomon Islands, followed by the third section, which briefly considers the development of the 'theology of Independence' and specific roles played by various Church leaders within the Independence movements. The fourth section discusses the more contemporary role played by these Churches. The fifth section discusses a wider consideration of the role of the Church in supporting nation-building and national identity, before the sixth section concludes the chapter.

## Historical Role of Church in Solomon Islands and Vanuatu

The early history of European contact in Vanuatu and the Solomon Islands is dominated by Christian missionaries. The first group of missionaries, from the London Missionary Society, arrived in the New Hebrides in 1839, with

Presbyterian missionaries assuming responsibilities for this work in 1849. Anglican missionary activity also began in 1849.[3] Under the leadership of Bishop Selwyn, the Melanesian Mission[4] held a theological position of 'true religion, sound learning, and useful industry' (Brown, 2009b) that underpinned its activities within Solomon Islands and Vanuatu. Thus, from its inception, the provision of education and skills was a central tenet in the mission's work undertaken in this part of the Pacific. The role of missionaries in providing education and health services in Solomon Islands and Vanuatu (or more correctly, New Hebrides, as it was at that time) is important to note (Hilliard, 1978). Not only did the missionaries provide basic welfare service in the absence of that provided by the colonial powers,[5] they also laid the groundwork for a cohort of educated Solomon Islanders and Ni Vanuatu that was essential to gaining independence. While the British colonial powers provided some basic services in Solomon Islands, there was an almost an entire dereliction of duty by the dual-ruling French and English colonial powers within Vanuatu, with direct involvement in the provision of health and education services not occurring until the mid-1960s.[6]

One of the early tasks undertaken by Bishop Selwyn was to establish a boarding school in New Zealand for Melanesian youth (later relocated to Norfolk Island). These young people, mostly boys but some girls, were brought from the New Hebrides, Banks and Torres islands, Santa Cruz and Solomon Islands (this was before any western political presence was established in these areas) for education and experience of the Christian life, to be sent back to their home villagers as teachers and, eventually, clergy (Brown, 2009b, p. 6).

Upon their return, many graduates tried to change the lifestyle of the village and replicate that which they had experienced at the boarding school. Indeed, the mission activity of the Melanesian Mission (in contrast to that of the Roman Catholic mission) centred around local schools—not missionary stations. While success was limited—given their age and lack of year-round presence of expatriate missionaries—this provision of education and health was an important stepping stone towards more substantial services being available across the region. Indeed, without the presence of these young people, no basic welfare services would have existed at this time in these villages.

Political autonomy was also important to the Melanesian Mission. In addition to health and education, the Anglican mission also supported autonomy (in church, culture and state), self-reliance and health (including improved maternal and child health) (Brown, 2009b). An annual gathering (*vaukolo*) of chiefs and teachers was established in 1887 by the Reverend John Plant in Gela (in Solomon Islands) to aid decision-making that affected the local communities. 'Various subjects were discussed, concerning dancing parties, heathen marriages, burial-grounds, coco-nuts, guns and dynamite, 'undesirables', the price of wives, and the abuse of tattooing' (Coombe, 1911, p. 315). This ability for 'power-sharing' between traditional leaders and church leaders aided the 'localizing' of the church. It also predated the establishment of the British Solomon Islands Protectorate by 6 years and thus served as a de facto national assembly with participants often numbering more than 1,000. Another important example of the self-autonomy practiced within the Melanesian Mission was the use of a local language as early as 1921 as the official language of the Synod. The role of the church in providing social services also predated any colonial presence. At this time, the church developed an industrial training school ('useful industry'), many new schools and the new theological college ('sound learning'), a Melanesian Liturgy and theological education resources ('true religion') and new clinics and hospitals ('good health'). It was assumed that all these activities would contribute to the increase of population (depopulation was still an issue) and prosperity of ordinary Melanesian Anglicans (Brown, 2009b, pp. 10–11). Indeed, the work of these missionaries laid the foundation for the social services that would follow. Given the early focus on autonomy—particularly within the Anglican missionary—much responsibility for this provision fell to local church members.

## Independence: Church Leaders and Theology of Independence[7]

The church in Vanuatu provided four important opportunities to local leaders that facilitated the independence movement within this region; (1) opportunities for higher education; (2) opportunities for leadership roles; (3) opportunities to utilize existing countrywide networks; and (4) opportunities to study and incorporate an evolving social justice theology into church teaching and outreach. It is arguable that without recourse to these four important resources, political independence of Vanuatu would not have happened: either at the time it did or in the form that it took. Sethy Regenvanu—Minister of State in the first Government of the Republic of Vanuatu—provides a suitable illustration of how the Church assisted the Pacific Islanders to form and lead independence movements.

While missionaries had provided education throughout Melanesia for over 100 years, access to upper secondary school education in the Pacific was quite limited during the 1950s and 1960s. Students were selected to attend higher secondary schools on a competitive basis, and this usually involved leaving their home islands and moving to either a regional centre or the capital city. For many, this was a very difficult move as their primary mode of self-identification was to their home village and island. There were few role models on which to base themselves with many being the first from their families, villages and islands to move away to continue their education. It was therefore a substantial break with the common experiences of their friends and communities. There was also a financial burden that was levied on these students' families. Not only did they have to pay the fees and associated living costs, but there was also the opportunity costs of having a family member unable to contribute to a household because of their absence. (At this time, many students at these high schools were in their late teens and even in their mid-20s.) In a traditionally cashless society, parents of students therefore had to undertake non-traditional farming tasks or work in order to enter the monetized economy—albeit in a limited manner—to be able to pay the fees and living costs in cash. As a result, not all those selected were able to continue their studies—either having no family support or finding the experience of moving to the boarding school too alienating.

Such barriers to participation resulted in those who successfully completed their study to more often than not be individuals with strong personalities and leadership abilities. The majority of upper secondary school graduates returned to work in their home villages as school teachers. For a minority though, their education continued within post-secondary training institutes so that they might receive the necessary theological and pastoral training to allow them to work as pastors in their local churches. The experience Sethy Regenvanu illustrates the opportunities provided to a new generation of Ni Vanuatu leaders.

Regenvanu undertook his education within missionary-run schools—first locally, than at the district level, before finally undertaking his final years of school in the capital city. However, the church also provided leadership opportunities that extended outside of Vanuatu. Regenvanu, for example, spent a year in Papua New Guinea at a youth leadership programme run by the Methodist Church of Australia and New Zealand. The purpose of this course was to 'learn about leadership, to prepare and conduct group studies, to conduct worship services, and to preach' (Regenvanu, 2004, p. 55). An (perhaps) unintended consequence was a political awakening. Mixing with fellow Pacific Islanders and discussing their own histories and political situation provided a new political perspective.

> As a result of my PNG experience, new meaning and purpose was added to my studies. I became more interested in national political and economic concerns, church affairs, and matters of wider public interest. I acquired a new vision of the future of Vanuatu (Regenvanu, 2004, p. 57).

It is reasonable to suggest that the opportunity afforded to Regenvanu by the church had direct consequences for Vanuatu's future Independence. This was further aided by his additional theological studies undertaken at the Pacific Theological College in Fiji. Again, this afforded not just the opportunity to acquire theological knowledge, but also opportunities to mix with fellow Pacific Islanders, participate in political discussions, witness the gaining of independence for Fiji and organize Pacific-wide cultural events. All of these experiences provided skills and knowledge that would assist with

Vanuatu's future independence movement. This personal opportunity for higher education also shaped Regenvanu's personal view of the importance of universal education across Vanuatu.

For his first church-appointment—after 17 years of study—Regenvanu began working in the Education Office of the Presbyterian Church based in the capital city of Port Vila.[8] Within this role, Regenvanu was able to direct education policy for the Presbyterian Church and also utilize the networks established by these Western church leaders to participate in pre-nationalistic discussions and planning. These networks included contacts with:

> key people in the government, private sector, the various local churches, United Nations, Pacific Conference of Churches and the New Hebrides Christian Council . . . I was included in this network and was able to make some very important introductions and contacts. It was an effective introduction to what was soon to become my increasing involvement in the political affairs of the country and in the service of the government (Regenvanu, 2004, pp. 88–9).

While it was entirely possible that a Ni-Vanuatu man might purposely be excluded from such networks by white men holding positions of power and influence, the willingness of certain leaders within the Presbyterian Church to provide an entry to these networks cannot be understated.[9] (This is not true of all Western missionaries though. The expatriate leadership of the Catholic Church opposed independence and ceded leadership to local Church leaders for a long time.)

By working closely with local Presbyteries (equivalents to dioceses), Regenvanu was able to focus the Presbyterian Church's education programme away from formal education (which the churches had just recently given responsibility for, to the government) and 'focus its attention on non-formal sectors: leadership development, vocational training, social justice and political awareness' (Regenvanu, 2004, p. 92). The approach taken within tasks was based on a liberation theology emanating from Latin America and the Tanzanian focus on self-reliance initiated by Nyerere. There is of course a long history of a theology of social justice within the region (see Brown, 2009b), with Bishop Baddeley (head of Melanesian Mission from 1932–47) very focused on the 'whole man'.

> . . . is profoundly concerned with men's lives here and now. It is concerned with the whole man, his body and his mind as well as the spiritual part of him. What's the purpose—'tis a sham—to tell people of harps in heaven when they are coughing their lungs out with T.B.; when leprosy has eaten away the limbs of one or other of the family, when you know that 40 percent of your babies will die within a few hours of birth, and no one seems to care! But the missionary does care—hospitals where

all may come for healing; doctors and nurses moving about among the bush and saltwater people; picked lads sent away to be trained as doctors; girls trained in mothercraft and maternity work able to help their people as white folk cannot in that climate and under the conditions of island life. And missionary work involves schools where lads and girls receive education to fit them to go to a Medical Training School or to an Agricultural Institute from which they may return to make their own contribution to their people's daily life, to fit them for better citizenship in a new world fast closing in upon them (Fox, 1958, pp. 95–6).

The churches of Vanuatu at this time also saw the value of working together and resenting a relatively common position on Independence—though the Catholic Church often stood outside of this inter-denominational cooperation. An unsurprising evolution of political parties occurred at this time, with the most influential being the New Hebrides National Party (NHNP) lead by Father Walter Lini (an ordain Anglican priest). Quite soon the leadership of the NHNP consisted largely of Church leaders as few other Ni Vanuatu had secular opportunities of education and leadership. The history of Vanuatu's colonial period and independence is worthy of much further discussion than space permits in this chapter (see Miles, 1998). However, an important aspect of this history is the role that Church leaders undertook within different denominations in garnering support at the local level for independence, input into the drafting of the constitution and providing the on-the-ground organization required for the ensuring political campaigns. Without the churches, Vanuatu 'would not have had the handful of educated indigenous people at the crucial stage to direct the country in its course towards political independence' (Regenvanu, 2004, p. 170). These included the ordained Anglican priests Father Walter Lini and Father John Bani; Presbyterian pastors Sethy Regenvanue, Willie Korisa, Jack Hopa and Jack Taritonga; Presbyterian Elders George Sokomanu, Thomas Reuban and John Naupa; Church of Christ pastor Samuel Bule; and Roman Catholic priest Father Gerard Leymang.[10] The support of overseas church partners—Pacific Conference of Churches, World Council of Churches, the Presbyterian Church of Australia, the Australian Council of Churches and the General Synod of the Church of Melanesia—also aided the achievement of Independence for Vanuatu (Brown, 2009a). Without opportunities for education, roles of leadership, access to national networks and acceptance of evolving theological teaching, it is quite likely that the Republic of Vanuatu would not have been achieved in the time or manner it did.

Of course, the involvement of the church as its leaders (and trained members) did not finish once independence was achieved. It has continued to play a very important role since then. It has continued to not only provide social services, but also advocate for good governance as well as support the development of a national identity within these countries.

## Contemporary Role of Church in Solomon Islands and Vanuatu

Gaining independence from British colonial rule was less difficult in Solomon Islands than that experienced in Vanuatu.[11] However, since this time, its political environment has been characterized by instability with 17 different governments over 30 years. Throughout this period, successive governments have been accused of corruption and the misuse of public office (UN, 2002). As a result, there have been low levels of public confidence in all government institutions since their inception (Roughan, 2004). Resentment towards successive governments is also linked to the perceived hoarding of power and influence to the capital city of Honiara, located in the Guadalcanal Province. Public sentiment held that resources were being removed from all other provinces and being invested in infrastructure and facilities in Honiara rather than being redistributed among the poor provinces. Successive governments had also been accused of fiscal irresponsibility through: (1) the inefficient monitoring of log exports resulting in the failure to capture potential revenue via duties and other taxes and (2) the provision of tax exemptions and duty remissions to various individuals and firms (UN, 2002; ADB, 2004; Allen, 2005).

So while Solomon Islands has been a nation for 30 years, these continuing political failings have exacerbated a lack of national identity that itself fuelled the recent civil unrest. Nationalism within Solomon Islands is limited as 'most people carry with them competing clan, island, province and nation identities—in that order' (UN, 2002, p. x). Basic allegiances remain to the family and clan, not to the nation (Mamaloni, 1985; Kabutaulaka 2005).

Political instability and perceived corruption in conjunction with this lack of a strong unifying sense of nationhood led to long-held ethnic-based rivalries and tensions to transform into bloody civil strife that lasted between 1999 and 2003 but continues to simmer to the present day. The immediate events igniting the period of civil strife involved a number of violent murders and retaliatory attacks between different ethnic groups in Honiara. However, the underlying causes have a longer history (see Bennett, 2002; Moore, 2004; Kabutaulaka, 2001 for further analysis of the civil strife). Resource ownership, resource use and poverty are central to both the longer smouldering of tension and more recent incendiary of violence (Roughan, 2005).

The civil strife had serious consequences for the country as a whole. Over 20,000 people fled the violence in Honiara to their home provinces, including many educated and senior bureaucrats (again adding to the disintegration of government services[12]).

> It was a situation in which state structures never completely collapsed but were subverted and utilized to serve the interest of a self-defined and

privileged few. Some people in the government, the police and the public service in general increasingly cultivated cliental relationships, used state institutions to serve their interest, and extorted money from the state coffers (Kabutaulaka, 2005, p. 292).

While the civil strife and violence was centred in Honiara, a general breakdown of law and order occurred in other provinces and rural areas as well.

Both during and immediately following the conflict, it was the churches that have both provided space for brokering peace and facilitated ongoing dialogue between different ethnic groups (Brown, 2009b; Pollard, 2000; Douglas, 2005). Importantly, the different Christian denominations worked collectively in this role. 'It was many of the churches and church groups notably the Solomon Island Christian Association (SICA) which played a significant role in maintaining cohesion and advocating for a resolution to the conflict' (Wallace, 2010, p. 134). Had the churches split along denominational lines, the tensions in Solomon Islands would have been significantly worse. By acting collectively, the church was able to provide an authoritative 'moral' voice with regard to the violence. On a more practical front, the churches were able to facilitate the release of prisoners held by either side of the conflict as they worked across the conflict lines and had a level of freedom in moving from one side of the conflict to the other (Brown, 2009b). This is not to say though that the church was immune to the violence. Seven Melanesian Brothers were killed as they tried to broker peace and work with local communities during this time (Brown, 2004).

The churches continue to play an important role in providing social services throughout Solomon Islands (Bird, 2004; Rhodes, 2007). It is important to consider the role that the churches played during this time in continuing to provide basic welfare and education services in the absence of governments. For example, the Christian Care Centre operated jointly by the Sisters of Melanesia and the Community of Sisters of the Church was open in the mid-1990s to provide a refuge for women and children to escape sexual and domestic violence. The Church of Melanesia—with funding from the New Zealand aid programme—now also provides various programmes across the country focusing on women's health, domestic violence, malaria prevention and care, HIV and AIDS care and prevention, family planning, adult literacy, etc. (see Brown, 2009b for an extended discussion of the history of church-related 'development' programmes in Solomon Islands). An important recognition of the role being played by the Church in working to build Solomon Islands is the recent increase in donor funding being funnelled through it. Most particularly is the 10-year programme (5 years each for phase one, 2004–9, and phase two, 2009–14)—Inclusive Communities Programme—which runs in all parts of Solomon Islands and is being implemented by the Church of Melanesia.[13]

# The Church and Contemporary Nation-Building in Melanesia

Nation-building refers to the cultural processes of forming a cohesive political community to support the development of a functional state. While the international community is preoccupied with post-conflict state-building (focused on issues of governance, institutions, accountability and the rule of law), many problems of political stability in the region attest to the challenges of nation-building (that is, community development, identity formation, national integration). Strong regional (Guadalcanal/Malaita in Solomon Islands, Papua highland/lowland, Vanuatu Anglophone/Francophone) divisions in Melanesian states testify to these ongoing challenges. These remain a key source of difficulty for domestic and international state builders in the region.

The challenges facing the fragile states in Melanesia derive from both a lack of a functional state and the absence of social cohesion and a sense of identity and community. The state must be effectively embedded in a socially cohesive national context, to ensure that the state enjoys legitimacy as a representative expression of the political communities it serves. Nation-building in the sense of creating the conditions for social cohesion, political stability and identity formation is therefore a neglected dimension of the state-building process.

Collecting data on the role of the church formed a smaller aspect of a larger research project on nation-building and national identity within Melanesia, undertaken in 2009 and 2010.[14] The national identity survey developed and implemented in this research is a modified version of the International Social Survey Program module on National Identity. As it is likely that the future elite of Melanesian countries will be current tertiary students, this survey focused on these students. Over 1,000 students were surveyed across Melanesia as the views of this cohort are an important predicator of future shifts within these nations.

The survey accumulated quantitative and qualitative data on key aspects of nation-building and national identity formation, including:

- Relative strength of civic or 'voluntarist' conceptions of national identity (which emphasize voluntary attachments to the nation, such as respect for political institutions and laws, or 'feeling' national belonging); and ethnic or 'objectivist' understandings of national identity (which emphasize notions of common descent and culture, such as being born in the national territory; being able to speak official languages, or belonging to a certain religion).
- Popular attitudes towards official conceptions of national identity such as official languages, respect for the constitution, secularism, pride national history.
- The extent to which institutionalized policies, collective mythologies and public discourses about national identity are reflected in the attitudes and beliefs of 'ordinary people'.

- Attitudes towards the relative importance of particular indicators of national identity.
- Gender, age, region of origin, self-identified language proficiencies of survey participants, to ensure representativeness within target profile and facilitate data analysis including cross-tab applications.
- The relationship between cultural identifications and particular understandings of citizenship and national identity.
- Assessing the relative strength or depth of affiliation, to the different levels and modes of identification within Melanesia: for example, kinship group; village; wantok-language group; island; district; denomination; nation; region.
- To better identify actual and potential social and political faultlines in post-independence national polities.

The research found that the church has played an important role in aiding nation-building within Melanesia. It is interesting to note that the role of the church continues to be highly regarded by these future elite across a range of measures. This suggests that the depth or authenticity of religious faith will remain a defining characteristic of Melanesian countries in the foreseeable future. As such, the role of the churches will not diminish significantly. This has consequences for both secular and sectarian leaders within these countries.

When asked to identify the importance of different aspects to be considered, for a Ni-Vanuatu, a Papua New Guinea or a Solomon Islander, being Christian ranked extremely highly across all countries. Nearly 80 per cent of all respondents in Vanuatu ranked being Christian as being 'very important', with another 11 per cent ranking it as important. Responses in Papua New Guinea and Solomon Islands were similar, with the respondents rating being Christian 'very important' were 75 and 86, respectively. This suggests that the long history of church's presence within Melanesia has resulted in a very authentic engagement.

In discussing the various groups that citizens belong to, religion ranked within the top five across all three countries. Possible groups that the respondents were asked to rank were: occupation, ethnic/language group, gender, age, religion, preferred political party, nationality, family and region of the country you live in. In Vanuatu, Solomon Islands and Papua New Guinea, the top five ranked groups were family, religion, occupation, ethnic/language group and nation—in that exact order across all three countries (see Table 5.1). It is therefore clear that religious identification is quite integral to these young tertiary students.

However, religious faith is not simply an issue of identification. The survey also tested the day-to-day influence of religion and churches. Of importance was the role assigned to churches by respondents with regard to them playing a very important role in mediating certain disputes. In Vanuatu, nearly 15 per cent of respondents suggested that the church should play a role in settling disputes between neighbours (see Figure 5.1). While

*Table 5.1 Top five groups of identification within melanesia (% Selected by respondents)*

| | Papua New Guinea | Solomon Islands | Vanuatu |
|---|---|---|---|
| Family | 57 | 34 | 44 |
| Religion | 18 | 20 | 23 |
| Occupation | 12 | 14 | 13 |
| Ethnic/language group | 5 | 11 | 7 |
| Nation | 4 | 11 | 6 |

this number was still lower than the role assigned to national police (28 per cent) and Customary leaders and chiefs (57 per cent), it is still quite significant—especially as only 5 per cent of respondents thought the church should mediate disputes concerning crimes against property and crimes against persons. Interestingly, in Papua New Guinea, 15 per cent of the respondents also saw the church having an important role in mediating disputes between neighbours (see Figure 5.2), compared to 45 per cent suggesting the national police and 40 per cent suggesting customary leaders and chiefs. Given the recent unrest, it may not be unsurprising that the role of the church in resolving disputes between neighbours was selected by 20 per cent of the respondents. The faith in the national police within Solomon Islands was less than in Vanuatu and Papua New Guinea, with only 30 per cent believing it had a role compared to 45 per cent choosing customary leaders and chiefs. The results in Solomon Islands show that 20 per cent of tertiary students believe that the church should mediate disputes between neighbours (see Figure 5.3). A strong argument could also be made that

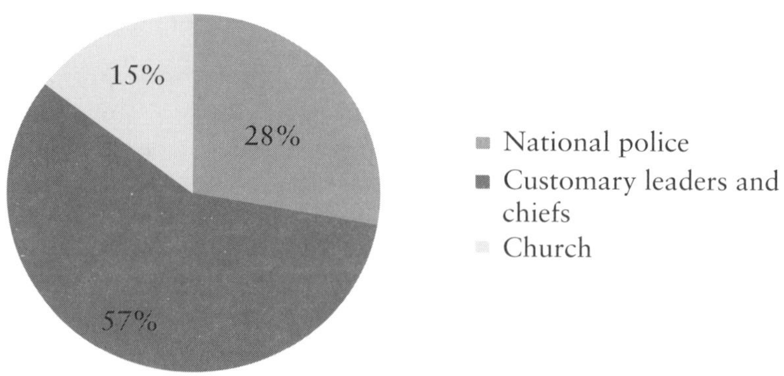


Figure 5.1 Who should resolve disputes between neighbours in Vanuatu.

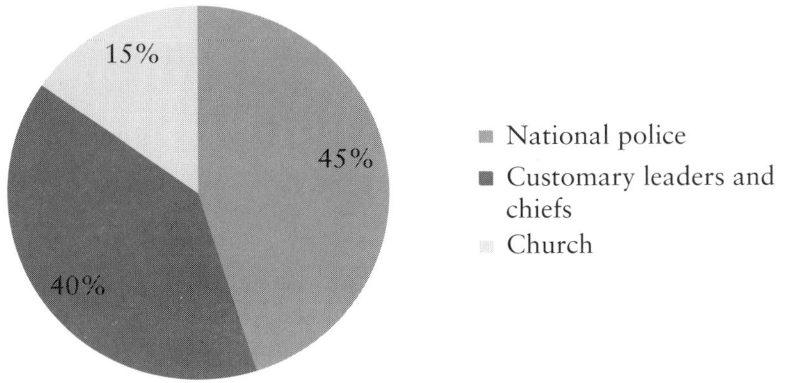


**Figure 5.2 Who should resolve disputes between neighbours in Papua New Guinea.**

many customary leaders and chiefs also play a leading role in local churches, therefore strengthening this civil society role required from churches by communities within these Melanesian countries.

Focus group discussion held with tertiary students across all three countries also provided evidence of the uniting role the churches have played in these countries. It was noted that one of important roles played by the churches was the development and dissemination of a common language (Tok Pisin, Solomon Pidgin, and Bislama—all forms of English creole). Through this common language, people from different ethnic groups across different islands were able to communicate more effectively and see themselves as being of one language. This facilitated not only trade, but also inter-marriage—which was highlighted as an important aspect of building a nation and breaking down traditional barriers to a common national identity.

While this larger research project focused on the views of the future elite (tertiary students) around building national identity within Melanesia, it

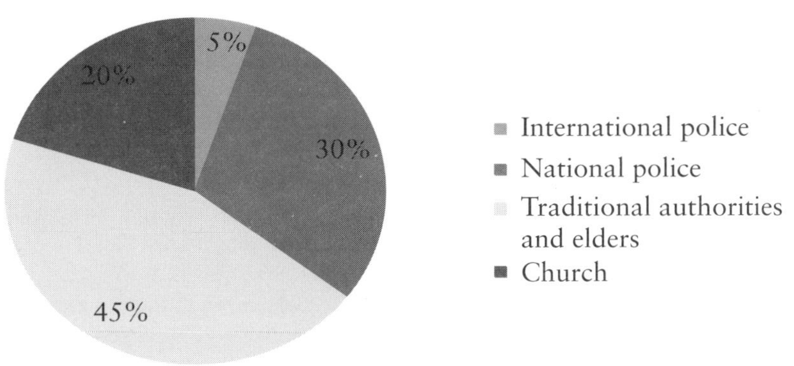


**Figure 5.3 Who should resolve disputes between neighbours in Solomon Islands.**

became clear that the role of churches remains important for these young people. This suggests that the consequences of a strong history of church and religion within these countries will continue into the (immediate) future.

## Conclusion

The purpose of this chapter was to describe the historical and contemporary role of the (Christian) churches within nation-building in Melanesia. Having had a presence that predates colonial rule, churches within Vanuatu, Solomon Islands and Papua New Guinea have provided social services (such as education and health) well beyond that provided by the nation state (or its colonial predecessor); have provided opportunities for leadership for local Melanesians within the church hierarchy that subsequently supported independence movements (including a theology of independence); and have continued to play an important civil society role since independence, worked closely with local communities to hold governments accountable, and initiate and support conflict resolution and reconciliation activities in times of civil unrest. When surveyed, the future elite of these countries still rank Christianity as an important characteristic of these nations and see the churches as having an ongoing and important role in social affairs. While Solomon Islands, Papua New Guinea and Vanuatu have been nations for between 30 and 40 years, national identity is still weak. Given the ongoing importance of nation-building within Melanesia, it is important that Christian churches be recognized by researchers, policy planners, those implementing social and economic programmes, donors and national governments as having played and continuing to play a central role in this endeavour.

## Notes

1 The relatively ecumenical manner in which these different denominations have worked together within Melanesia over such a lengthy period of time and the almost complete absence of non-Christian religious beliefs held by Melanesians, the different Christian denominations will be referred to collectively as 'the churches'.
2 East Timor was also included in this research project.
3 Other denominations played important roles in the provision of basic welfare services, but for the sake of space are discussed in this Chapter (see Gardner, 2006).
4 The Anglican Church of Melanesia is the largest church in the Solomons and the second largest church in Vanuatu (being smaller than the Presbyterian Church and of similar size to the Catholic Church) (Brown, 2009b).
5 See Miles (1998) for a description of the Condominium Government established between the English and French in 1907 and the dual control prior to this.

6 Though they did financially support some missionary-run activities, for example, supporting various Anglican-run hospitals from the mid-1930s (Brown, 2009a).

7 This section focuses largely on Vanuatu's independence that occurred in 1980.

8 Regenvanu's appointment as the first Ni-Vanuatu Director of Christian Education within the Presbyterian Church followed a year after the General Assembly (led by George Sokomanu—the first President of the Republic of Vanuatu) passed a motion—Declaration Concerning Independence—calling for the two colonial powers to cede power and prepare the country for self-determination.

9 Institutional inequality between expatriate and local church leaders was still persistent at this time, which included provision of hot running water in their bathrooms, separate dining arrangements (and menus), better accommodation, etc. (Regenvanu, 2004).

10 A similar list of church-trained leaders of the early Solomon Islands Government would include Francis Bugoto, Mostyn Habu, Will Betu and Lily Poznanski (Brown, 2009a).

11 Largely a factor of the different positions taken by the Anglophones and Francophones and the respective British and French colonial powers (see Miles, 1998).

12 A benefit of this return to home provinces was that many that returned had skills and expertise that did not previously exist in these provinces, thus lifting local capacity.

13 An Inclusive Communities Programme—based on this model—is now being implemented within Vanuatu.

14 This research was undertaken in conjunction with Dr Michael Leach (Swinburne University), Associate Professor Simon Feeny (RMIT university), Dr Heather Wallace (Deakin University) and James Scambary (Swinburne University). The research is funded by AusAID through the ADRA Scheme and is entitled 'Understanding Attitudes to National Identity in Melanesia'.

# References


Allen, M. (2005), 'Greed and grievance: the role of economic agendas in the conflict in Solomon Islands', *Pacific Economic Bulletin*, 20(2).

Asia Development Bank (ADB) (2004), *Country Strategy and Program Update (2005–2006): Solomon Islands*. Manilla: ADB.

— (2005), *Asia Development Outlook 2005*, Manilla: ADB.

Bennett, J. (2002), 'Roots of conflict in Solomon Islands', *State, Society and Governance in Melanesia Working Paper 2002/5*, Canberra: Australian National University.

Bird, C. (2004), 'Blowing the conch shell: a baseline survey of churches engaged in service provision and governance in the Solomon Islands', report to AusAID, <www.anglicancommunion.org/provincialnews/melanesia/client/news/client_news_detail.cfm?naid = 1534>.

Brown, T. (2004), 'The role of religious communities in peacemaking: Solomon Islands', *Anglican Religious Life Journal,* 1, Canterbury Press. <http://anglicanhistory.org/academic/brown_religious2003.pdf>.

—. (2009a), *The Anglican Church and the Vanuatu Independence Movement*, unpublished mimeo, Melbourne: Deakin University.

—. (2009b), *Reflections on the History of the Theology and Practice of 'Development' (Past and Present) in the Anglican Church of Melanesia in Solomon Islands and Vanuatu*, unpublished mimeo, Church of Melanesia, Honiara.

Coombe, F. (1911), *Islands of Enchantment*. London: Macmillan.

Douglas, B. (2005), *Christian Custom and the Church as Structure in 'Weak States' in Melanesia*, paper given at the Civil Society, Religion and Global Governance: Paradigms of Power and Persuasion, 1–2 September, Canberra, Australia.

Feeny, S. and Clarke, M. (2009), *The Millennium Development Goals and Beyond: International Assistance to the Asia-Pacific*. London: Palgrave-MacMillian.

Fox, C. (1958), *Lord of the Southern Isles*, London: Mowbray and Co.

Gardner, H. (2006), *Gathering for God: George Brown in Oceania*, Dunedin: Otago University Press.

Hilliard, D. (1978), *Gods Gentlemen: A History of the Melanesian Mission 1849-1942*, Brisbane: University of Queensland Press.

Kabutaulaka, T. (2001), 'Beyond ethnicity: the political economy of the guadalcanal crisis in Solomon Islands', *State, Society and Governance in Melanesia Working Paper 2001/01*, Canberra: Australian National University.

—. (2005), 'Australian foreign policy and the RAMSI intervention in Solomon Islands', *The Contemporary Pacific*, 17(2), 283–308.

Mamaloni, S. (1985), 'A political struggle for rural development', in Kinika, B. and Oxenham, S. (eds), *The Road Out: Rural Development in Solomon Islands*, Suva: University of South Pacific.

Miles, B. (1998), *Bridging Mental Boundaries in a Post Colonial: Identity and Development in Vanuatu*, Honolulu: University of Hawaii Press.

Moore, C. (2004), *Happy Isles in Crisis: The Historical Causes for a Failing State in Solomon Islands, 1998–2004*, Canberra: Asia Pacific Press.

Pollard, A. (2000), 'Resolving conflict in Solomon Islands: the women for peace approach', *Development Bulletin*, 53, 44–6.

Regenvanu, S. (2004), *Laef Blong Mi: From Village to Nation*, Suva: University of South Pacific Press.

Rhodes, D. (2007), 'Analysis of the "community sector" in Solomon Islands', report to AusAID, <www.ausaid.gov.au/publications/pdf/Community_Sector_in_SI_May_08.pdf>.

Roughan, J. (2004), 'The villager, poverty reduction and NGO links', paper presented at Solomon Islands *Government Development Partners Consultative Talks*, Honiara, 15–19 November 2004.

—. (2005), 'Getting rid of poverty', *Scoop Independent News*, 30 May, retrieved 5 November 2006, <www/scoop.co.nz/stories/HL0505/S00364.htm>.

United Nations (UN) (2002), *Common Country Assessment: Solomon Islands*, Office of the United Nations Resident Coordinator, Suva.

Wallace, H. (2010), 'The Solomon Islands: conflict and capacity', in Kenny, S. and Clarke, M. (eds), *Challenging Capacity Building*, London: Palgrave.

# 6

# The God Factor: Adventism, Medical Missionaries and 'Development' in Papua New Guinea

Brad Watson

## Introduction

The 1995 Copenhagen Declaration on Social Development described poverty as, 'a condition characterised by severe deprivation of basic human needs, including food, safe drinking water, sanitation facilities, health, shelter, education and information' (cited in Hughes, 2008). Issued at the United Nations (UN) World Summit for Social Development, this definition excluded intangibles such as love, happiness, access to natural resources and social connectivity. However, it highlighted growing international consensus over the material dimensions of relative disadvantage later formalized within the Millennium Development Goals (MDGs). As troublesome as their classification and motives may be, a critical question is to what extent faith-based organizations (FBOs) have contributed to poverty reduction. Are 'faith', 'religion' and 'poverty reduction' linked in a beneficial, symbiotic relationship? This chapter discusses the Seventh Day Adventist (SDA) Church in Papua New Guinea (PNG) as an agent of change since 1908. It argues that the SDA church is an important service provider, which has contributed to the development process. Among others, medical missionaries may be seen as pioneering humanitarian workers.

Gibbs (2004) argues that there are four main religious blocks in PNG, the first of which includes the mainstream churches such as the Catholic, Lutheran, Anglican and Uniting. Collectively they exert pressure for good governance, also participating in the PNG Council of Churches, Church Education Council (CEC) and Church Medical Council (CMC). The second block consists of the Evangelical Alliance and includes Baptists, Nazarean and Salvation Army. The third block, largely non-political and the newest to PNG, consists of Pentecostals such as Four Square and Assemblies of God. Interestingly, the SDA church is identified as a fourth and separate block.

> . . . the Seventh Day Adventist (SDA) church constitutes a separate block as they have kept a distinct profile throughout their nearly 100-year-presence in PNG. They did not join the former Melanesian Council of Churches, founded in 1965 (now known as the PNG Council of Churches, PNGCC), out of a concern that they would be drawn into political debates and have to adopt positions not in accordance with their faith. (Hauck et al., 2005.)

Growth of the SDA church has been substantial. In 2010, church membership reported in the SDA Church Yearbook (GC, 2010) exceeded 242,900 individuals in over 870 churches. A PNG census conducted in 2000 found that 10 per cent of the adult population was affiliated with the SDA Church, a proportion exceeded at that time by the United Church (12 per cent), the Evangelical Lutherans (20 per cent) and Roman Catholics (29 per cent) (PNG Census, 2000). In the South Pacific Division of SDAs, PNG stands out as the country with the highest proportion of SDAs, a surprising outcome, given the late arrival of Adventism in PNG, the small scale of early missionary endeavour and the slow growth of the missions prior to World War Two.

The SDA Church is an important service provider in PNG. In 2010, it operated one university (PAU), one college (Sonoma), three senior secondary schools, four junior high schools and ninety-three primary schools. According to the associate education director of Adventist schools, it supported 21,000 students, a number that is rapidly increasing. In addition, the church runs six day clinics, one flying clinic and thirty-two aid posts and dispensaries. By some accounts, SDA MPs have held 25 per cent or more of seats in PNG parliament at times in the past decade. Clearly then, the SDA church has influenced not just service provision but also the nation-building and political process itself.

## SDA Mission History Prior to World War Two

SDA work in Papua began modestly in 1891, with a small shipment of religious literature conveyed up Australia's east coast and through the Torres Straight on London Missionary Society (LMS) boat the John Williams (Hook, n.d.). Active in the Pacific since 1797, LMS workers had spearheaded missionary work throughout Polynesia, moved westwards to Melanesia and arrived in Papua in 1871, where they eventually established mission stations at intervals of roughly 150 kilometres along Papua's coastline (Schwarz, 1985). Sending printed literature to Papua via the interdenominational LMS, was, at that time, the only viable outreach option for the fledgling SDA Church. In 1899, church membership in Australia consisted of just 1,782 individuals (GC, 1889). Although church leaders had planned to send a missionary family to Papua in 1895 (Albert and Hattie Read), the plan was personally scuttled by Dr John Harvey Kellog (Founder of the Kellog TNC) who wrote,

> They have been designated to go to New Guinea to work among the cannibals, and in a field where no missionary thus far has been able to get a foothold. I was distressed enough when I heard of it. I did not learn of it until I found they were just on the eve of starting . . . after several days hard work succeeded in getting the matter reconsidered. (cited in Hook, n.d.)

SDA church leaders visited several Papuan coastal villages briefly between 1902 and 1905, commenting on the prevalence of disease, unhygienic living conditions, tobacco use and betel nut chewing. However, 13 years had passed between the first shipment of literature and the arrival of three pioneer missionaries in 1908. Septimus W. Carr, an Australian and his New Zealandar wife Edith, landed at Port Moresby with high hopes constrained by limited human and physical resources. Where the first LMS pioneers had arrived with eight Loyalty Islanders and a troop of Samoans (Schwarz, 1985), the Carrs were assisted by just one Fijian missionary, Benisimani (Beni) Tavodi. This combination of Australian and Pacific Islander missionaries was not unusual. In her overview of Adventist missionaries to Papua during the period 1908–42, Anderson (cited in Ferch, 1991) notes that the combination of Western and Pacific Island missionaries had been pioneered by other evangelical Christian groups and was in keeping with '. . . the pattern of Christian missionary venture throughout the Pacific . . . '. In the years to come, Pacific Islanders from Fiji, the Solomon Islands and the Cook Islands played an important role as SDA missionaries to Papua, as did at least three Aboriginal Australian couples.

The SDA trio found their work challenging. There were 75 other European missionaries scattered along the Papuan coast, representing approximately one-tenth of the total European population (Hook, n.d.).

LMS had been active in Papua for 37 years and the Catholic Church for 23 years. As relative latecomers, the Carrs discovered that the British protectorate had already been divided into 'spheres of influence' in a comity agreement. With the encouragement of the then governor, William MacGregor, the LMS, Wesleyans and Anglicans had agreed in June 1890 to allocate boundaries among themselves. The LMS was to focus on the southern coast of Papua; the Methodists, the eastern islands including the Milne Bay region; and the Anglicans, part of the north coast. In agreeing to this division, MacGregor sought to minimize fractious competition between Christian groups while maximizing their 'civilising influence', especially with regard to their peacemaking role in areas characterized by tribal warfare. Although MacGregor and subsequent governors did not legitimize the comity agreement through law, ' . . . he and his successors simply respected it by refusing to cede land anywhere round the coast to missions other than the parties to the compact' (Garrett, 1982).

Like the Catholics, who had arrived somewhat earlier in Papua and also found themselves unwelcome due to the comity agreement, the SDA trio sought to establish a mission station inland; however, in their case it was 40 kilometres from the coast on the Sogeri Plateau. Chapman (in Ferch, 1991) asserts that here Septimus Carr, despite stringent objections from the LMS, leased 150 hectares of land for 'agricultural and pastoral uses, and for school and general mission purposes'. The land had been purchased by the Government, a decision that apparently delighted the villagers. By one account Bisiatabu meant ''holy' or 'sacred' because the locals thought the devil lived there'. (Hook, n.d.). As was the case with other churches, the overwhelming imperative was conversion; however, this required a well-equipped 'base'. With contracted labour, the Bisiatabu mission took shape and evangelistic endeavours were begun. However, the local Koiari people, well known for their independence and mistrust of foreigners, proved resistant to the evangelistic efforts of the new missionaries. Anderson (in Ferch, 1991) notes that the station workers, signed to 1-year contracts, changed frequently. Although a week of prayer in 1913 resulted in 11 plantation workers declaring an intent to convert, it seems that none were baptized.

Although Carr was successful in establishing a small mission station and rubber plantation consisting of 800 trees, he presided over one baptism during his 6 years of mission service. The late SDA historian Noel Clapham (n.d.) notes that no sooner had the boy been converted than his angry father intervened and removed the child. The second baptism in Papua occurred in 1920 and Adventist mission work on the gulf coast progressed slowly. While the mission offered paid plantation work and opportunity to learn some English, it seems that there were few incentives for local people to join. In 1921, Pastor and Mrs Griffiths F. Jones were appointed to Papua and soon afterwards the energetic pioneer embarked on a walking tour of

27 isolated villages in the Astrolabe Mountains. There his group treated and prayed for the dying son of a village chief who promised to send two boys to the mission school after his son was 'healed'. In 1922, the mission school at Bisiatabu opened with 26 students, much to the approval of Jones who wrote, 'The school is doing well considering we have a lot of untamed, undisciplined, savage, larrikin youth . . . ' (Anderson, cited in Ferch, 1991).

While the growth of some other Christian groups surpassed that of Adventism between the wars, it should be noted that the number of Adventist missionaries was relatively small. In 1923, Adventists could declare just three missionaries. A year later, in 1924, the Bisiatabu SDA Sabbath School, still the only one in Papua, declared a membership of 37 (Anderson, cited in Ferch, 1991). According to Pech (cited in Schwarz, 1985), there were 158 overseas missionaries in Papua in 1927; however, the 1927 SDA Yearbook (GC, 1927) records the presence of just ten SDA ministers or licensed mission staff.

In December 1923, the SDA Australasian Union Conference's Executive Committee allocated additional funds for the existing Bisiatabu school and for establishment of new schools (Chapman, 2003), formalizing an attempt to broaden service delivery. The possibility of expanding the Solomon Islands work into New Britain also received attention. However, discussions between G. F. Jones and the Lieutenant Governor resulted in the warning that SDA expansion would be 'blocked by the other missions and the Commonwealth grant of land'. Heeding the warning, yet determined to expand the SDA church work in Papua, Jones undertook a different approach. Rather than requesting a land grant, and challenging the comity agreement, he approached the people of Efogi directly to 'carry forward our work in their own land' (Chapman, 2003). After lengthy discussion with enthusiastic local landowners, an agreement was made to establish Efogi School.

G. F. Jones' decision to establish small mission stations in villages and William Lock's arrival in 1924 are seen as turning points in Adventist mission in Papua, and perhaps the origins of service delivery approach that characterized later work. According to Clapham (n.d.), 'The school was much admired by government officials, who urged the Adventists to commence work along the coast in both directions from Port Moresby'.

Colonial administrators, keen to reduce violence between warring clans, and encourage enterprise, embraced Christian missionaries as a civilizing, development influence, a role that sat easy with SDA missionaries. The 1918 edition of the Appeal for Missions (Australasian Union Conference, 1918) confidently asserted, 'The most thorough investigation shows that the gospel of Christ lifts all classes of people who receive it, to a new life. It Christianizes them, and that makes them a truly civilised people'. Such a discourse emphasized the backwardness and primitiveness of the 'other', reinforcing the idea of 'heathenism', a concept used often in mission literature. Although there is relatively little discussion in SDA historical literature on such matters, Anderson (cited in Ferch, 1991) notes the cultural impact of the arrival of Nafitalai, a Fijian SDA missionary and his wife at Efogi in 1924, 'Nafitalai had a part in the first burial service at Efogi, an occasion of significance as the Efogi people traditionally placed the dead body in a tree'.

The year 1928 represented a turning point after which more significant SDA church resources were focused on both Papua and, increasingly, in New Guinea. In Papua, SDA mission outposts, made possible with the collapse of the comity agreement, had been established along the coast at Vailala, Korela and Aroma. They may be seen as 'the beginning of a vast network of mission stations which began to multiply rapidly in the late 1920s' (Hook, n.d.). Aroma, approximately 170 miles east of Port Moresby, was staffed by Mrs Alma Wiles, a widow and veteran of mission work in New Hebridies where her husband Norman had died in 1920 from Blackwater fever. These outposts typically consisted of a small school building, church and, in some cases, a rudimentary clinic used to dispense medicine and treat tropical disease.

Illness often took a toll on the early missionaries and its consequences revealed the latent hostility that often existed between missionaries and local spiritual leaders. When Beni Tavodi, the first Fijian SDA missionary to Papua, died from snakebite in 1918, angry sorcerers claimed credit for his death (Anderson, cited in Ferch, 1991) by arguing that they had weakened him with sorcery while he was in prayer. Interestingly, the consequences of Tavodi's death have resonated for almost a century and resulted in an emotional reconciliation ceremony held in June 2008 between descendents of the Taburi clan in the Koiari district and the grand nephew of Beni Tavodi. 'It is believed that Mr Tavodi was killed by sorcerers of the Taburi clan whilst on his knees praying one Sabbath morning' (Naivaluwaqa, 2008). While Adventists have been reluctant to acknowledge the role of sorcery in the deaths of early missionaries, the Taburi clan have blamed it for the deaths and consequently for their historic lack of progress and political clout. Opposition to missionaries has come to be seen as opposition to progress, resulting effectively in a curse.

In 1925, Ratu Tevita Daivalu and his wife Liviana began work at Bisiatabu School, earning a reputation among the church leadership for effective spiritual leadership, good classroom teaching and efficient coconut production. Tevita, however, died of Blackwater fever in 1928, an event interpreted by local people as also resulting from sorcery. Tevita, opposed to pigs for hygiene reasons, had evidently killed a pig that had uprooted his garden and in unrepentantly doing so may have alienated some of the villagers (Anderson, in Ferch, 1991). For the most part, the Bisiatabu mission struggled to impact on the local people who showed little interest in their teachings.

On a pragmatic level, the death of Beni and Tevita is a reminder of the stark dangers faced by early missionaries in Papua, resulting from isolation, lack of health-care, overwork, disease and the inevitable collision of cultures, economic systems and world views that often took place with the arrival of missionaries. Compared to other religious groups, SDA missionaries fared well. In 1901, the pioneering LMS worker James Chalmers, and young Congregational minister Oliver Tomkins, nine students and two others had attempted to land on Goaribari Island. The party of 13 were killed and eaten. Chalmer's first wife Jane had passed away prematurely in 1879 after years of patiently enduring malaria, dysentery and loneliness. His second wife, Lizzie had died in 1900, after repeated health breakdowns and recurrent tropical illnesses (Garrett, 1997).

The Methodists also experienced tragedy in New Guinea. Well before New Britain was annexed by Germany, 83 Fijian Wesleyans had volunteered to join George Brown who was en route to Melanesia. The leader of the six married couples and three single men who were finally selected, Aminio Baledrokadroka, assured Fijian administrators that ' . . . no one has pressed us in any way; we have given ourselves up to do God's work, and our mind today, sir, is to go with Mr Brown. If we die, we die; if we live, we live' (Garrett, 1997).

After establishing mission stations in New Britain, all the original Fijian women died, two of the Fijian children perished and Brown himself suffered from recurring, debilitating fevers. Angry over disruptions to local trade networks, a powerful trading chief intercepted and killed Reverend Sailasa Naucukidi and three other Fijian men, consuming them as was customary for warriors in that area. Despite punitive raids led by Brown, he and the chief responsible for the attacks later became 'friends' (Garrett, 1997). Although this incident may be seen as the coercive outcome of a power-play between missions and chiefs, we must keep in mind that these instances are rare and precede decades of coercion by the secular colonial administration as it sought to impose Western law, especially under the Kiaps in the Highlands prior to independence. For SDA missionaries, there are no recorded incidents of direct conflict, use of weapons or physical coercion.

In 1933, the SDA church headquarters was established near Port Moresby. However, the growth of SDA church in British Papua prior to World War Two remained slow compared to its growth in the former German territory of New Guinea. 'By 1940, Adventist missions had been active in Papua for thirty-two years, with a total of 1,780 converts. By contrast, sixteen years' effort in the Territory of New Guinea, where Christianity had previously been almost unknown, had produced an enthusiastic membership of 4,000' (Clapham, n.d.). The 1939 SDA Yearbook (GC, 1939) provides a tantalizing clue, noting that in New Guinea there were 100 island teachers and missionaries. No such listing is made for Papua. It is important to note that church growth occurred fastest where local people had little or no previous experience with Christianity, had a shorter history of direct contact with traders, were when exposed to Islander missionaries able to contextualize and indigenize religion, and where missionaries provided significant social services or made displays of technological power and wealth. Success was also evidenced in social groups that were under considerable economic or health-related stress.

## SDA Mission and Social Work After World War Two

Like the staff in other church denominations, SDA expatriate missionaries were evacuated in 1941 and 1942 and were not to return in numbers until 1946 and 1947. Their return in the period 1945–7 was accompanied by a degree of urgency also evident in other denominations. However, in 1945, PNG experienced profound change. German administration for New Guinea was relegated to a historical fact. Throughout the Second World War, large portions of the coastal fringe had been occupied by either the Japanese or the Allies and indigenous people had witnessed, for the first time, brutal conflict between the soldiers of industrialized countries. To the surprise of many indigenous people, the troops were sometimes godless. The fantastic wealth and power exhibited by military forces, resulted in 'religious reactions' including the appearance of cargo-cults. Additionally, the rapid influx of Missionaries in the post-World War Two years may have unconsciously 'added to the impression of many New Guineans that cargo and money were guaranteed by Christian faith and worship' (Garret, 1997).

Pastor Lester and Freda Hawkes arrived in Papua in 1947. In that year, according to the SDA Yearbook (GC, 1947), there were 80 SDA churches and 1,267 SDA members in Papua and New Guinea, with an unknown number of individuals in regular attendance. The Yearbook does not state the number of mission schools or clinics; however it does note the existence of 150 native teachers (GC, 1947). Tellingly, of the 49 missionary staff listed, 12 were ordained ministers, 16 were licensed ministers, 17 were licensed as missionaries and just 4 were licensed as medical missionaries (Mrs L. Hawkes, Mrs. T. F. Judd, Mrs. H. W. Nolan and Mrs Alma Wiles). Lester Hawkes who was classified as a probationary minister, however, considered himself a medical missionary and functioned as such, bringing the total to five. Others may have classified themselves as humanitarians of sorts, a reality not reflected in the classifications used by the SDA church at that time.

Medical missionaries in the SDA church were expressly supported as an integral part of the church's social gospel, also evident in other churches of the era and in the tradition of Christians such as Walter Rauschenbusch in the early 1900s. However, the one individual who exercised the most profound impact on the SDA's social gospel work was

Ellen G. White. In her massive body of writings, she repeatedly urged the church to combine education, health care and gospel preaching. For example, she wrote:

> I wish to tell you that soon there will be no work done in ministerial lines but medical missionary work . . . . You will never be ministers after the gospel order till you show a decided interest in medical missionary work, the gospel of healing and blessing and strengthening . . . . I wish to say that the medical missionary work is God's work. The Lord wants every one of his ministers to come into line. Take hold of the medical missionary work, and it will give you access to the people . . . . Medical missionary work, ministering to the sick and suffering, cannot be separated from the gospel (cited in Nelson and Van Dolson, n.d.).

The impact of White's advice is evidenced in the establishment of a dedicated department for medical missionary work at the General Conference of SDAs (active throughout the 1920s and 1930s) and the classification of some Australian missionaries in the post-World War Two period (1946–53) as medical missionaries whose primary task was to witness through humanitarian, medical-oriented action.

While Lester and Freda Hawkes were motivated by the Great Commission enunciated in Mt. 28:18-20, they differ from missionaries of that era who were motivated primarily by evangelical zeal and the finance of their endeavours through trade. As 'medical missionaries', Lester and Freda Hawkes may be seen as the forerunners of the later NGO workers who formed the Seventh-day Adventist Welfare Service (established formally in 1956) and eventually the religiously neutral Adventist Development and Relief Agency. Inspired by the words of Ellen G. White, they embraced her claim that 'Christ, the great medical missionary, is our example. He healed the sick and preached the gospel. In His service, healing and teaching were linked together. Today they are not to be separated' (White, 1923).

Lester's memoirs are refreshingly non-judgemental. Indeed they are often supportive of local culture and critical of Western practice. Summarizing the practice of a male using a string to draw up his scrotum to modestly cover his penis, Hawkes states ' . . . the men wore nothing more than one string skilfully arranged to satisfy their standards of modesty and practicality'. In commenting on the Fore practice of consuming their dead relatives, he asserts, 'Fore mothers and fathers love their children and relatives just as much as do those of "civilised" countries. They may express it differently, perhaps. But when they lose a loved one they are just as upset. Under no circumstances whatsoever would they think of placing the loved one in the dirt where insects, and worms, and even pigs could feast on them . . . . Instead, the Fore made the loved one a part of themselves'. Although critical of practices where jealous husbands would bite the noses off their wives, allow twins to die or abandon the ill to a painful death, Hawkes also expresses concern for introduction of prostitution, alcoholism and Western greed during the colonial era. Missionaries also draw attention as he expresses concern over the banning of traditional dancing, lack of appreciation for traditional music and blanket imposition of church rules, such as refusal to baptize a man with more than one wife.

Interestingly, when asked in conversation to define heathen, the prevailing term used by missionaries in his era, Hawkes responded by saying, 'A heathen is anyone who doesn't understand Christ or heaven's plan for him. It is a spiritual term'. When asked to identify the consequences of heathenism, he argued that it included tribal fighting, bad treatment of women, poor hygiene, spirit worship and ill health or avoidable death. Consequently, 'God's plan is a better life. A more abundant life. A more satisfying life in the earthly sense. It is freedom from spirits, from disease and health problems, from antagonism. The gospel is a unifying focus'. As a medical missionary, Lester viewed Christianity as a liberating force that can and did actively reduce poverty and add dignity to human life. In this sense, we may acknowledge that the commonalities shared with the modern humanitarian agenda, which also seeks increased longevity, better health, education, gender equality and human empowerment. The difference for medical missionaries, and arguably for many Melanesians today, is their valuing of religion as the primary pathway or motivational factor in achieving these ends. Religion may thus been seen as a bridge, one that indigenous people often welcomed, and sometimes resisted, in their quest for social and economic improvement.

Of interest to scholars is the close alignment with the social gospel that was discussed briefly above and the contemporary message of what might be referred to, somewhat controversially, as the 'evangelical humanitarian gospel'. It is suggested that both may be positioned as evangelical discourses or change that have been adapted to motivate and justify interventions. In the Table 6.1, one may see a degree of evolution of terminology from left to right, especially as utilized by Christian development organizations with non-religious focus in their work.

***Table 6.1 A Comparison of 'mission' and 'humanitarian' terms***

| Social gospel of christian mission | Humanitarian agenda of Contemporary NGOs |
|---|---|
| Heathen | Poor |
| Primitive/savage | Disadvantaged |
| Medical missionary | Humanitarian or development worker |
| Missionary organization | NGO |
| Gospel message | Human rights message |
| Evangelism | Modernization |
| Civilized | Empowered |

Half a century before the MDGs were adopted by the United Nations Development Program, Lester and Freda were building schools, providing primary health care, improving water sources, attempting to improve diet, curbing violent tribal conflicts and mitigating against cultural practices that are today contrary to our contemporary idea of universal human rights. The stories of Lester Hawkes reveal missional synergies with the MDGs including the goals of eliminating extreme *poverty and hunger,* reducing *child mortality,* promoting *gender equality*, achieving *universal primary education,* improving *maternal health,* combating *HIV/AIDS, malaria and other diseases,* ensuring *environmental sustainability* and developing *networks for development.* This fosters human flourishing (Petersen, n.d.).

Of course, the MDGs were more than half a century away when Lester arrived in Papua in 1947. However, in discussion, he was asked to reflect on medical missionary work and the current MDGs. He states, 'I am not sure that the term HIV/AIDS was even coined when we worked out there. We knew nothing of it, nor did we meet it'. When asked in November 2010 if he knew about the MDGs, Lester grinned, shook his head in the negative, paused and then asserted wryly that they 'sounded like a very good idea'. In consequent conversation, Lester noted that,

> People in the Highlands had pretty good nutrition. They were often healthy. Later, the problem was western food and habits. Pig Bel was a big problem. We didn't do a great deal with hunger although we did teach about healthy food.

In the early years, education was provided to train the missionaries rather than out of a desire to provide universal education for the sake of it. At virtually all mission stations, a school venue of some sort was built as a matter of priority, generally after construction of housing for the missionaries had been completed. While the formal education consisted of reading and writing, with scriptural classes, Lester asserts that 'Girls were trained to support their husbands in ministry'. This is graphically described by Pastor Hawkes in one incident where ministerial trainees 'kidnapped' their future wives and returned to the mission station, in direct contravention of local custom, to the delight of the girls involved and with the eventual blessing of their relatives who, Lester argues, had felt bound by custom but were secretly pleased with the arrangement and eventual outcome. Lester states that 'Over time many schools were established where there had been none. Schooling was a very important part of the work'.

It should be acknowledged that some SDA Appeal for Missions literature was, at times, less than respectful of women in Melanesian culture and prone to gross exaggeration. A particularly critical example is found in the 1927 Appeal for Missions publication:

> Women in heathenism have few enjoyments in life, and are sold in marriage like pigs and dogs. A Heathen values his daughters for their financial

> gain he can make out of them. Before marriage they are prostitutes, after marriage they are slaves in all but name.

Interestingly, Lester argues strongly that the work of SDAs liberated women, resulting in health and hygiene improvements, and evidenced in the formation of women-only Dorcas groups, which, in some cases has led to large rallies, demonstrations of women's solidarity and increased status as welfare providers in their communities. He says, 'Yes. It gave women confidence, improved their feelings about themselves. It gave them better status. The gospel does lift and build confidence'.

In interviews with both Lester and Freda, both stress that they worked very closely with women, especially Freda. Freda gave girls medical classes, sewing classes and taught them to make money. Western music was introduced, healthy habits like using a handkerchief were introduced and instruction was given on mother and infant health. The enormous pride that indigenous women garnered from this interaction is expressed in the anecdote over a visit to PNG in the early 1990s in which Freda met with one of her students, dressed more than 30 years later in a garment sewn at the mission station and kept carefully in all the years that followed as a prized possession, status symbol and arguably, as a sign of liberation or affluence. Lester asserts that:

> At Omaura (in the highlands) most of our nurses were men. Most girls could not break free from custom. This was a part of our medical work. We spent a lot of time with women. We trained mothers to bathe their babies and give them good food. Freda made maternal health a very important part of her work. She assisted with deliveries, obstructions, post-birth complications. At Omaura there was a heavy emphasis on women's health.

In the context of Seventh Day Adventism, Lester and Freda provide a case study into the approach, motivation and contribution of medical missionaries in PNG. Their voice is surprisingly moderate, being characterized by concern rather than criticism. They were active in key areas highlighted by the current MDGs and established some of the earliest services in their area in PNG, especially in the Highlands in the 1960s. Although their commitment to a social gospel is not unique in Christianity, it is indicative of a powerful agenda that peaked in mainstream Adventism in the 1960s and culminated with the establishment of the Adventist Development and Relief Agency (its predecessor was SAWS in 1956). However, a preview of key ADRA websites and their 'about us' and history sections does little to acknowledge the important humanitarian work evident in this era. For example, the ADRA USA website does little to recognize the ongoing nexus between church mission and 'development', perhaps in an effort to distance it from its roots in 'mission' for marketing and government compliance purposes. It blandly

*Table 6.2 Role of medical missionaries as humanitarian workers*

| SDA Medical Missionaries | FBO Humanitarian Workers |
|---|---|
| Desire to convert and change the world (Isa. 58). Abundant life and health | Desire for global justice and materialistic poverty reduction MDGs |
| Missionaries as change agents sharing the benefits of religion and Western medical knowledge | Humanitarian NGOs as change agents sharing the benefits of scientific knowledge and resources |
| Motivated by social gospel | Motivated by a humanitarian gospel informed within FBOs by a social gospel |
| Funded largely by church members in rich countries and sending churches | Funded largely by donors in rich countries and sending NGOs or governments |
| Premised on external change agents as a Civilizing influence | Until recently premised on external change agents bringing benefits of the West |
| Gospel and social pioneering work as a provider of health care, education and economic development gospel as liberation | Development and human rights as a gospel of liberation |
| Holistic mission, spiritually based mission | Materialistic, needs-based 'mission' |
| Impartiality 'loving ministry to men and women of all classes irrespective of creed or society' (Hon, 1948) | Often religiously and politically neutral |

states, 'ADRA is an independent agency established by the Seventh-day Adventist Church. The church's involvement in organized humanitarian assistance goes back nearly 80 years' (ADRA USA, 2010).

The role of medical missionaries as humanitarian workers leads to comparisons with contemporary faith-based NGO staff. There are indeed similarities as shown in the Table 6.2.

# Conclusion

There is no doubt that in PNG, Christian missionaries have profoundly affected the social, economic and value systems adhered to by those whom they sought to convert, at a time of concomitant, radical change under the powerful, colonial regime. Unfortunately, generalizations about the historical failures of Christianity do little to inform the contemporary debate about the power of 'faith' and 'religion' to engender and nurture poverty reduction. It is argued here that the introduction of Christianity to Melanesian society in PNG should be seen as a complicated process, open to interpretation and multiple perspectives. It involves:

> . . . historical, cultural, social, and often political considerations that are differently tangled, making each case unique in important respects. In addition, colonialism, a frequent concomitant of missionization, further complicates the ways in which new ideas are introduced, attributed, and interpreted locally. On the other side of the dynamic are local factors such as indigenous cosmologies, social organization, and destabilizing influences (out-migration, epidemics, government contacts) that make the society being missionized receptive to change or, occasionally, ready to radically reinterpret or reject it (Schieffelin, 2002).

A balanced view of historic Christian missionary endeavour and its impact on people, individually and collectively, must acknowledge the diversity of missionaries, their denominations, personal arrogance and the state of societies at the time of impact/contact. For example, the Anglicans in Papua were motivated by the belief that Western 'civilisation' would wreak havoc on Papua's indigenous people, as it had done on Australian Aborigines. Further, village Papuans were contrasted with all that was wrong in war-torn Europe. According to Wetherell (1997), 'In Anglican writing, island society was nearly always represented as loftier than European society- the paradise lost'. Whiteman (1983) argues that although the ideal of indigenous Christianity was often undermined by the reality of confused syncretism (as indigenous people fused new, culturally disparate beliefs and teachings with tradition), the Anglican Missionaries were generally positive and empathetic towards Melanesians, were relatively tolerant towards indigenous customs and succeeded in providing vernacular translations of their texts. Whiteman concludes that although they exhibited a degree of paternalism, ' . . . wholesale condemnation of missionaries as cultural destroyers is both superficial and inaccurate' (Whiteman, 1983).

Whiteman (1983) suggests that analysis of missionaries as agents of change (cultural brokers versus cultural destroyers) must: be based on a case-by-case basis; be evaluated in terms of the historical context in which they operated (by not comparing the paternalism in colonial and post-colonial eras); must consider the cultural milieu in which missions operated (for example their persuasive influence when PNG was administered by a coercive regime); in the context of indigenes as 'innovators' rather than 'passives'. He suggests that 'It is in the transactional strategies employed by indigenous innovators that we find the real locus of change- not in what the missionary advocates' (Whiteman, 1983). In short, the impact of missionaries and their religious beliefs on indigenous people must be kept in perspective, and as much as possible critique should come from indigenous people who adopted, adapted and rejected 'change'. Perhaps the activities of contemporary churches should be critiqued in the same way.

What missionaries themselves advocated is nonetheless important. A 1928 Church of England study book (cited in Hilliard, 1978) provides an interesting insight into a social gospel mindset, which predates the modern humanitarian movement, itself richly influenced by Christian teaching.

> . . . the Christianising of the world involves the creation of sanitary conditions, of an educational system, of social, economic, and political welfare, in which life and life abounding may come to its full personal and corporate development . . .

The Methodist missionary to Fiji in 1902, John Wear Burton, stated that he was not motivated by a desire to save heathen from eternal damnation, rather by the 'unhappy condition of people who, ignorant of the good news were living without the joy and happiness that Christ alone could give' (in Hilliard, 1978). While one may question Burton's assumption that the only pathway to joy and happiness was Christian theology, he nonetheless focused on non-material well-being, an important dimension of poverty and disadvantage yet to be fully explored.

Christianity is an important part of the national identity in PNG and is embraced within the constitution. In 2011, when the world president of the SDA church visited PNG, he was invited personally to pray with the Prime Minister Sir Michael Somare. Gibbs (2004, p. 3) notes that Papua New Guineans have a holistic worldview ' . . . within which empirical and non-empirical, sacred and secular, are distinguished but not separated. Thus dreams and visions, rituals and spells, blessings and misfortune, and public professions of faith are all considered quite compatible with power and politics . . . '

The consequence is that, at times, political campaigns share uncanny likenesses to evangelical crusades in which politicians claim moral superiority and restorative power. Despite the blatant corruption practised by some self-proclaimed Christian MPs, it is acknowledged that mainline churches play an important role in drawing attention to corruption; for example, a 1999 incident in which comments by Brian Barnes, Archbishop of Port Moresby, over shameful political conduct, contributed to the resignation of the prime minister (Gibbs, 2004).

Recognition is growing nationally and internationally that the churches are not just service providers, they are also able to mobilize significant social capital, influence good governance, form bridges across conflict-driven communities and provide a unifying influence in a culturally fragmented environment. The authors of Ringing the Church Bell (Hauck et al., 2005) point out that there are 150 missions, sects and free churches in contemporary PNG. Ninety-nine per cent of the population identify with Christianity. Christian groups collectively provide 50 per cent of all health services, co-manage 40 per cent of primary and high schools and run two of the nation's six universities. They are deeply involved in public policy, social justice, health/education and reconciliation/peace building. Additionally, they have a significant ability to bridge, mobilize and advocate for good governance. Among these churches, the SDA church is an important member.

There is clearly a strong social gospel component to SDA church work in PNG, evidenced in the provision of education and medical care. This is not unexpected, given Gerard Clarke's (cited in Bano and Nair, 2007) observation that in the late nineteenth and early twentieth centuries, FBOs worked extensively with states to provide health and education services in developing countries, a role that declined in the post-colonial period. However, in the case of PNG, it is clear that the importance of this service provision role has actually grown since 1975. The church has and continues to contribute to nation-building and development through delivery of essential services. Personal accounts, such as those from Lester Hawkes, are a welcome addition to SDA church history and provide the reader with fascinating insights into the mindset of medical missionaries as they engaged with the social justice issues of their time. In the absence of highly effective governance and government resources, a balanced development approach in PNG will view churches as necessary, key partners for the realization of human development goals.

## References


ADRA USA (2010), *FAQs*, retrieved 1 December 2010, <www.adra.org/site/PageServer?pagename = faqs_general>.

Anderson, M. (1999), *Do No Harm: How Aid Can Support Peace, or War*. Boulder, CO: Lynne Rienner Publishers.

Australasian Union Conference (1918), *An Appeal For Missions*. Warburton Victoria: Signs of the Times Publishing Company.

Bano, M. and Nair, P. (2007), *Faith-based Organisations in South Asia: Historical Evolution, Current Status and Nature of Interaction with the State. Religions and Development*. Working Paper 12, International Development Department, University of Birmingham.

Chapman, A. G. (2003), 'Breaking new ground – part 6 Efogi mission: entering New Guinea. *Journal of Pacific Adventist History*,' 3, 2.

Clapham, N. (n.d.), *Seventh-Day Adventists in the South Pacific 1885–1985*. Warburton, Victoria: Signs Publishing Company.

Ferch, A. J. (ed) (1991), *Journey of Hope: Seventh-Day Adventist History in the South Pacific 1919–1950*. Warburton: South Pacific Division of Seventh-day Adventists.

Garrett, J. (1982), *To Live Among the Stars*, WCC Publications, Suva.

—. (1997). *Where Nets Were Cast: Christianity in Oceania Since World War II*, Suva and Geneva: Institute of Pacific Studies.

General Conference of Seventh day Adventists (GC) (1889*), General Conference Bulletin: Summary of Statistics of Conferences and Missions for the Year Ending December 31, 1899.*

—. (1927), *Seventh-day Adventist Yearbook*, Hagerstown, MD: Review and Herald Publishing Association.

—. (1939), *General Conference Bulletin: Summary of Statistics of Conferences and Missions for the Year Ending December 31, 1939.*

—. (1947), *Seventh-day Adventist Yearbook,* Hagerstown, MD: Review and Herald Publishing Association.

—. (2010), *Seventh-day Adventist Yearbook*, Hagerstown, MD: Review and Herald Publishing Association.

Gibbs, P. (2004), *Politics, Religion, and the Churches: The 2002 Election in Papua New Guinea,* SSGM Working Paper No. 2. Goroka: Melanesia Institute.

Hauck, V., Mandie-Filer, A. and Bolger, J. (2005), *Ringing the Church Bell: The Role of Churches in Governance and Public Performance in Papua New Guinea,* European Centre for Development Policy Management.

Hillard, D. (1978), *God's Gentlemen: A History of Melanesian Mission 1849–1942*, QLD: University of Queensland Press.

Hon, E. W. (1948), 'Medical evangelism', *Australasian Record*, 14 June 1948, Warburton: Signs of the Times Publishing Company.

Hook, M. (n.d.), *Lotu Bilong Sevenday: Early Adventism in Papua New Guinea*, South Pacific Division Department of Education.

Hughes, D. (2008), *Power and Poverty: Divine and Human Rule in a World of Need*, USA: Intervarsity Press.

Naivaluwaqa, T. (2008), 'Tribesman confess to killing missionary', *Harina*, 25(11), 3.

National Statistical Office of PNG (2000), *PNG Census 2000*, retrieved 1 December 2010, <www.spc.int/prism/country/pg/stats/2000_Census/census.htm>.

Nelson, W. K. and Van Dolson, L. R. (n.d.), *Health Education in the Seventh-day Adventist Church School of Public Health*, Loma Linda University.

Petersen, R. L. (n.d.), *Strategies for Holistic Mission,* retrieved 1 December 2010, <http://webmail.bostontheological.org/assets/files/10a_petersen.pdf>.

Schieffelin, B. (2002), 'Marking time: the dichotomizing discourse of multiple temporalities', *Current Anthropology*, 43, (Supplement), August–October.

Schwarz, B. (ed), (1985), *An Introduction to Ministry in Melanesia: A Handbook for Church Workers,* PNG: The Melanesian Institute.

Wetherell, D. (1977), *Reluctant Mission: The Anglican Church in Papua New Guinea, 1891–1942*, Queensland: University of Queensland Press.

Whiteman, D. L. (1983). *Melanesians and Missionaries: An Ethnohistorical Study of Social and Religious Change in the Southwest Pacific*, USA: William Carey Library.

# PART THREE

# Case Studies: Mission Organizations and Development

# 7

# The Micah Mandate: An Evangelical View

Steve Bradbury

## Introduction

Watch what God does, and then you do it, like children who learn proper behaviour from their parents. Mostly what God does is loving you. Keep company with him and learn a life of love. Observe how Christ loved us. His love was not cautious but extravagant. He didn't love in order to get something from us but to give everything of himself to us. Love like that (Eph. 5.1-2, The Message).

Faith-based non-government development organizations (FBNGDOs) are working in interesting times. Times, it would seem, when development has discovered religion. Even though 'western official donors have traditionally been ambivalent about the relationship between faith and development and the activities of faith-based organisations' (Clarke, 2007, p. 79), there is an increasing recognition in official development circles that such organizations 'are important players in many spheres of development, with broadly and deeply established roots as key, and sometimes, sole providers of essential services—notably health and education—and community mobilisers' (Marshall and Keough, 2004, p. 1). Towards the end of his tenure as president of the World Bank, James D. Wolfensohn concluded that 'the engagement of faith communities in the fight against poverty is vital to success in achieving the Millennium Development Goals' (Marshall and Keough, 2004, p. xii). FBNGDOs, embedded and deeply rooted in these communities, and sharing the same holistic world view in which all of life is viewed through a spiritual lens, can play a pivotal role in the struggle against greed and injustice.

In a language highly unusual in the academic discourse on development, Michael A. Edwards, the influential development practitioner and author of numerous papers on the work of NGDOs, argued in a conference address in 2003 that 'the future of the world depends on how successful we are in developing a new science of love' (Edwards, 2003). He explains that more than 20 years of 'evaluating individuals and organisations that work for peace and social justice' has convinced him there is 'a missing link in many of these efforts that holds back their effectiveness and achievement, and this missing link is love, or more precisely the failure to use love as the basis for the functioning of the organisation and its work'. In his reflections on the connectivity between spirituality and social transformation, Edwards openly draws inspiration from the example of Martin Luther King Jr.,[1] the Baptist pastor and iconic civil rights leader, and concludes that 'marrying a rich inner life dedicated to the cultivation of loving kindness and compassion with the practice of new forms of politics, economics and public policy is . . . the key to social transformation' (Edwards, 2003). This is a language and yearning that FBNGDOs can fully subscribe to. Nevertheless, Edwards' cautionary note regarding those faith-based groups 'that carry with them more than a whiff of fundamentalism', is another reminder of the need for open and constructive dialogue between FBNGDOs and senior development officials, and a commitment to search for mutual understanding.

A further reason for dialogue is the capacity of FBNGDOs to engender significant community support for anti-poverty programmes. In this they are proving to be valuable allies to government international development departments, such as AusAID (Australia) and DFID (United Kingdom). In recent years, these departments have benefitted from a steadily growing slice of their national budget pie as a result of the policy changes flowing from effective community lobbying. To give an Australian example, the Jubilee 2000 campaign, mounted by a coalition of Christian FBNGDOs and spearheaded by TEAR Australia, was a revelation to both the government and the participating agencies as to their community mobilization capacity. An evaluation of the campaign conducted by Janet Hunt concluded that 'the campaign petition, which was signed by 24 million people worldwide, and some 457,000 people in Australia—the largest ever foreign policy petition presented in Australia—was itself an indication of the reach of the campaign in the community' (Hunt, 2002, p. 10). According to Hunt (2002, p. 10), the significant cancellation of debt owed to the Australian Government by Nicaragua and Ethiopia during the period of the campaign was in large part due to the impact of Jubilee 2000 on government policy.

The very positive experience associated with the achievements of Jubilee 2000 in Australia paved the way for Micah Challenge, which as a direct consequence was able to, far more easily, persuade a number of FBNGDOs to join together in coalition to campaign around the Millennium Development Goals (MDGs). Micah Challenge Australia has further demonstrated the mobilizing capacity of these agencies through its very effective galvanizing of many thousands of individual Christians and hundreds of local churches to lobby federal politicians in support of the MDGs. This campaign was an undoubted factor in achieving a significant increase in political commitment to overseas aid by all major parties in the last two Australian federal elections.[2]

However, even when the substantial contribution of their direct development interventions is added to their achievements in lobbying for increased official aid, a deep-rooted suspicion regarding the motivation and agendas of FBNGDOs continues to linger within the ranks of the development establishment.

Most governments still view development as a secular enterprise. They want to engage with the institutional forms of faith (the religious institution), but remain suspicious about the spiritual dimensions of faith (belief in God). Not surprisingly, secular donors still would like a sanitized separation between the institutional and spiritual elements (James, 2009, p. 5).

The Archbishop of Canterbury, the leader of the worldwide Anglican Communion, directly addressed this recently in his closing keynote lecture in the seminar series on 'New Perspectives on Faith and Development', sponsored by the Tony Blair Faith Foundation, DFID, Islamic Relief, World Vision and Oxfam. Dr. Rowan Williams acknowledged:

> At best, communities of religious conviction have the potential to be serious and effective allies in the struggle against privation. But on the other hand, there is a long-standing suspicion towards faith in many quarters of the development establishment . . . . There is always going to be the shadow of suspicion that they will favour their own instead of working for universal benefit, or that they are using aid and development as a vehicle for propaganda on behalf of their convictions, a cloak for proselytism (William, 2009).

Clarke refers to the same anxiety when he notes that 'the prospect of donor support of organisations committed to active proselytising and/or the denigration of other faiths in some of the poorest and most culturally sensitive countries in the world' will continue to be a challenge to DFID (Clarke, 2007, p. 91). Evidence of this ongoing concern can be seen in current DFID protocols governing eligibility for DFID grants, which explicitly address this issue. For example, the current application guidelines for DFID's Civil Society Challenge Fund (2010) stress that 'we will not consider projects that contain any element of evangelising or proselytising'.

## Mission and Donors

The regulatory framework governing AusAID's operations demonstrates that DFID is not alone in this precautionary and pre-emptive behaviour. The Australian Government's Overseas Aid Gift Deduction Scheme, which sets the criteria for tax-deductible donations for overseas aid, states very clearly that:

> Evangelism (also called proselytism and missionary work) is the practice of attempting to convert people to another religion or faith ... Tax deductible funds cannot be used for evangelistic purposes nor for missionary activities. Missionary activities include evangelism but also extend to activities designed to build up the knowledge and faith of believers including theological training and training in and study of works of religious wisdom such as the Koran, Torah or Bible. The building and maintenance of places of worship are also ineligible (AusAID, 2010a, pp. 10–11).

The AusAID-NGO Cooperation Program (ANCP) Guidelines are succinct: 'Approval will not be provided for activities which subsidise evangelism or missionary outreach'. The length and detail of the accompanying explanatory notes, however, give testimony to the depth of concern. They stress that AusAID funds must be used 'to assist in strengthening an organisation's or a community's development capacity or socio-economic situation', and not to strengthen the 'religious witness' of a church or religious organization. While recognizing that 'in many situations this may not be an either/or question' they recommend that in such cases, where there is a mix of objectives, AusAID funds should not be used. Under the very specific sub-heading of 'evangelical activities', the explanatory notes state:

> AusAID and NGOs recognise and agree that AusAID funds are not to be used for programming that is designed to convert people from one religious faith or denomination to another or from one political persuasion to another. Nor should AusAID funds be used to build up church, ecclesiastical or political structures except in circumstances where those structures are specifically designed to provide relief and/or development assistance. In this context, church, ecclesiastical and political structures include not just infrastructure, but could also extend to training or organisational activities (AusAID, 2010b, p. 5).

The use of the terms 'religious witness' and 'evangelical activities' in this AusAID document provides supportive evidence for Archbishop William's conclusion that 'a deepening fluency in the language of religious discourse, to understand the intention and nuance behind religiously inspired definitions of mission and human development' could help reduce suspicion within the development establishment regarding the activities and intent of FBNGDOs.[2] The theological framework within which Christian FBNDGOs operate, or their world view, to use a more secular term, deems their development and humanitarian aid work as genuinely religious activity of the kind described in many a biblical exhortation.[3] This is so regardless of whether or not it is accompanied by other 'spiritual' or church-based liturgical activities. Viewed through this theological lens, their practical responses to human need are expressions of the justice and compassion of God. In and of themselves, they are a profound 'religious witness', a 'witness to the transforming grace of

Jesus Christ', (Micah Network, 2010) and an indispensible element of the *evangelion* (good news) that Jesus proclaimed and demonstrated. What they do and how they do it is a direct outworking of, and inseparable from, their religious convictions. As a consequence, their descriptions, explanations and justifications of their work to their natural constituencies will frequently use the language of religion. Such language can often be understandably mystifying to secularists, sometimes disturbing, and sometimes even alienating. Greater effort to explain language and religious concepts on the one side and to understand them on the other, and more effort to explain and understand the nature of religious motivation in the work of justice and compassion, would encourage higher levels of faith literacy in official development agencies. This is turn could reduce unease and suspicion, increase levels of trust, and result in stronger partnerships between those agencies and some FBNGDOs.

What follows is a window into the struggle for deeper understanding and fluency within the Micah Network, a loose alliance of over 330 evangelical Christian relief, development and justice organizations. In recent years, it has provided a forum where its members have together wrestled with many of the issues confronting them, in the process seeking greater theological clarity and have been working hard to bring their actions and behaviour into closer alignment with relevant biblical principles. First, however, some analysis of a recent and tragic event will serve to illustrate at least some of the relevant issues.

## (Mis)understanding Mission

On 5 August 2010, ten people, two Afghan nationals and eight expatriates, returning from an International Assistance Mission (IAM) health camp, were murdered in a remote part of Afghanistan. The following day, Zabihullah Mujahid, purporting to be a Taliban spokesman, told the AFP news agency that these women and men were killed because 'they were Christian missionaries', that is, their purpose for being in Afghanistan was to persuade Afghan Muslims to convert to Christianity. He also accused them of being American spies (BBC, 2010). A few days later, Qari Malang, a senior spokesman for the Taliban shadow governor of Nuristan, in an interview with the Afghanistan Analysts Network (2010), strongly denied the Taliban's involvement and condemned the murderers:

> We have checked the facts regarding these foreigners and our people in the area have confirmed that they were bona fide aid workers and had been providing assistance to the population. Furthermore, we have learnt that among the killed foreigners was Dan Terry, who had a long history of helping our people, including in Kunar and Laghman provinces and that he had previously provided welfare assistance to the families of those civilians martyred in bombardments . . . . We pass on our condolences

> to the families of those killed . . . . We regret these killings and strongly assert that this is not the work of the Taliban who will never do harm to genuine aid workers . . . . as soon as we manage to apprehend those responsible for this act, we shall subject them to whatever punishment our laws prescribe.

This tragic incident illustrates and highlights two significant points of relevance to this chapter. First is the significant contribution that Christians are making towards economic, social and human development in many of the world's most difficult and challenging places. The Nuristan province in north-east Afghanistan is an extreme example of such a place. Most of the ten murdered people were expatriate Christians, and when explaining why and what they do, women and men such as these inevitably point to their faith. Their motivation runs deep, fuelled and sustained by profoundly held convictions regarding the nature and character of the God they worship and how that God wants the church to engage with a suffering humanity. This is not to suggest that there is complete uniformity in how they understand and express these strongly held beliefs. Moreover, just as there are differences in theology between individuals, who from the outside may appear to speak a common language, so are there differences within and between evangelical Christian FBNGDOs.[4] It is no easy task to recognize and understand these sometimes subtle but often significant differences from the outside. However, if Archbishop Williams is correct in his surmising, then it is possible that more effort on the part of evangelical Christian FBNGDOs to explain how they understand the faith/development interface, in particular the evangelism/development interface, may allay unnecessary and unhelpful suspicions.

The second issue is that of the motivation and agenda of evangelical Christian FBNGDOs. Regardless of the authority of Zabihullah Mujahid, his accusations against IAM were illustrative of the suspicion felt by many secularists and people of other religious faiths towards evangelical Christian FBNGDOs. Whatever the declared intent of these organizations in working for the social and material welfare of the poor, is not their real purpose, at worst, that of religious conversion, and their development work merely a cover for proselytizing? Or, at best, while they may have a genuine commitment to a development agenda, are they not equally committed to an evangelistic agenda and, therefore, run the danger of blending and compromising the two agendas? Given the controversial nature of the place and role of evangelism and witness in the work of evangelical Christian FBNGDOs, it is illuminating to examine the IAM's stated position within the context of broader discussions within and between other Christian FBNGDOs.

In an interview with the BBC on 7 August 2010, less than 48 hours after the killings, Dirk Frans, Executive Director of IAM stated:

> As to us spreading Christianity, this is simply not true. We are a Christian agency, we are registered as such. In fact, we have been registered as

> such from the very beginning, since 1966. The Taliban know we are a Christian agency, and still they allowed us to work because they actually saw what we did.

In a press release issued the following day, Frans (IAM, 2010) elaborated:

> IAM is a Christian organisation—we have never hidden this . . . . Our faith motivates and inspires us—but we do not proselytize. We abide by the laws of Afghanistan. We are signatories of the Conduct for the International Red Cross and Red Crescent Movement and NGOs Disaster Response Programmes, in other words, that (sic), 'aid will not be used to further a particular political or religious standpoint.' But more than that, our record speaks for itself. IAM would not be invited back to villages if we were using aid as a cover for preaching. And in particular, this specific camp (was) led by Tom Little, a man with four decades' experience in Afghanistan, (and) has led eye camps for many years to Nuristan—and was welcomed back every time.

Belquis Ahmadi, an Afghani women's rights advocate currently working with the International Human Rights Law Group in Washington, DC, was head nurse/administrator for the International Committee of the Red Cross in Kabul from 1988 to 1994, during which time she worked closely with Tom Little. Her testimony, given shortly after his death, collaborates IAM's claim that it is not a proselytizing agency:

> I had the privilege to travel and work with Tom on several occasions. His professionalism, and compassion for those most in need, was unrivalled . . . . I have known and interacted with both Tom Little and Dan Terry (one of the other slain aid workers) since the 1970s. None of us have ever been given a Bible or any other form of Christian literature, or were invited to convert (AAN, 2010).

Dr Abdullah Abdullah, a contender in Afghanistan's 2009 Presidential election, provides similar testimony: 'Knowing Tom personally, he was a Christian, but he was not preaching Christianity, at least I never saw anything, nor did I hear anything from the people of such activities'. Dr Abdullah went on to say:

> I have seen the missions helping the people who don't have access to any other care and giving them hope for the future. In areas like Nuristan, people don't even know they can be cured. So when this sort of team goes to a village and people start coming to them, there will be hundreds of cases where blindness can—and is—prevented and people who are considered blind will see the light again in their own life (AAN, 2010).

In its 2009 Annual Report, IAM (2010) describes itself as 'an international association of Christian organizations serving the people of Afghanistan with compassion and excellence in the name and spirit of Jesus Christ through training and capacity building that fosters wholeness and transformation'. Glenn Lapp, a Mennonite Central Committee volunteer and one of those so tragically killed in Nuristan, epitomized this approach to Christian mission. In a report to his sending body, he wrote:

> The main thing that expats can do is be a presence in the country, treating people with respect and with love and trying to be a little bit of Christ in this part of the world .... My hope is that MCC can .... continue to help this country work toward peace on many different social, ethnic and economic levels (Hurst, 2010, p. 7).

Clearly, IAM is utterly transparent about its Christian faith identity and the centrality of this faith in motivating its work. Equally clear is that IAM has not been persuaded that the legal constraints preventing it from proselytizing within Afghanistan de-legitimizes in any way its mission and witness as a Christian agency. Within the framework of its own faith identity and theology, it is able to fully justify its ongoing presence in Afghanistan and commitment to a development agenda, even though it is not engaged in urging those who benefit from its programmes to change their faith status. Without such an understanding, and the powerfully deep commitments it generates, it is highly unlikely that IAM would have had the resilience and determination to faithfully remain at its post in Afghanistan throughout for more than four decades of almost unceasing armed conflict. Official development agencies can respect sacrificial endeavour such as this, even if false accusations of proselytizing may still jangle latent suspicions. However, how does IAM's perspective and theology of mission sit within the broader 'community' of evangelical Christian FBNGDOs? A look at some of the discussions and reflections within the Micah Network, as it has wrestled with this and other issues along the faith/development interface, can shed some light on this question.

Membership of this young network, which began in 1999, is restricted to agencies who are active in integral mission and able to wholeheartedly endorse the aims of the network and its statement of belief. They range in size from small local operations to large international NGDOs such as World Vision Australia and Tearfund UK. The great majority of them are indigenous organizations in low-income countries. The network describes itself as a 'global evangelical Christian response to the needs of poor and oppressed communities', and its statement of belief places it firmly within the evangelical Christian tradition (Micah Network, 2010). The aims of the network, also available on their website, are threefold: to strengthen the capacity of member organizations to make a 'biblically-shaped response to the needs of the poor and oppressed'; to be an effective and strong voice into the Church 'regarding the nature of the mission of the Church to proclaim and demonstrate the love of Christ to a world in need'; and to be a prophetic voice, 'calling upon and influencing the leaders and decision-makers of societies to 'maintain the rights of the poor and oppressed and rescue the weak and needy (Psalm 82)'.

The second of these aims needs to be understood in the context of a strangely persistent controversy among evangelical Christians regarding the Church's social responsibilities, a controversy that has spawned a library of papers and books. The authors of one of the more recent publications offer a usefully brief explanation:

> Evangelical Christianity has long been plagued by a dichotomy. In the last century liberals reduced the mission of God to social action and in response evangelicals reduced it to making individual converts by proclaiming the 'gospel'. This was a case, common in the history of theology, of a bad argument being countered by an equally bad one . . . . Theologians bear a heavy responsibility sometimes! The polarization of evangelism and social action was hardly ever complete but enough heat and suspicion was generated for social action to be damned by many evangelicals for its association with liberalism and for proselytizing evangelism to be damned by liberals for its association with obscurantist fundamentalism (Grant and Hughes, 2009, p. 11).

One consequence of this dichotomy has been the need for many member organizations of the Micah Network to justify to their evangelical Christian constituencies the theological validity of their work as an authentic expression of Christian mission. It was this that prompted the leadership of the network to set integral mission as the focus of its first global consultation, held in Oxford, UK, in September 2001.[5] The crafting of a short theological rationale for integral mission was one of the consultation's primary outcomes. As with any document produced by a strongly participatory process involving well over a hundred people, theologians and development practitioners from 50 countries, the Micah Network's Declaration on Integral Mission involved compromise.[7] Nevertheless, it was enthusiastically embraced by all who participated in its creation and has proved to be a significant and influential document well beyond the network's membership.

Embedded in the heart of the declaration is a short definition of integral mission, incorporating a brief explanation of the interconnectedness of evangelism and social action:

> Integral mission or holistic transformation is the proclamation and demonstration of the gospel. It is not simply that evangelism and social involvement are to be done alongside each other. Rather, in integral mission our proclamation has social consequences as we call people to love and repentance in all areas of life. And our social involvement has

> evangelistic consequences as we bear witness to the transforming grace of Jesus Christ. If we ignore the world we betray the word of God which sends us out to serve the world. If we ignore the word of God we have nothing to bring to the world. Justice and justification by faith, worship and political action, the spiritual and the material, personal change and structural change belong together. As in the life of Jesus, being, doing and saying are at the heart of our integral task.

This definition of mission and the overall declaration have served the Micah Network well in encouraging much wider acknowledgement among evangelical Christians, of social action as a legitimate and necessary dimension of Christian mission. An important and recent example of this was the inclusion of a paragraph from the document in the concluding statement of the Third Lausanne Congress (October 2010), a gathering of 4,000 evangelical Christian leaders from 198 nations. However, as will be explained below, the declaration can be understood in such a way as to devalue the commitments and achievements of an organization like IAM in Afghanistan. Moreover, it fails to take into account and address the complexities and sensitivities of verbal proclamation in the context of unequal power and influence. Were this to be done at some future stage, it may help alleviate lingering secular and other-faith suspicion regarding the work of some Christian FBNGDOs.

Vinoth Ramachandra, a member of the Micah Network International Panel of Reference, argues that the Micah Network's definition of integral mission

> is often taken to mean that there can be no authentic Christian social action that is not accompanied *at the same time* by the verbal proclamation of the Gospel, just as there can be no authentic proclamation that is not accompanied *at the same time* by social action . . . . This creates tensions for those who work in situations of human suffering where the open proclamation of the gospel is not possible or where the latter is likely to be so misunderstood (perhaps because of a history of bad practice—so-called 'unethical conversions') as to lead to the suppression of all works of compassion initiated by Christians (Ramachandra, n.d.).

Ramachandra (n.d.) has identified a major weakness in the declaration—one that inadvertently de-legitimizes so much of costly and sacrificial Christian development work as expressions of the integral mission, such as that being done by IAM. I am confident this was never the intention of the declaration's architects, who were primarily concerned with demonstrating to those with a passion for evangelism that social action in response to human need is an integral part of the Biblical mission agenda. I am equally confident they would happily amend its declaration in order to prevent such a reading.

The second and more complex issue is that of the place of verbal witness and evangelism in the context of humanitarian relief and development programmes. The Micah Network's Declaration on Integral Mission is absolutely unequivocal in affirming evangelism as an essential dimension of the church's mission, not surprising, given the network's evangelical roots and identity. A passion for evangelism is a vital part of this identity, at least in theory if not always in practice. However, what the declaration lacks, perhaps because of its brevity or its original purpose and intended audience, is any acknowledgement of the sensitivities and ethics of evangelism in contexts of human vulnerability and dependence, or any attempt to address them. There could be great value in the Micah Network developing a set of relevant guidelines to remedy this, not only because of continuing concerns in official development circles about the possible misuse of development aid in the pursuit of a religious conversion agenda, but also to heighten awareness and sensitivity to these issues within the network.

All development and humanitarian programmes necessarily involve transactions between people of greater or lesser dependence on the one side and those who are the conduit for essential resources or services on the other. Within the context of these transactional relationships, there is an inevitable imbalance of power, regardless of how much care is exercised and regardless of the humility or otherwise of the development or aid workers. Given this, the potential for misunderstanding and manipulation, even unintentional, is considerable. Therefore, it is critical for evangelical Christian FBNGDOs to wrestle vigilantly and honestly with these tensions that abound along the evangelism/development interface. The added vulnerability of children adds to the complexity and controversy of this process for child-focused organizations, as well as to the degree of vigilance required.

While there is no attempt to address them within the context of its foundational declaration on integral mission, the Micah Network has given brief consideration to these tensions in another context—in its current multi-year project to build the resilience of local communities to respond to disasters. Major humanitarian disasters, of course, create heightened vulnerability, hence the greater urgency to develop clear guidelines regarding evangelism or proselytizing within those situations. In 2007, staff from several Micah Network members came together in Thailand to examine the potential and desirability of the network developing a collaborative approach to disaster management. Emerging from these deliberations was a discussion paper on proselytizing.[6] Drawing heavily, perhaps even exclusively from a current Tearfund UK policy document, the discussion paper carefully differentiates between evangelism and proselytism. Furthermore, in claiming that 'members of various religious traditions and of the international development community and media have come to understand "proselytism" as involving unjustified manipulation or use of coercive techniques or force to achieve conversion' (Micah Network, 2007, p. 1), it is suggesting that this distinction between evangelism and proselytism is commonly held. How widely this distinction is understood or accepted within official development circles is a topic worthy of careful research. The DFID and AusAID documentation referred to above indicates that these two organizations continue to treat evangelism and proselytism as synonymous. Hence the need for more nuanced and careful discussions between Christian FBNGDOs and the official development sector.

The Micah Network discussion paper on proselytizing provides insight into important and fundamental convictions commonly, though not universally, held by evangelical Christians working in aid and development. Right up front it expresses the evangelistic 'longing to see people coming to a personal faith in Jesus Christ', but in the same breath utterly rejects 'manipulative or coercive proselytism as a way of propagating the Christian faith' (Micah Network, 2007, p. 1). Using the strongest of language it states: 'It is absolutely abhorrent to us to exploit people's vulnerability in order to put pressure on them to convert to our religion'. It adds, 'Conversions gained in this way are often superficial and bring no credit to the converts or the Christian faith in general' (Micah Network, 2007, p. 1). Indeed! The people who are truly compromised in such circumstances are not the exploited who convert, but those who wittingly or unwittingly take advantage of human vulnerability to push a conversion agenda. The statement also stresses that providing humanitarian relief should never be an evangelistic strategy, saying that 'we are not involved in giving relief to the needy so that we can evangelise, but because it is our Christian calling to give relief to the needy' (Micah Network, 2007, p. 2).

A similar attempt to distinguish the obvious wrongs of proselytism from broader Christian witness is found in World Vision's 'Ministry Policy on Witness to Jesus Christ', adopted by their international board in September 2006.[7] The policy immediately states in its opening paragraph that 'witness to Jesus Christ is an integrating principle in all that we do', and that this witness will 'be expressed in holistic ways through its ministries of relief, development, advocacy and public awareness'. The policy clearly allows World Vision to fund what it calls 'religious activities' while recognizing that some funds they receive cannot be used for such purposes, in which case such activities will be financed with funds sourced elsewhere. But proselytism is not acceptable:

> World Vision's support of religious freedom requires that we do not proselytise. Proselytism takes place whenever assistance is offered on condition that people must listen or respond to a message, or as an inducement to leave one and join another part of the Christian church and/or one religion to join another religion. Respecting the dignity of those with whom we work, World Vision does not exploit vulnerability or use the power of development and humanitarian programmes to coerce conversion.

What is clear from all this is that the abuse of development interventions and humanitarian aid in giving greater leverage to an evangelistic agenda—sugar for the evangelistic pill—is utterly unacceptable, not just to secularists but also to many if not most evangelical Christian FBNGDOs. However, does this mean that Christians serving the poor and vulnerable communities must always remain mute about the very thing that motivates and sustains them in their work? Is it never legitimate and even appropriate to give verbal witness to the profoundly relational faith that burns deeply within us? Surely not. In fact, in the great majority of cultures within which most development agencies are hard at work, genuine religious motivation is much more understandable than atheistic or agnostic secularism, and it should perhaps be noted that the latter is not without its aggressive disciples. In these communities, respectful sharing of faith, which by definition will be devoid of any coercive pressure to convert, is more often than not perfectly acceptable. Moreover, the Biblical imperative to communicate the good news of God's love, uniquely expressed in the person, work, death and resurrection of Jesus Christ, is clear, and the longing to see others experience that love is deeply embedded in evangelical Christians.

Ronald J. Sider (1993, p. 123), one of the most influential evangelical Christian social activists of the last three decades, poignantly expresses this yearning:

> The most important reason for evangelism is God's astounding, overflowing love for a lost and broken world. This mission is not primarily ours. It is God's. It is because God so loved the world that we follow in the divine steps seeking to share that love . . . . If one has been sought and embraced by transforming Love, how can one fail to lead others to that same embrace?

Sider's example illustrates how both the desire to seek justice for the poor and the motivation to share the message of the gospel that is indeed 'good news to the poor', have the same root—an ongoing and personal experience of a just and loving God. But the question remains, how can these two legitimate objectives be worked out in a context of power inequality, vulnerability and dependence?

## TEAR Australia

TEAR Australia, one of the founding members of the Micah Network, is another Christian FBNGDO that has wrestled hard and long with this difficult question, and its current position may offer some useful guidance. Since its origins in 1971, TEAR Australia has been explicit about its purpose of raising funds for practical programmes designed to alleviate the suffering of the poor, and not for programmatic evangelistic activities.[8] Its current 'Guidelines For Development and Relief Assistance' explain the motivation and mission of the organization and spell out what it will and will not fund. In the section on underlying principles, the motivation of the organization is described in the language of faith:

> TEAR Australia is motivated by its understanding of God, the words and actions of Jesus, and the mission that he passed on to the Church. We believe that God loves all people and offers them new life in Christ. The Bible shows us the values and characteristics of the Kingdom of God. The world falls far short of these standards. We believe that God seeks to involve us in the work of the Kingdom. This involves working for justice and hope with and alongside people living with poverty, and advocating for just social and political structures that promote the dignity and security of all people. We are aware of the interconnectedness of human society with the whole of creation and acknowledge our responsibility to respect and care for it.

This expresses very clearly the connectivity between core convictions regarding the character and values of God, and the practical work of justice and hope that flows out of these convictions. The guidelines then define the organization's mission, and what is very clear from this definition is that the entire focus and agenda are on development (including advocacy) and relief:

> TEAR Australia works to enable opportunities for people living with poverty to engage in processes to change their lives and their circumstances. These include development, relief and advocacy projects that give priority to the rights, interests, needs and capacities of the poorest and most marginalised people. We seek to address both the symptoms and the causes of poverty through projects that produce tangible, lasting changes. We hope to strengthen individuals and communities in their efforts to address their own development priorities into the future.

The last but definitely not the least of TEAR Australia's underlying principles is that of faith, and it is here that it specifically addresses the tensions associated with the evangelism/development interface.

TEAR Australia and its partners see their development work as an expression of God's love and as a statement of God's justice. TEAR does not fund or subsidize proselytizing activities. Neither will TEAR support the use of relief and development activities to recruit people into the church. We believe that work conducted with this objective lacks integrity, undermines the Gospel and exploits vulnerable people. TEAR only supports projects that are based on development objectives, not on religious, sectarian or political grounds. TEAR does, however, rejoice when people's lives are enriched by their encounter with Christ. Wherever possible, TEAR encourages its partners to work with and strengthen the Church in its ministries of justice, compassion and community-building.

In its categorical rejection of proselytizing, TEAR Australia shares common ground with World Vision, Tearfund UK and many other evangelical Christian FBNGDOs, as it does in its yearning to see people enriched through an 'encounter with Christ'. However, TEAR adds a further clause opposing the use of 'relief and development activities to recruit people into the church'. This additional note was designed to discourage any suggestion that a growth in church membership is a required outcome of TEAR-funded development projects. This does not mean TEAR is anti-evangelism, far from it, and it does rejoice when it sees the evidence of lives transformed through an encounter with Christ. It has not bought into a secular atheistic materialism. Nevertheless, it recognizes that evangelistic objectives programmatically integrated into a development or relief programme can too easily be misunderstood, and unintended coercion of those who feel obligated may be the very unfortunate consequence. This same concern to avoid unintended coercion can be seen in the 'Development and Evangelism Policy' of CBM Australia (2008), another member of the Micah Network, which states: 'Evangelism is omitted from development practice because promoting a faith may impose conditions or obligations on individuals, families or communities seeking participation or access to development activities or services'.

TEAR Australia, World Vision Australia and CBM Australia are all members of the Australian Council for International Development (ACFID), Australia's peak body for aid and development NGOs, and signatories of its Code of Conduct. Clause 2.7 of the code requires that 'Funds and other resources designated for the purpose of aid and development will be used only for those purposes and will not be used to promote a particular religious adherence or to support a political party, or to promote a candidate or organiation affiliated to a political party' (ACFID, 2009, p. 12). In its guidelines to the code, ACFID elaborates:

> Funds raised for aid and development purposes are only to be used in programmes which in no way exploit the people and communities who are vulnerable and do not place any conditions or obligations on recipients in terms of religious or political outcomes that would affect their access to services being offered.

However, in somewhat of an understatement it acknowledges 'that applying this clause will be quite difficult in some situations and some level of judgment may be necessary (ACFID, 2009, p. 12)'. Difficult indeed, for surely it is impossible to objectively measure the degrees of coercion or prove the absence of coercion in an individual's conversion.

One solution may be to distinguish between programmatic evangelism, that is, specifically designed evangelistic and church-building activities, and the informal sharing of deeply held 'spiritual' beliefs. In effect, this is the practice TEAR Australia has adopted. The former, when integrated into a relief and development programme as part of a total package, run the very real danger of introducing a pressure to convert. The latter, however, occur within the natural boundaries of respectful human intercourse and relationships, in which personal convictions, motivations and experiences are shared and explained.

Informal sharing of this nature is far less likely to lead anyone to think that access to the aid on offer may be enhanced by a pretence of conversion. Genuine conversion, arising out of the conviction that what is being experienced is God's love mediated through his people at work in a development programme, is an entirely different matter from the pragmatic 'conversion' that a vulnerable person may offer in the hope of further support or preferential treatment. The one involves a deep matter of the spirit, the other the economics of despair.

## Conclusion

One of the greatest strengths Christian FBNGDOs have is their capacity to work in partnership with local churches, and in many regions these churches are already proving a huge resource for development. In Sub-Saharan Africa, for example,

> in every community—from the smallest, most remote village, to the largest urban centres, there is an institution that is always present. It can muster tremendous human resources; it has an infrastructure in place; it is truly 'grassroots'; and it can influence behaviour, politics, and social justice. In fact, in many instances it has changed the course of human events. I am referring to faith-based institutions in general and the church in particular (Okaalet, 2002, pp. 274–5).

Well beyond Africa, 'the church network extends into the darkest city slum and the most remote rural areas, beyond the reach of state structures or even an NGO's most robust 4×4' (Boyd, 2009, p. 12). Moreover, 'often the local church is the poor: its members endure famine and live with the effects of HIV like everyone else' (Boyd, 2009, p. 12).

By working in partnership with these local churches in such a way as to 'strengthen the Church in its ministries of justice, compassion and community-building' (TEAR Australia), Christian FBNGDOs can enhance Christian witness that is relational and respectful. As a general rule, the neighbour-to-neighbour evangelism of local congregations embedded within communities is more likely to be respectful and less likely to be coercive. However, care will still be needed to ensure that funds designated for development or relief activities are used solely for that purpose. Moreover, care will also be required to ensure that local congregations or local church-based development agencies do not exclude people outside their church communities from their aid programmes. Clearly such practice is contrary to core Biblical, love-your-neighbour values.

Before concluding, it is important to give some consideration, albeit briefly, to the content of the gospel, the proclamation of which has been so strongly endorsed in the Micah Network's Declaration on Integral Mission. It is very clear in the declaration that the gospel as understood by the Micah Network is indeed good news to the poor.

We call one another back to the centrality of Jesus Christ. His life of sacrificial service is the pattern for Christian discipleship. In his life and through his death, Jesus modelled identification with the poor and inclusion of the other. On the cross God shows us how seriously he takes justice, reconciling both rich and poor to himself as he meets the demands of his justice. We serve by the power of the risen Lord through the Spirit as we journey with the poor, finding our hope in the subjection of all things under Christ and the final defeat of evil. We confess that all too often we have failed to live a life worthy of this gospel.

Through their work with the poor, and their exposure to the circumstances of those who are systematically oppressed and exploited, or persistently ignored and deemed of little value, the reflective practitioners of the Micah Network are constantly reminded that it was among people such as these that the gospel was first proclaimed and first experienced. It was the weak and the powerless in a much maligned and oppressed corner of a ruthless empire who first embraced the liberating power and transformative hope of Jesus' gospel. Proclaiming a gospel such as this is a far cry from much of the evangelism associated with the churches that inhabit the world's more affluent and comfortable neighbourhoods. Bearing witness to a gospel such as this 'does not mean giving an isolated, personal testimony to individuals from an abstract and historical situation. On the contrary, bearing witness involves a joyful public declaration by one who has experienced abundant life in Jesus Christ and participates in his passionate commitment to the poor, the powerless and the oppressed. Only from within such a transforming experience and radical commitment can there be an authentic evangelistic witness' (Costas, 1982, p. 184). Could it be that this 'transforming experience and radical commitment'—a commitment to act lovingly, pursue justice, resist greed and value each and every person as an individual made in God's own image—is the very force that Edwards has identified as the missing factor in secular development?

Within the membership of the Micah Network are many reflective and theologically astute practitioners of integral mission. As a consequence, it is well placed to help evangelical Christian FBNGDOs wrestle with the critical and complex issues that inhabit the development/justice/faith/evangelism interface. Its regular regional and occasional global forums provide excellent opportunities to share vital experience and learning and to define more fully their understanding of good operational practice in integral mission. The challenge of developing a set of guidelines for ethical and Biblically informed evangelism in the context of vulnerability and powerlessness is something it is ideally positioned to embrace.[9] In such ways the Micah Network can richly contribute to the dialogue between FBNGDOs and official development agencies, a dialogue that will undoubtedly continue to 'challenge secular desires for a clear division between faith and development work' (James, 2009, p. 7). Hopefully, it will also serve to further demonstrate that Biblically shaped faith can be a potent force for both global justice and good development in poor communities.

# Notes

1 This is explored more fully in Edwards, Michael A. and Post, Stephen Garrard (2008), *The Love That Does Justice: Spiritual Activism in Dialogue with Social Science*, New York: Unlimited Love Press.

2 The Hon Bob McMullan, the then Parliamentary Secretary for International Development Assistance testified to the significant role of Micah Challenge in an address to the World Vision staff early in 2008. This can be viewed at www.youtube.com/watch?v = g0xD92ztWEg.

3 op. cit.

4 See, for example, James 1:26–27; Micah 6.8.

5 Nor is it to suggest in any way that only Christians have a monopoly on self-sacrificing compassion or commitment. Such a proposition is clearly ludicrous.

6 The Micah Network leadership had earlier recognized the need to develop a common vocabulary and had decided to adopt the term integral mission, originating in Latin America, as the most suitable.

7 As Chair of the Micah Network (1999–2009), the author participated in the writing of this declaration.

8 Several national expressions of World Vision are active members of the Micah Network.

9 It is worth noting that this policy predates by 13 years the organization's first and successful application for AusAID funding.

# References

Afghanistan Analysts Network (AAN) (n.d.), *Ten Dead in Badakhshan 6: Local Taliban Say it was Murder*, retrieved 15 September 2010, <www.aan-afghanistan.org/index.asp?id = 986>.

— (n.d.), *Ten Dead in Badakhshan 4: Afghan Reactions (UPDATED)*, retrieved 22 September 2010, <http://aan-afghanistan.com/index.asp?id = 971>.

AusAID (2010a), *Overseas Aid Gift Deduction Scheme Guidelines*, retrieved 2 November 2010, <www.ausaid.gov.au/ngos/pdfs/oagds_guidelines.pdf>.

— (2010b), *AusAID-NGO Cooperation Program (ANCP) Guidelines*, retrieved 2 November 2010, <www.ausaid.gov.au/ngos/pdfs/ancp_guidelines.pdf>.

Australian Council for International Development (ACFID) (2009), *ACFID Code of Conduct*, retrieved 1 November 2010, <www.acfid.asn.au/acfid/code-of-conduct/acfid-code-of-conduct>.

BBC (n.d.), *Foreign Medical Workers Among 10 Killed in Afghanistan*, retrieved 15 September 2010, <www.bbc.co.uk/news/world-south-asia-10900338>.

Boyd, S. (2009), *In the Thick of It: Why the Church Is an Essential Partner for Sustainable Development in the World's Poorest Communities*, UK: Tearfund.

CBM Australia (2008), *Development and Evangelism Policy*. CBM Australia.

Clarke, G. (2007), 'Agents of transformation? donors, faith-based organisations and international development', *Third World Quarterly*, 28(1).

Costas, O. (1982), *Christ Outside the Gate: Mission Beyond Christendom*. Maryknoll, NY: Orbis.

Department for International Development (2010), *Civil Society Challenge Fund Application Guidelines*, retrieved 22 October 2010, <http://www.dfid.gov.uk/Documents/funding/CSCF-application-guidelines-2010.pdf>.

Edwards, M. A. (2003), *The Love That Does Justice*, retrieved 14 October 2010, <http://futurepositive.org/docs/The%20Love%20That%20Does%20Justice.pdf>.

Grant, J. A. and Hughes, D. A. (2009), *Transforming the World: The Gospel and Social Responsibility*. Nottingham, UK: Apollos.

Hunt, J. (2002), 'The Jubilee 2000 campaign in Australia: an evaluation', *Internal Jubilee 2000 Report*.

Hurst, M. S. (2010), 'Seeking the Shalom of Afghanistan', *TEAR Target*, 4.

International Assistance Mission (IAM) (2009), *Annual Report 2009*, retrieved 23 September 2010 <www.iam-afghanistan.org/sites/default/files/IAM_Annual_report_2009.pdf>.

— (2010) *On the Death of 10 of the 12 Nuristan Eye Camp Team Members*, retrieved 16 September 2010, <www.iam-afghanistan.org/what-we-do/eye-care/outreach/press-release-1-اعلامیه-مطبوعاتی->.

James, R. (2009), *Handle With Care: Engaging with Faith Based Organisations in Development*, retrieved 1 October 2010, <www.intrac.org/resources.php?action = resource&id = 625.

Marshall, K. and Keough, L. (eds) (2004), *Mind, Heart and Soul in the Fight Against Poverty*. Washington, DC: World Bank.

Micah Network (n.d.), *The Micah Network Declaration on Integral Mission*, retrieved 9 November 2010, <www.micahnetwork.org/en/integral-mission/micah-declaration>.

— (n.d.), *Our Beliefs*, retrieved 1 October 2010, <www.micahnetwork.org/en/about-us/our-beliefs>.

— (2007), *Disaster Management Working Group Papers*, retrieved 27 October 2010, <www.micahnetwork.org/en/page/papers-2007-south-asia-micah-network-disaster-management-working-group>.

Okaalet, P. (2002), 'The role of faith based organizations in the fight against HIV and AIDS in Africa', *Transformation*, 19(4).

Ramachandra, V. (n.d.), *What is Integral Mission?* retrieved 20 October 2010, <www.micahnetwork.org/sites/micahnetwork.org/files/WhatIsIntegralMission_IMI-THE-001.pdf>.

Sider, R. J. (1993), *One-Sided Christianity: Uniting the Church to Heal a Lost and Broken World*. Grand Rapids, MI: Zondervan.

William, R. (2009), *New Perspectives on Faith and Development*, retrieved 21 October 2010, <www.archbishopofcanterbury.org/2605>.

# 8

# Palms Australia: Missionaries, International Development Volunteers and Beyond: Prophetic Wisdom for Cross-Cultural Engagement

Roger O'Halloran

## Introduction

This chapter examines the evolution of a programme, from its birth in 1961, as the Paulian Association Lay Missionary Secretariat (PALMS) to the eve of its Jubilee (fiftieth year) from a mission-sending programme to an International Development Volunteer (IDV) programme. This chapter considers influences on the vision, mission, values, philosophy, policies, process and practice that have taken the programme beyond simply being either a missionary service or an international development programme.

Emphasis will be given to the influences during a key transition period from the 1990s until 2010 with a particular spotlight on the refinement of the programme in the decade 1995–2005.

The chapter draws largely on the author's experience over 18 years as a volunteer in the field, employee, president and executive director of the association that runs the programme. Most of the analysis is reliant on that experience and of all who in that time have shared the experience of their involvement. The chapter also outlines external pressures for change in organizational practice, invites the reader to explore ideas from literature and research that inspired transformational thinking in both mission and development and refers to subsequent research that has examined the results of change and suggests further organizational refinement.

The Paulian Association came into existence as a Sydney-based lay movement within the Catholic Church in 1956 (Paulian Association, 1981). The first meeting of PALMS was held in July 1961 and the first lay missionaries were sent in January 1962. For at least the first 30 years it would have been fair enough to characterize these lay missionaries as Catholics volunteering to be sent (qualified or not) to help in education, health, building and other programmes and to reinforce the evangelistic and proselytizing mission of the Catholic Church to 'natives' in the developing world.[1]

By 2002, in light of the fact that PALMS had become the central programme and the only name of the association recognized outside Sydney, the membership renamed and reconstituted the Paulian Association as Palms Australia (Palms). In the subsequent desire to articulate a clear emphasis on development, Palms produced the following:

> An economic, social, cultural, spiritual and ecological process which encourages the empowerment and wellbeing of individuals, communities and organisations to reduce poverty, enjoy basic human rights and work towards a future of interdependent and ecological sustainability (Palms, 2010a).

It remains the introduction to Palms Australia's development philosophy today.

## Prophetic Wisdom Enlightens Development: Some Basics

While Palms Australia has abandoned its missionary roots as those of a bygone era, the contemporary prophetic wisdom of missiologists, theologians and other prophets continues to animate a 'dynamic' (Georgeou, 2010, p. 7) IDV programme. Those who engage cross-culturally with a narrow focus (many missionaries, development 'professionals' and academics) find

Palms extraordinarily eclectic and conceptually complicated. Volunteers and host communities and others more intimately engaged with Palms suggest that it embodies the successful integration of developments in mission with the mission of development.

This chapter highlights the intellectual thought and scholarship of missionaries, theologians and other contemporary prophets, whose reflections on cross-cultural engagement have reinforced Palms' understanding that development is inseparable from culture and beliefs, and show how this principle underscores Palms entire approach. This approach, which means that the priority for Palms IDVs is to build relationship and learn from their hosts rather than operating out of a narrow focus, such as a Western neo-liberal development focus (Georgeou, 2010, pp. 44–51), is uncritically adopted by most North-South volunteers by virtue of their enculturation.

It probably needs to be understood that Palms has a vision to achieve much more than one-way host-community development. The integration into the programme of contemporary prophetic thinking on building cross-cultural relationship creates a unique opportunity for IDVs to achieve superior mutual benefits. In fact it is an approach suitable for those in government, environment, economic and other sectors seeking authentic cross-cultural dialogue and may be the only way to advance peaceful and sustainable global solutions in any cross-cultural engagement.

Unfortunately, there is an absence of rigorous study demonstrating how successfully IDV programmes achieve their outcomes over the longer term. There is, however, a long tradition of cross-cultural missionary movement from churches in the North to the South, and in that sphere there has been a significant reflection on outcomes. Palms has found that tapping into this rich source of understanding has provided comprehensive insights into the dynamics of cross-cultural relationships and some very sound underpinnings for effective development practice.

The faith outcomes that missionaries have attempted to achieve might be dismissed as very different to the more economic and social, or more recently, ecological and governance outcomes, set for IDVs. However, with the mission of both conceived out of Western tradition and thinking and applied using processes and symbols from that starting place, the barriers to success are fundamentally the same. An ill-prepared IDV from a completely different culture is as much without knowledge of critical success factors as will be missionaries from the same tradition.

Another reason for Palms turning to particular prophetic pilgrims that they have is that these are missionaries who have frequently stayed longer in host communities than any IDVs or anthropologists. Furthermore, they are also not missionaries who have let their zeal to plant their faith override their reflection on the merits of their approach. Indeed, true to the call of their faith, they are deeply reflective on their experience of relationship with people of a culture different from their own.

As indicated, this chapter later identifies the particular prophets and the influence their thinking on cross-cultural relationships has had on the Values, Vision, and Mission statements, which express the key concepts at the heart of Palms' procedures, particularly in the preparation and support of Palms IDVs. Next, however, it is worth putting some of the catalysts for change into perspective.

## Catalysts for Change: Incongruence and External Pressures

By the 1990s, PALMS had sent around 1,000 missionary volunteers, primarily to teach, build, nurse and help administer Catholic Church missions in some 35 countries. It was, no doubt, a proud achievement. It may have differed little from other international volunteer sending agencies (IVSAs) operating in the 'development age' (Georgiou, 2010, pp. 32–44)[2] except that, as a lay missionary organization, PALMS had the added dimension of serving the interests of the Catholic Church.

> The Paulian Association is a work of the Lay Apostolate established under the authority of His Eminence Cardinal Gilroy. The task that P.A.L.M.S. has set itself is . . . (3) To place P.A.L.M.S. at the disposal of Monsignor Thomas (National Director, Catholic Mission), The Vicars Apostolic and all Missionary Orders (Boylan, 1961, p. 1).

In the early 1980s, PALMS began receiving a small annual grant from the Australian Government, persuaded perhaps that PALMS volunteers, while named lay missionaries, were fulfilling similar objectives to the fully funded Australian Volunteers Abroad. PALMS subsequently also joined the Australian Council for Overseas Aid (ACFOA),[3] the peak body for all agencies engaging in overseas aid and development. Was PALMS beginning to consider assignments beyond the jobs in Catholic missions unable to be filled by locals? Was it considering a mission more significant and better able to exploit the capacity of qualified professionals now presenting for mission? Not yet.

Despite being at the forefront, globally, of lay missionary movements and volunteer sending in 1961, in 1990s' Australia, PALMS began to appear somewhat anachronistic even to some within its Catholic Church base. Much anecdotal evidence suggests that after the death of the Paulian Association's creative and inspiring founding Director, Roy Boylan, in 1979, significant directional conflict had arisen. While some volunteers were still indicating a rewarding individual experience, the PALMS vision, and the living out of it, did not evolve much beyond a vague 'doing good' to help the church provide for the 'oppressed and dispossessed' living in 'third world' communities.

Right through until the 1990s, PALMS struggled to deal with internal unease regarding the ability of an increasingly dated and compromised mission philosophy to provide direction in a new era. The understanding of the terms in the acronym, let alone the acceptance of the message, was very different 30 years after the founding. Part-time chaplains and other associated religious missionaries would suggest new mission paradigms for cross-cultural dialogue within changing cultural contexts such as globalization. Unfortunately, a sustained attempt to map a path forwards seemed to be beyond the capacity of the voluntary executive, management (with other programmes dominating attention) and a small staff stretched to implement the recruitment preparation.

By this time, the Australian Government, which had become the key funder, did begin to seek the articulation of a clearer and more relevant development message. Until this time, they had been satisfied with the rhetoric in PALMS acquittal of funds indicating that volunteer placements were relieving poverty, but AusAID had begun to shift emphasis to volunteers sustainably achieving poverty reduction through the transfer of skills. In most PALMS volunteer placements, if the capacity of individuals and local communities was being developed, it was unintentional, as if by osmosis, and, no effective audit was done in the country to see that the rhetoric matched practice.

Perhaps inspired by the Government's new interest in monitoring the activities of volunteer agencies, or maybe seeing the need to relieve some stress of the staff workload, in the early 1990s, the PALMS co-ordinator implemented a renewal of organizational procedures. While valuable, it was more about systems than direction. Discussion of the relevance, scope and intention of PALMS' mission still only really occurred through presentations by the missionary religious at PALMS courses for the preparation of departing missionaries. Speakers from Australian Catholic Relief (later Caritas) did give a brief introduction to their work (including ideas around Catholic Social Teaching and development) at the same courses; however, PALMS, as such, had neither a documented development philosophy, nor a set of strategies with a clear direction to volunteers about how such might be achieved.

The Church 'missions' being served overseas, primarily in the Pacific, and in particular in Papua New Guinea, understood PALMS volunteers as missionaries faithfully building, teaching, nursing or doing whatever it took to grow the reach of the institutional church. Clearly education and health facilities being developed by the church demonstrated an interest in the welfare (Georgeou, 2010, pp. 35–7)[4] of its flock. However, it could at best be described as 'loving welfare' rather than the capacity building of which AusAID were beginning to conceive.

While the communities being served were undoubtedly better off for having replicas of first world clinics and schools and even general stores, in a few cases, they did not have the capacity or cultural predisposition to run them. Such facilities were 'successful' to the extent that religious missionary congregations and PALMS and other lay volunteer missionaries were available to fill all the major positions, and funds from the Church in the North poured in to help achieve the missionary effort. Among a number of the missionary leaders who set up the facilities, there appeared to be an accepted wisdom that embarking on a training programme to develop the capacity of the local community would be a waste of time, or worse, eventually leading to movement of locals so trained away from the service of the mission.

PALMS was being pulled in different directions by AusAID, the expectations of church hierarchies in Australia and overseas and a growing scepticism within the Australian church and society about the efficacy of traditional mission practice. Until this period, expression of a need to change had been met with strong resistance internally, characterizing any change as pulling PALMS away from the mission for which it was established. This might be explained by the fact that the director of the Paulian Association at the time, had worked for, or been a volunteer with PALMS, since inception in 1956 and still had a strong passion for the inspiration of the charismatic first director who had died in the job in 1979.

Perhaps weariness with resistance to change coincided with the appointment of this author as PALMS co-ordinator late in 1995. Recognizing the need for change by the beginning of 1996 and citing the question: 'What new directions do you think Palms might take?' (O'Halloran, 1996a, p. 3) from his job interview, the new co-ordinator launched a 'Review of Life for PALMS' in the quarterly PALMS POST, which was distributed to all host communities, volunteers, returned volunteers and others in the Australian network. It built a case to 'renew and revitalise' PALMS approach to mission opening with the words of Franciscan theologian Richard Rohr:

> How many times must one turn around? How can the Gospel ask for repeated, ongoing turning around? The answer lies in our very human tendency to find another comfort zone. We faced one shadow, we're proud of our effort, and we think we're converted for good . . . Then the Gospel orders us again, turn around. Again? We're addicted to this self-image we worked so hard on and want to keep it. All right so we build another castle and settle down. Then the Gospel says once more, turn around. It's always about letting go, a perpetual series of turning around (Rohr, 1994, pp. 131–2).

By mid-1996, Jim Knight (SVD), a former PALMS chaplain, arranged a visit to Australia by missionary priest, Father Anthony Gittins (CSsP). He inspired an intimate group of the Paulian Association Executive and staff that PALMS mission needed to be about the radical ministry of Jesus to remove cultural structures of sin. Assisting the oppressed had been Palms rhetoric for some time; however, Gittins provided a theory offering a new inspiration for thinking about mission that could also underpin an important rational for engagement in more effective community development.

Gittins was the first of many from the Chicago Theological Union (CTU) to give a spine to PALMS' mission that assisted those within, previously resisting change, to see him as providing a link to their mission. It also inspired others internally with a direction forwards that better clarified some of the rhetoric floating around PALMS. It opened the door to increased congruence with AusAID, although it fitted perhaps more than they would be comfortable with the dynamic politicization model of development (Georgeou, 2010, pp. 39–42). Also, volunteers exposed to Gittins' concept would start to experience less congruence in some more traditional mission placements. In Gittins' model, the traditional mission placement could be more easily interpreted as being part of a structure that was reinforcing oppression, rather than being an opportunity for authentic sustainable community development, as Palms would come to define it.

Gittins' model also challenged PALMS to educate the Australian Church, particularly the more conservative in the institutional hierarchy, who only perceived lay missionaries as serving the mission of the institution. Jim Knight also had expressed a view that as laity it might be more appropriate for PALMS volunteers to be working out of community-based organizations rather than directly for the institutional church. Tension about such was always evident, but without a robust rationale for another model, PALMS had been reluctant and lacked capacity to have an open conversation about where they stood.

Being muted in this way made it difficult to clearly promote the mission to those interested to participate in mutual development[5] rather than conventional and patronizing models of mission or development. The qualified and experienced professionals in their fields now ready to volunteer were coming from a social milieu that was less tolerant of traditional religious-lay hierarchy. There were alternative secular agencies able to place them where they might make a relevant contribution to community development.

This fitted with Bishop Geoffrey Robinson's claim (May 1996) that many Catholics no longer shared a common imagining. Leading up to and after Vatican II there was fresh discussion by theologians and members of the Church about different conceptions of their Church. The Catholic Church had become different things to different people.

To better appreciate PALMS' dilemma vis-à-vis its approach to mission, it will be useful now, as it was for the organization after the Gittins visit, to locate PALMS within a framework or model of mission. The next section draws largely on a paper by this author (O'Halloran, 1996b, pp. 3–5) and a presentation by Jim Knight (SVD) at a Palms Orientation Course.

## Models of Mission and Church

A decade after Vatican II, Avery Dulles (1974), using a similar approach to Marcello De C. Azevedo, S. J. (1985, pp. 601–20), provided a classifying system for distinguishing various models of church; Church as: 'Institution', 'Herald', 'Servant', 'Sacrament' or 'Communion'.

## Mission Supporting Church as Institution

This model was dominant in the Catholic Church globally until the 1960s. It implies a vertical relationship from God and Christ through Pope, bishops and priests to the laity. It is a model characterized by the notion that 'Father is always right'. Leadership is represented by strong intervention, a high degree of direction and correction and high dependence by followers.

While some claimed the Paulian Association was leading the laity to a new model of church, such rhetoric was unconvincing with evidence in 1997 still pointing to an obsequious relationship with the hierarchy. There was a perceived need for the support and recognition of the Australian Catholic Bishops, many of whom remained conservative in their expectation of deference to the institution. To some degree this explains why for many years PALMS evolution seemed somewhat caught or paralyzed between encouraging an authentic mission for laity and the mission of the institution.

In sending people into the field, PALMS had always worked within institutional church structures establishing links between the Catholic diocese from which the volunteer had come and the one within which they go to live. The Paulian director's claim in 1997 that '. . . rather than encouraging institutional power over the organisation, or its volunteers, this procedure was designed to build faith across cultures and provide a network of support for volunteers . . . '[6] may not have been understood by all within the institution. On one occasion in 1997, after hearing that PALMS had sent a volunteer to work in a refugee programme run by a Buddhist organization on the Thai/Burma boarder, the director of Catholic Mission challenged that the funding provided by them might be threatened. This was despite the fact that the substantial funding for PALMS placements, and all funding for this one, came from AusAID.

PALMS had always selected a missionary priest as chaplain because it was mainly the priests who had the opportunity to study and gain experience in theology, pastoral ministry and mission. In one sense, this gave priests power, but rather than attempting to exercise control, it would seem that most have provided PALMS with selfless service. One outcome of the 1996 PALMS 'Review of Life' was that not only the priests might serve as spiritual advisers; however, it was interesting that when the Paulian Association tried to appoint a lay chaplain a few years later, the Archbishop of Sydney advised that this would not be acceptable.

Concerned not to perpetuate a model in which it felt stymied, this author's 1996 paper announced that while PALMS remained keen to maintain association with individual clerics and Bishops and organizations of the church, such relationships should be seen as akin to the fellowship described in Acts of the Apostles (Acts 2:44–46), rather than as supporting a vertical concept of power or a wish to reinforce a model of institutional church.

## Mission as Herald

This model suggests a role as herald or messenger of the word of God. Lay Catholic access to theological colleges and biblical interpretation was not greatly encouraged until well after Vatican II. Lay heralds proclaiming the word by street corner preaching was not a tradition with which either the laity or the hierarchy was comfortable.

Paulians had, however, practised the more circumspect 'See, Judge, Act' process of Joseph Cardinal Cardijn and the Belgium Workers movement. This process encouraged members to identify issues in their society where people appeared to be disadvantaged, to seek discernment through theological reflection and to take relevant action within the community in relation to the word of God. In doing so, one would express values and a position vis-à-vis the culture of the world within which we live and through such action may be seen as a herald.

Boylan's commitment to '. . . place P.A.L.M.S. at the disposal of Monsignor Thomas The Vicars Apostolic . . .' did support the Church as herald model. There was evidence in a number of missions, still in 1997, that expatriate lay missionaries were there to simply strengthen the infrastructure of the institution, which in some cases supported little other activity in the community than preaching. In one case at an Australian mission, a volunteer's attempted engagement with the local community, outside of the mission, was criticized by the priest on the grounds that that was not the volunteer's purpose for being there. In 2001, a volunteer, at a mission in PNG where no training was provided, discovered that his free labour as a printer, threatened the viability of a local enterprise.

Simply supporting church enterprise, without community engagement, or through unfair advantage at the expense of a community enterprise, is not a model of mission as herald supported by Palms. Azevedo (1985, p. 611) identifies that: 'The word and its proclamation are not meant to reinforce confessional, institutional, social or political positions, or to abet the expansion of the Church as society'. While empowered to animate the word through Cardijn methodology, Palms understood its work by 1997 to be much bigger than mission as herald.

## Mission as Servant

This model at least opens one to the world than the above models, which are inclined to see the church as an exclusive society. We allow ourselves to be challenged by and, in turn, challenge the world in our example of service. It fits somewhat with the social teaching of the church around the preferential option for the poor. 'The disposition of the whole Church is one of universal service to humanity as such, which is now seen as one big family or indeed as the People of God' (Azevedo, 1985, p. 615).

This position taken by Vatican II represents a positive outlook on the capacity of the church to save the world. However, given the paternalistic institutional model by which the Catholic Church has been known, it becomes a difficult model to adopt convincingly. In this author's 1996 paper it was said: 'Providing members are willing to acknowledge their human frailty, the ideal, which this model represents should sit very comfortably with the work undertaken by PALMS' (O'Halloran, 1996a, p. 3).

A booklet sent to PALMS applicants in 1997, stated, '. . . lay people (have) as important a role to play as religious, and could add an extra dimension to the service of developing communities'. It was referring to volunteers having a variety of other qualifications, put at the service of communities, to train local people where they may want training and so develop capacities beyond simply spiritual needs. This is a good model of mission as servant, provided we are careful to ensure that it is the local community that identifies such needs.

PALMS had experienced similar difficulties to the rest of the Catholic Church in offering service not conceived as a need by the local community. While keen to serve, the only model of church that early PALMS missionaries knew, and took with them into the field, was institutional and Western. In many cases it was a religious missionary from Europe or Australia, also grounded in the model of institutional Western church, who had requested and welcomed them.

If the request is not one made because of a need recognized by the local community, it may be no more than paternalistic and probably inappropriate thinking about saving the world with 'developed world' knowledge and proficiency. While it may be well intended, service is at risk of meeting the agenda of the giver's need to be needed and resultant paternalism may produce unintended outcomes. Dependence rather than interdependence can be encouraged, which is does not fit with the principles of sustainable development.

In 1997, Palms was already clear that if this method alone were to provide the theological basis for the work of PALMS, volunteers could easily oppress the 'objects' of their service by 'working for' rather than 'working with' the poor.[7]

## Mission Supporting Church as Sacrament

Traditionally, the clergy have been predominately responsible for administration of sacraments.

> Already in the second half of the second century, a relationship between the bishop and the eucharist was fixed in many places; henceforth, priest's function will be gradually determined by his relationship to the eucharist Schillebeeckx (1983–4).

Like the model of church as institution '. . . the focus is on the ordained, on those whose primary duty is towards service of the community of believers through liturgical and other ministries . . .' (Lennan, 1995, p. 11). As laity, volunteers have limited authority to administer sacraments and as such are limited in their ability to reinforce this model of church as sacrament if this is how church as sacrament is accepted.

Vatican II expressed a broader position: 'Church exists in Christ as a sacrament or sign and an instrument of intimate union with God and of the unity of the whole human race' (Paul VI, 1964, p. 1). Many volunteers work in ways that will be seen as a sign of the visible presence of Christ and in 1997 PALMS' guidelines spoke of seeking the unity of the earth community. While PALMS' members are not ordained priests and can only administer some sacraments in '. . . special and grave circumstances . . .' (John Paul II, 1989, Footnote 72), it was identified in 1997 that PALMS' work in light of Lumen Gentium was very much in keeping with this model.

## Mission for Community

This model of 'church in communion' would appreciate diversity in its unity, but clearly is not achieved while there is oppressive poverty destroying human dignity. Structural poverty, the 'structure of sin' (John Paul II, 1991)[8] created by human beings yet to be liberated from their worldly focus, must be removed before this model of church is complete. In 1997, it was stated thus:

> It is the model of church (and mission) in which PALMS most strongly identifies its theology and development philosophy. For PALMS to play its part in achieving this model of church as acclaimed by Vatican II, it will require, what has been identified as: 'a counter cultural example with those who seek the same communion' (Gittins, 1996; O'Halloran, 1996c, pp. 1–3).

By this model, volunteers do not work 'at the disposal' of a church hierarchy; they take part in the ultimate sacrament of communion with the earth community; they do not arrogantly simply preach the word as heralds and they avoid serving the needs of the culturally oppressed paternalistically. To see everyone as sons and daughters of God, sharing the bounty of the earth responsibly, makes a significant difference that enables solidarity and appropriate sustainable development in all communities. Indeed, it is a model of mission intrinsically linked to a mission of mutual sustainable development.

This model, where mission and development are one, provides authentic and fitting engagement for lay volunteers. It is a collective search for love, justice and peace where no one is more or less important and as such requires prophetic formation. In particular, it requires that volunteers used to Western lifestyles be prepared for greater vulnerability (O'Halloran, 2001; Joyce, 2009) than if they were engaged in other models of mission and this is where contemporary missiologists provide such good guidance.

## Prophetic Wisdom Enlightens Development

This section highlights Palms' documents and procedures, and the particular thinking and reflection of the missiologists and other prophets that were brought to bear on them, as well as examining the subsequent ways in which we expect an IDVs approach to development to be influenced.

*Values statement*: Solidarity has been a key expression of Palms for probably as long as it has existed, but was only ever documented clearly since the organizational restructure. What was a vague notion that, no doubt, meant different things to different people, became a comprehensive statement and diagram on the basis of a presentation by Donal Dorr (1991, p. 62) where he interprets Micah (6:6–8) to underline a Christian mission. Solidarity is the ideal, but Dorr's statement and representation highlight the values that one must strive to achieve if one is to approach that ideal.

The values statement accords with the position PALMS took in 1997 when identifying most closely with a model of mission as a sacrament of unity in the world. It should underpin for IDVs that volunteering is not an opportunity to teach others, but an opportunity to interdependently achieve solidarity. If the vision statement describes the place we want to reach and the mission statement says what we are doing to get there, the values tell us the attitude of mind we need to have to do that mission and achieve that goal.

Formation of IDVs in the enabling values spelt out in the statement is '. . . a formation in solidarity and readiness to offer others not simply material aid but their very selves' (Benedict XVI, 2006, Sec. 30b). What Palms attempts to achieve with the formation of IDVs in these values (which also underpin the volunteer ethos discussed at the beginning of the chapter) is an attitude of mind that accepts that: 'The one who serves does not consider himself superior to the one served, however miserable his situation at the moment may be' (ibid, Sec.35). Paulo Freire (1970, p. 72) provides the link from these values to the way in which Palms encourages IDVs to undertake their mission of development: 'Education must begin with the solution of the teacher-student contradiction, by reconciling the poles of the contradiction so that both are simultaneously students and teachers'.

Mission statement: (Palms, 2010d) Palms mission statement is in three parts. There is no order of importance, but there is sequence for IDVs, which should assist to achieve the reconciliation of the contradiction identified in Freire's pedagogy. The first aspect of the mission is expressed in a direct quotation from CTU missiologist Roger Schroeder (2000, pp. 147–61): 'Advance mutually enriching and challenging relationships of understanding, acceptance and care, to the point of sharing worlds of meaning in the deepest sense, with people of a culture different from one's own'.

This suggests that the relationship between the volunteer and the host becomes one of deep reciprocity and Palms recognizes this as the building block to the second part of its mission identifying what AusAID would recognize as the development mission: 'Build the capacity of individuals and strengthening institutions through knowledge and skill exchange between Palms global volunteers and communities seeking their assistance'.

An authentic sacrament of unity, requiring mutual relationship, is difficult to achieve while parts of the same body are prevented from developing their full capacity. Many Catholic missions where PALMS went to work did not use knowledge and skill 'exchange' to build the capacity of both the volunteer and host communities, and building institutional capacity was often more about building the institution of a Western church, and associated infrastructure, rather than identifying that dialogue and exchange provided opportunities for learning where all might 'become human together'.[9] Palms offers two advantages over religious missionaries for being able to achieve the development mission.

First, it is able to offer to lay volunteers with a broad variety of qualifications, skills and experience. Indeed, Palms engages an even broader range of talent for this important aspect of its mission by following Papal teaching:

> In proclaiming the principles for a solution of the worker question, Pope Leo XIII wrote: 'This most serious question demands the attention and the efforts of others' . . . This affirmation has become a permanent element of the Church's social teaching, and also explains why Pope John XXIII addressed his Encyclical on peace to 'all people of good will' . . . and, as I have written in the Encyclical *Sollicitudo rei socialis,* there is a reasonable hope that the many people who profess no religion will also contribute to providing the social question with the necessary ethical foundation. . . . Indeed, openness to dialogue and to cooperation is required of all people of good will, and in particular of individuals and groups with specific responsibilities in the areas of politics, economics and social life, at both the national and international levels (John Paul II, 1991, Para. 60).

Secondly, as Jim Knight points out, lay volunteers, not identified as part of the Institutional Church, live closer to the experience of the host community and are able to be identified more easily by local communities as sharing similar joys and struggles. The religious in many host communities, where life is more hierarchical, are frequently deemed to be on a higher plane, making unity and mutuality more difficult to achieve. While this provides a rationale for Palms IDVs living more closely with communities, and working in community-based organizations, rather than in institutional church structures, it is not all that needs to be done to achieve the desired mutual 'skill and knowledge exchange'.

In 2003, AusAID were using the term skill transfer as a means of development assistance. As Freire indicates, if skill transfer is the mission, there is a significant imbalance of power; a temptation to egotism, which Georgeou's (2010, p. 167) paper pointed out as a significant motivating factor of volunteers: 'In imparting technical skills and knowledge, volunteers tended to take on the role of 'leader' and expressed a desire for control in relationships with locals'.

It was within the 2003 debates around accreditation that Palms introduced 'knowledge and skill exchange' as preferable, given the mutuality it believed was important in cross-cultural volunteering. Skill exchange is a process where the volunteer and host communities explore possibilities together, without the implication of 'transfer' suggesting that the volunteer has superior understanding. In Freire's (1970, p. 54) words:

> No pedagogy which is truly liberating can remain distant from the oppressed by treating them as unfortunates and by presenting for their emulation models from among the oppressors. The oppressed must be their own example in the struggle for their redemption.

Secondly 'exchange' implies that volunteers have something valuable to learn. Emphasizing 'knowledge and skill exchange', and only slowly building relationships, gives the volunteer the opportunity to learn:

1. Language and culture that help one to (a) understand the structures (Why are conditions this way?) and (b) to earn the respect in the local community required for the host to trust a stranger (volunteer) (Gittins, 2002, Ch. 2).
2. That technologies and approaches employed in the West may not be development solutions in the host community; '. . . the only Christian solution I can see is the adoption of a different model of development from the one which lies at the heart of the present Western way of life . . .' (Dorr, 1991, p. 59).
3. Humility, as one comes to recognize that the hosts may have a lifestyle incorporating skills and knowledge needed by the West in order to pursue a more sustainable and peaceful future. 'Development volunteers commented that what they gained from their experience abroad affected their attitudes and behaviour towards others once they returned to Australia. Lisa said that she had gained a better appreciation of living in another culture and empathy for the experiences of migrants in Australia' (Georgeou, 2010, p. 222).

Also reliant on the success of the first is the third aspect of Palms Mission: 'Engage Australian communities and host communities through Palms global volunteers so that each increases their awareness and enthusiasm to encourage just, sustainable, interdependent and peaceful development'.

Georgeou's (2010, p. 225) research found that:

> Volunteers are pivotal in linking the Australian community to the volunteer's host community. In line with Spence (2001; 2005), this study also found that volunteers contributed to friendship networks which cross cultural divides, contributing to different understandings of being which are important to peace building'.

Peace is identified in Palms' Vision, and Deep Peace (Shalom) in Palms' Values, as the ultimate realization of mission as a sacrament of unity in the world. Georgeou's (2010) research and Australian Government Volunteer Program (AGVP) Review (Kwitko and McDonald 2009) both point to the need to assist friends and families to develop a conceptual framework and understand the day-to-day life of a volunteer in placement as well as formalize opportunities for the volunteer to share the learnings from their experience, after returning home.

It is the combination of the three aspects of Palms' Mission that underscores why the model of Church as a Sacrament of Unity is where Palms best fits. Being a sacrament of unity cannot be achieved, where structures of sin, as explained by Gittins, exist. First, justice requires that opportunity is shared so that all can develop their capacities. This can only happen if mutual and trusting relationships are developed and understanding across cultures is facilitated.

## Conclusion

The founding of PALMS was somewhat ground-breaking in the Catholic Church of 1961, prior to Vatican II identifying a greater engagement of the laity in the mission of the church. However, at the time, individual lay people were going off to the missions without training and formation 'and many received a tremendous shock', so the obvious need was similar to what it is today. At that time of course it was not at all surprising that Roy Boylan as the founding director subjugated the activities of PALMS to the hierarchy of institutional church.

From time to time there were tensions around how much authority the hierarchy was exercising, but up until the time of Roy's death in 1979, there was no significant pressure for change in the original mandate, or how it was implemented. In the 1980s when Palms needed to respond to significant social change and changes in the way the mission of the church was being interpreted, it struggled. By the mid-1990s its mission from the 1960s that took it comfortably enough through the 1970s was irrelevant to almost all stakeholders.

Palms would only find relevance again when pressure from the major funder, AusAID, forced it to identify and seriously consider the model of mission by which it could undertake authentic mutual development. Spending time considering the wisdom of the missiologists in the second half of the 1990s brought about the realization that the mission they were describing was integral to or even the same as the development in which IDVs could appropriately engage. And although its major funder was starting to push along a different path of development at the beginning of the new millennium, Palms had become inspired and confident in the expression of its development mission.

Palms uses the wisdom emanating from all sources previously cited. These are the missiologists, theologians and other prophets who assist to prepare IDVs to be vulnerable, so that they might take their ego off the tower we in the West are encouraged to erect for it and achieve the solidarity required. For it is only in such solidarity that we can be liberated together.

These missionaries, theologians and other prophets assist the preparation of pilgrims, are able to negotiate transition and are open to transformation. Observance of their messages, identified in Palms' values, vision, mission, volunteer ethos and development philosophy puts IDVs in touch with their own creative spirit and prophetic self, assisting them to question the taken-for-granted in their own cultural tradition, and not to leave a careless footprint on the sacred ground of others. Volunteers open to the wisdom of these prophets are prepared to be humbly animated by the insights of those with whom they go to work; and share, again with humility, skills that they have had the good fortune to develop, knowing that this mutual animation is the substance of collective liberation.

Palms is the intermediary endeavouring to bring the message through a more secular language to the broader public, because, as Popes for over 100 years have noted, all are a part of the solution. This is why the more fundamental religious will be heard to comment that much of the language of Palms does not clearly state anything to do with Mission. Indeed, it is hard to say that many in the church appreciate a mission that integrates poverty reduction and sustainable global development as necessary adjuncts to achieving the Vatican II model of church as a sacrament of unity in the world. In Australia, as in many countries, mission and development are still divided between two church bodies. The Pontifical Mission Societies do mission (in its various models) and Caritas with a rationale from Catholic Social Teaching takes on the various constructs of development as they evolve over time.

Equally many in secular society are still to appreciate what contemporary missiologists, theologians and other prophets have identified. A consultant engaged for AusAID once remarked that Palms' vision was not something AusAID had instruments for measuring. He would be recognized by Georgeou (2010) as having a managerial/instrumental approach to development. However, while Georgeou identified some of the conceptual influences of prophets like Freire, cited above, and is able to suggest this as the reason for Palms fitting somewhat within a dynamic politicisian model of development, her secular academic perspective also fails to identify the missiologists, theologians and other prophets who enlighten Palms' approach to development.

For the development academics and clerics such separation is the norm and, as said by way of introduction, any who engages cross-culturally, with a narrow focus, will find Palms extraordinarily eclectic or conceptually complicated. On the other hand, those who choose Palms as volunteers, or supporters, while identifying some of the tensions mentioned by Georgeou's research, also find in Palms' expression of the integration of mission and development a strong calling to solidarity. A solidarity that is more than 'a vague sort of compassion, or shallow distress at others' misfortune, but involves a liberation of victims, oppressors and 'innocent' bystanders, allowing all life to live to the full. This is why the conclusion that Palms embodies the successful integration of developments in mission with the mission of development is reached.

Palms, as a learning organization, does need to address a number of tensions identified by Georgeou. Doing so will create an even stronger programme. And given that, Palms might well be correct that a programme integrating their processes for achieving authentic cross-cultural dialogue is required for the success of all, in every sector, who seek sustainable solutions to address global challenges.

## Notes

1 The first lay missionaries went to Papua New Guinea and later to other parts of the Pacific and the world.

2 Georgeou's (2010, pp. 32–44) discussion of an historical overview of development volunteering from the development age to the end of the Cold War is a recommended reading for providing the 'fashionable' global development models influencing the approach of Palms and other IVSAs at this time.

3 Later renamed Australian Council for International Development (ACFID).

4 Georgeou (2010, pp. 35–7) characterizes this model as the Charity/Welfare Model of development.

5 Georgeou (2010, pp. 39–42) characterizes this as an aspect of the Politicization Model of development.

6 Mary Gilchrist in conversation with the author.

7 Georgeou (2010, pp. 40–1) for a discussion of 'working for' vis-à-vis 'working with'.

8 Also see Australian Catholic Bishops' Conference (1992).

9 Columbian missionary Father Noel Connolly developed this idea at Palms Orientation courses 2001–4.

# References


Australian Catholic Bishops' Conference (1992) *Common Wealth for the Common Good: A Statement on the Distribution of Wealth in Australia.* Collins Dove, North Blackburn, Victoria.

Azevedo, M. (1985), 'Basic ecclesial communities: a meeting point of ecclesiologies', Theological Studies, 46; 601–20.

Benedict XVI (2006), Deus Caritas Est. Sec. 30 b, <www.vatican.va/holy_father/benedict_xvi/encyclicals/documents/hf_ben-xvi_enc_20051225_deus-caritas-est_en.html>.

Boylan, R. (1961), 'The task that PALMS has set itself', PALMS POST, 1, 1.

Dorr, D. (1991), 'A spirituality of justice', A paper presented to the Turning Point Conference: *Celebrating the Centenary of RERUM NOVARUM and the Future of Catholic Social Teaching;* Shinnick, D. (1992) Archdiocese of Adelaide (October, 1991).

Dulles, A. (1974), Models of the Church: a Critical Assessment of the Church in All its Aspects, Garden City, NY: Doubleday.

Freire, P. (1970) *Pedagogy of the oppressed.* New York: Herder and Herder.

Georgeou, N. (2010), 'Australian Volunteers Abroad in the Asia/Pacific Region: Altruistic and Egoistic Desire in a Neoliberal Paradigm (2006–2009)', unpublished Doctoral thesis, University of Wollongong.

Gittins, A. (1996), 'Mission and culture: removing the structures of sin', Talk sponsored by Divine Word Missionaries, Palms, Croydon Park, NSW, 4 March, 1996.

—. (2002), 'Strangers in the place—learning to be', Ministry at the Margins, Maryknoll, NY: Gittins Orbis Books.

John Paul II (1989), The Vocation and Mission of Lay Faithful In the Church and in the World, <www.vatican.va/holy_father/john_paul_ii/apost_exhortations/documents/hf_jp-ii_exh_30121988_christifideles-laici_en.html>.

—. (1991), Centismus Annus . . . In Everyday Language, <www.vatican.va/holy_father/john_paul_ii/encyclicals/documents/hf_jp-ii_enc_01051991_centesimus-annus_en.html>.

Joyce, B. (2009), 'Embracing Vulnerability in an Age of Fear', retrieved November 2010, <www.palms.org.au/about/papers>.

Kwitko, L. and McDonald, D. (2009), *Australian Government Volunteer Program (AGVP) Review.*

Lennan, R. (1995), *Redefining The Church; Vision & Practice*, Alexandria, NSW: EJ Dwyer.

O'Halloran, R. (1996a), 'Review of life for PALMS', *PALMS POST*, Summer.

—. (1996b), 'PALMS: what model of church?', *PALMS POST*, Winter.

—. (1996c), 'Counter-cultural visitors inform our review', *PALMS POST*, Autumn.

—. (2001) 'Achieving solidarity with international neighbours', The idea of the Vulnerable Volunteer was initiated in a paper for Volunteering: NGO Conference for the International Year of Volunteers. Melbourne, May 2001.

Palms Australia (2010a), *Development Philosophy*, retrieved November 2010, <www.palms.org.au/about/papers>.

—. (2010d), *Our Mission*, retrieved November 2010, <www.palms.org.au/about>.

Paulian Association (1981), *Paulian Association: First 25 Years*, Sydney: Paulian

Association.
Paul VI (1964), *Lumen Gentium*, 1, retrieved November 2010, <www.vatican.va/archive/hist_councils/ii_vatican_council/documents/vat-ii_const_19641121_lumen-gentium_en.html>.
Rhor, R. (1994), *Quest for the Grail*, Crossroad, New York.
Robinson, G. (May 1996), *Nothing so Beautiful, Nothing so Ugly*, Sydney.
Schillebeeckx, E. (1993), 'The changing meaning of ministry', *Cross Currents*, Winter, 1983–4.
Schroeder, R. (2000), 'Entering someone else's garden: cross-cultural mission', in Bevans, S. Doidge, E. and Schreiter, R. (eds), *The Healing Circle: Essays in Cross-Cultural Mission*, Chicago: CCGM Publications.

# 9

# Blurring Mission and Development in the Mennonite Central Committee[1]

Philip Fountain

## Introduction

For much of the past 60 years there has been scant sustained attention by mainstream development actors and scholars to questions on the relationship between religion and development. Observing this situation, Ver Beek (2000) has characterized spirituality as a development 'taboo'. Similarly, Marshall (2001, pp. 368, 340) has called religion a 'blind spot', which has been 'strikingly disarticulated' by mainstream development actors. Together with Keough, Marshall (2004, p. xv) has also noted the paucity of academic literature documenting the work carried out by religious communities and actors.[2] Within the last 5–10 years, however, this situation has begun to change in perhaps the most important and far-reaching transformation in the discipline of development studies. Religion is now back on the mainstream research agenda to an unprecedented extent. In his writing, only a few years after the authors cited above, Hovland (2008, p. 171) notes the extraordinary recent 'surge of interest' in religion and development. But this surge is not constrained to academia. Balchin (2007, pp. 532–3) has suggested that the 'f-word' ('faith-based') is so 'policy-sexy' right now, and that it has become an almost obligatory buzzword for those seeking to get ahead in international development policy.

The return of religion is reflected in recent shifts by many major official development agencies around the world, including: George W. Bush's 'faith-based initiative' in the United States (Firoz and Matthews, 2003), the United Kingdom's Department for International Development's sponsorship of the Religions and Development programme housed in the University of Birmingham (Rakodi, 2007), the Australian government's funding of the Church Partnership Program in Papua New Guinea (Hauck et al., 2005; Hauck 2010), United Nations Population Fund attempts to engage with faith-based organizations on HIV/AIDS (UNFPA, 2007) and initiatives by the World Bank to partner with Christian churches in Africa (Belshaw et al., 2001). The realization that 'faith matters' (Clarke, 2006), it seems, while coming late to development industry and academe, has nevertheless hit with considerable force. Religion, as Deneulin and Rakodi (2011, p. 48) have argued, is 'no longer avoidable'.

Yet, both the ignoring of religion and the celebration of its new-found celebrity status have tended to obscure a more complex history. The world of international aid and development has long been haunted by the spectre of religion. The impact of 'religion'[3] has been pervasive even in its apparent absence. One of the most important ways in which religion has left its mark has been in the repeated and sustained attempts by mainstream actors to expunge it from the work of development. This is particularly apparent in the attempts made to create a sharp demarcation between 'mission' and 'development', with the former freighted with religious associations and the latter commonly imagined as a domain of technical and scientific intervention. This dichotomy is so firmly inscribed in policy documents throughout the development industry that it should be regarded as a core dogma of development orthodoxy.

## Separation of Mission and Development

One example comes from the Canadian International Development Agency (CIDA), which has a reputation for being a progressive and forward-thinking development institution (Morrison 1998, p. 19). In 1993 and 1994, CIDA engaged in an early foray into debates on 'religion and development' with Canadian churches and Christian NGOs, an initiative that was well ahead of its time. A follow-up report articulated a response to these dialogues in 22 points (CIDA, 1995). While authored by CIDA, the document was widely circulated and discussed by other participants. Remarkably, there is a strong affirmation of the role of 'spirituality' with the recognition that 'there is a spiritual dimension to the development process' and that '[e]fforts to create a rigid separation between religion and developmental processes are often inappropriate, and may be counter-developmental'. However, a few paragraphs later, a rigid division is re-asserted:

> It is natural and appropriate that Christian NGOs integrate the spiritual dimension into their relief and development programming, and do so in ways that a *secular state agency* can not . . . . Christian NGOs recognize and agree that CIDA funds are not to be used for programming designed to convert people from one religious faith to another, or to build up church and ecclesiastical structures apart from relief and development programming . . . The promotion and development of a particular religious faith is not part of CIDA's mandate. Funding for this type of activity should come from church-related sources and not the state. This is not an area where CIDA and Christian NGOs share common goals and objectives, and the funding of these activities should be kept separate (my emphasis).

In this excerpt, it is clear that CIDA seeks to expel certain aspects of religion from its funding chain. To do so, CIDA explicitly identifies itself as a 'secular' agency and locates this identity in opposition to the 'religious' identity of Christian NGOs; while rarely stated quite so openly, this assumption undergirds much contemporary official development assistance (Deneulin and Bano, 2009, p. 110). However, neither 'secular' nor 'religious' is given definitional clarity; a notoriously complicated endeavour in the discipline of anthropology (Bowie, 2006, pp. 18–22). Instead, it simply assumes that everyone *knows* what is being talked about and that a secular-religious split can (and should) be taken for granted. While it is surmised that common ground between CIDA's secular agenda and religious actors exists (and therefore the possibility of partnership), there are also clearly areas of incommensurability. CIDA carves out a cluster of activities associated with church assistance and religious proselytizing, which it deems illegitimate for funding. As a secular agency, CIDA aims to contribute only to secular development, even if it occasionally makes use of religious actors to do so.

In mainstream development circles, church assistance and religious proselytizing are the default activities captured by the notion of 'mission'. CIDA's discursive demarcation between its development activities and those of 'mission' is illustrative of a widespread tendency among development donors to appear to rehabilitate religious actors, or at least render them amenable for 'partnership', while at the same time, keeping the religiosity of such actors at an arm's length. This bounding of religion, a 'policing of the sublime' (Milbank, 2006, pp. 101–44), remains a key domain of development governmentality. This imagining of a secular realm devoid of religious association is, crucially, itself an intervention into the religious, that is, a religious intervention. CIDA's insistence on a mission–development binary is a radical disciplining and re-construction of religion and should be seen as a potentially transformative attempt to re-work religious subjectivities in ways that run parallel to explicit proselytizing. Far from being neutral, CIDA's policy, therefore, implicates it directly in the politics of transcendence.

In presenting the case of the Norwegian Agency for Development Cooperation (NORAD), which has instituted similar sorts of divisions as CIDA, Hovland (2008, p. 177) has argued that the 'distinction between 'development' and 'mission' is clearly marked by the perception of 'faith' that has come to the fore in post-Enlightenment secularized society' in which 'religion' is seen as 'a separate (and declining) compartment of life, distinct from other areas'. Here, Hovland exposes the ideological project on which divisions between development and mission are premised. This work of constructing a secular-religious dichotomy has been a fundamental, if long ignored, aspect of development discourse. The attempt to propagate and promote 'parochial' and 'particular' religions has been widely viewed as the antithesis of ethical and effective development. This expulsion of mission from development has been part of the mythos, which enables development practitioners to imagine that their values, ethics and practices are valid and applicable *transculturally*. It also facilitates an imagination that displaces consideration of ways in which 'development' can itself be proselytizing (Henkel and Stirrat, 2001; Pandian, 2008; Salemink, 2004) or premised on genealogies intimately interwoven with missionary ideas and practices (Rist, 2009, p. 77; Manji and O'Coill, 2002; Clarke, 2006, p. 845; Parfitt, 2009). Recent genealogies of secularism (for example, Asad, 2003; Milbank, 2006; Taylor, 2007) have challenged and problematized the idea that it is either as autonomous from the religious or as universal in reach as is often imagined. Hovland (2008, p. 177) too submits that the secularity of development is an extremely tenuous proposition and that 'it is far easier to draw the line between development and mission in theory than in practice'.

Following Hovland's suggestion that practices reveal considerable fluidity than is often assumed in policy, this chapter interrogates the intersections between mission and development in the work of a particular NGO in Indonesia. As Hovland also points out, it is not only the self-consciously secular development organizations that draw such distinctions. Accordingly, this chapter focuses on the Mennonite Central Committee (MCC), a North American Christian organization in the Anabaptist-Mennonite tradition, which carries out programmes in over 50 countries around the world.[4]

## Mennonite Central Committee

MCC is a relief, development and peace-building agency 'supported by and accountable to' Mennonite and Brethren in Christ Churches in Canada and the United States (Epp Weaver, 2007, p. 13). In fact, I was frequently told by MCCers that, on account of MCC's intimate connections with these churches, MCC should be understood less as an NGO than as a 'peoplehood movement' of North American Mennonites.[5] MCC emerged from the Mennonite peoplehood and, in some ways, more closely resembles a social movement than it does as a formal NGO with the boundaries between the constituency and MCC being notably fluid and porous.

MCC was founded in the United States in 1920 as a Mennonite agency bringing together diverse Anabaptist groupings to channel aid to Mennonite co-religionists in Ukraine suffering from famine, the carnage of World War One, and the turmoil of civil war and the eventual victory of the Bolshevik Red Army (Unruh, 1952, pp. 11–40).[6] Though it underwent a hiatus during the 1930s, MCC was re-born during World War Two due to a confluence of pressing needs (Toews, 1996, pp. 120–83; Bush, 1998, pp. 90–128; Miller, 2000, pp. 3–8). As one of the historic peace churches, Mennonites have long taught that non-resistance and pacifism are central to a correct understanding and praxis of the Christian faith. The demands of total war, including particularly mass conscription, intruded upon Mennonite churches in the United States and Canada and threatened their faith commitments. In response, American Mennonites entrusted MCC with the task of facilitating Civilian Public Service (CPS) camps for Mennonite conscientious objectors.

As conscription continued after the end of the Second World War, MCC played an ongoing role in providing opportunities for alternative service. The demands of war and heightened patriotism in both Canada and the United States during this time also led many Mennonites to conceptualize non-resistance as passivism, an inadequate expression of their peace theology in the face of total war. This led to a widespread shift from 'quietism' to 'activism' (Driedger and Kraybill, 1994). Less content to enjoy a separated existence as *Die Stillen im Lande* (the quiet in the land), Mennonites sought opportunities to proactively embody their ideals of peace and service, including volunteering for service in war-torn Europe and, later, further afield (Unruh, 1952; Dyck and Dyck, 1991; Yoder et al., 2004, pp. 46–56). MCC became one of the primary channels through which this more engaged Anabaptist identity was expressed resulting in a dramatic expansion of MCC's work into Indonesia and elsewhere around the world. By 1995, MCC had over 15,000 alumni in the United States and Canada, who had served in formal assignments, many overseas, and over 50,000 volunteers contributed each year to MCC's fund-raising and supporting roles (Kraybill, 1996, p. 24). The numbers have only continued to increase since then. Such figures, however, only begin to scratch the surface of MCC's engagement with North American Mennonites. In her history of MCC in Ontario, Marr (2003) has argued that MCC has been a transformative driver of identity change among Ontario Mennonites, bringing diverse Mennonite groups together in a common enterprise and expanding Mennonite horizons through an increasingly globalized outlook.[7] Moreover, MCCers have often seen themselves as playing a prophetic role in encouraging Mennonites to become more politically active, as is particularly apparent in Marr's discussion of long-time MCC Ontario leader Dave Worth, who described his work with MCC as being a 'peace evangelist' to Ontario Mennonites by bringing them the 'good news' about 'the gospel of peace' (Marr, 2003, p. 267).[8]

This church constituency is also the primary donor source for much of MCC's finances, though not all. Since 1968, MCC Canada has channelled CIDA funds to particular projects throughout the 'developing' world (Marr 2003, pp. 205–6). This relationship has always been controversial not least because of the split that CIDA imposes between development and mission. However, the distinction between development and mission is also drawn by North American Anabaptists as well as MCC staff themselves. This is perhaps most apparent in the division of labour between MCC as a 'service agency' and the various 'mission boards' associated with particular Mennonite conferences. This latter collection of organizations is mandated by their sponsoring churches to engage in missionary activity in ways in which MCC is not.

## Planting Churches in West Kalimantan

During my research in North America, I interviewed Elizabeth Detweiler,[9] a staff member in the MCC Ontario office in Kitchener. In her introduction to the organization, I was told that MCC's church connections remain strong. Pointing to the Christian Scriptures, specifically Mt. 25, she summarized MCC's central purpose as: 'being Christ to other people'. MCC was deeply concerned with feeding the hungry, giving water to the thirsty and welcoming the stranger. However, while MCC did not try to hide its Christianity, it is 'not there to convert'. While MCC was fulfilling a Christian commission, this was disassociated from evangelistic intent. Similarly, at an orientation for new international volunteers at MCC's head office in July 2008 at Akron, Pennsylvania, those heading to Latin America were told that while the term 'missionary' was often used on their visas, they should avoid using that signifier in their everyday work. Instead, they should identify themselves as 'development workers' with their colleagues, friends and neighbours; a term that was felt to have more positive connotations. An interview in Winnipeg with an MCC staff member put the issue more explicitly. In the midst of negotiations with Chinese officials over setting up programmes in mainland China, the question was raised as to whether MCC would seek to carry out evangelism as part of its work there. The MCCer told me that he had responded in the following terms:

> MCC has been working in Bangladesh for forty years and there has never been a single convert as a result of its work there. We want communities to advance themselves and if they do so within their own faith tradition, then that is fine with us.

All these formulations of MCC's theological identity resonate with a comment written in the early 1990s by Ray Brubacher (1991), at the time the director of MCC's Overseas Services, in an internal MCC newsletter in which MCC is described as a 'church organization that does not plant churches'.

In Indonesia, both expatriate and Indonesian MCCers would largely have concurred with these sorts of framings. In interviews and casual conversations, I frequently encountered the view that many had volunteered with MCC rather than a mission organization because they did not want to actively engage in evangelistic work, although they still wanted to carry out a distinctively Christian service. Still, while it may be true that MCC did not gain any converts to the Christian faith as a consequence of their work in Bangladesh (though it is unclear how this could be empirically confirmed), the same could not be said for Indonesia. A series of conversations with Howard Miller, a former MCCer who had worked in Indonesia during the 1970s, alerted me to a period in which MCC Indonesia carried out evangelistic work in West Kalimantan (1977–84); over this period, MCC became a *church-planting* organization. During his time with MCC Indonesia, Howard had worked as MCC's Country Representative and so had been closely involved in setting up the programme in West Kalimantan.

A review of three consecutive MCC Indonesia Annual Reports paints a picture of the emergence of the idea of evangelistic work in West Kalimantan. In the 1975 Annual Report, Howard wrote that in the past MCC had sought to clearly articulate to the Indonesian Mennonite churches that its work was distinct from that of mission boards. Howard questions, however, as to whether MCC is 'only interested in social services and not in the churches' evangelical witness'. He goes on to note that specific efforts were being made by MCCers in Indonesia 'to identify more closely with the churches in their total witness to Indonesian society'.

The implications of this identification are spelled out more clearly in the following year's Annual Report (1976) in which, in addition to the ongoing medical, relief and agricultural development work, MCC's objectives for the year included the goal: 'to support, encourage and facilitate the expansion of the witness and ministries of the Mennonite-related churches of Indonesia'. A handwritten note on the otherwise typewritten report elaborates that one of the Indonesian Mennonite churches, Gereja Kristen Muria Indonesia (GKMI), was in the early stages of planning 'mission work' in West Kalimantan 'encompassing evangelization as well as community development including attention to health, education and agriculture'. GKMI had invited MCC to support the program 'especially in the community development aspect'.

Expatriate and Indonesian workers were still being sought to staff the proposed project by the time the 1977 Annual Report was written. However, the lead partner in the project, PIPKA Foundation,[10] the GKMI mission board, which had been founded in 1965 modelled after North American examples, had already sent an 'evangelist' to West Kalimantan. The area of mission is identified as Kapuas Hulu near Putussibau, the reason being that no other 'missions' were located in the area. The report further outlines:

> The Dayak people in our focus area are still quite primitive compared to other areas, for this reason the nature of our ministry in this area is very different from our ministry in Java and Sumatra. It is comprehensive. The aspects of ministry which we want to carry on together are spiritual, educational, agricultural, health and others with spiritual being first and foremost.

The consecutive reports therefore highlight a gradual shift in framing MCC's work in the West Kalimantan project. Prior to committing to a specific project, there was an explicit attempt to create space, both imaginative and practical, for associating with the 'total witness' of the Indonesian churches (Mennonite Central Committee, 1975). This moved into the formulation of a concrete plan for MCC to provide support 'especially in community development' (Mennonite Central Committee, 1976), which, the year after, had MCC actively engaging with a mission organization to undertake 'spiritual [ministry] first and foremost' (Mennonite Central Committee, 1977). The key issue is not where the line between 'community development' and 'spiritual ministry' was to be drawn, but rather that MCC had actively engaged in a partnership with an organization that had an intentional and explicit evangelistic goal. The provision of staff and finances to PIPKA was never going to easily fit into clearly demarcated categories.

Later in 1977, two expatriate staff were seconded to MCC from Eastern Mennonite Missions (EMM), the mission board of the Lancaster Mennonite Conference, to participate in the work in Kalimantan (Yoder 2006, pp. 302–3). They worked alongside Indonesian PIPKA staff carrying out a range of tasks including Bible teaching, agricultural development, literacy training and infant health care. By 1984, the expatriate MCC staff had completed their assignments and left the country (Mennonite Central Committee, 1985), though Indonesian PIPKA staff continued working in the area. Towards the end of the 1980s, American Mennonite missionary Stanley Shenk (1988, p. 106) reported that there were 13 Mennonite congregations established in West Kalimantan as a result of PIPKA and MCC's work.

This example of evangelism by a 'religious NGO' contrasts with examples provided by Kroessin and Mohamed (2008) of the da'wah activities of Saudi Islamic NGOs in Somalia or the 'holistic' and 'lifestyle evangelism' strategies deployed by Christian NGO workers in Zimbabwe analysed by Bornstein (2002; 2003, pp. 45–66). In both these examples, the proselytizing work is described as being pervasive; it is not an option in which the NGO involved choose to enact or otherwise, but rather is woven into the very fabric of the Good, which these Islamic and Christian organizations seek to achieve. The case of MCC, however, is that of 'a church organisation that does not plant churches' that is here planting churches. Church planting is not an inherent or ubiquitous aspect of MCC's work but an option chosen, a wilful (and temporary) departure from business-as-usual. This evangelistic turn is intriguing because it was an aberration in the history of MCC's work in Indonesia. The key question, therefore, is how MCC came to perceive the planting of churches in West Kalimantan as a legitimate activity.

Crucially, while the evangelistic turn can be regarded as an anomaly in MCC's praxis, it was not an entirely unique deviation. Toews (1996, p. 208), a Mennonite historian, has pointed out that the work of MCC and Mennonite mission boards 'often converged'. He argues: 'Mission programs brought in MCC programs, and MCC's relief work brought Mennonite missionaries. In Taiwan, Ethiopia, India, Vietnam, Japan, Hong Kong, Uruguay, Puerto Rico, and Belize, MCC relief and development efforts preceded the establishment of Mennonite congregations'. While Toews does not examine in detail whether it was MCCers or only the mission boards who contributed to the church planting, it is clear that the possibility of crossing the mission/development line was available to MCC in other contexts. A more explicit discussion of MCC evangelism is provided by Glick (1985, p. 29) in her brief history of MCC in Bolivia. Glick describes the active involvement of North American MCCers who contributed to the Bolivian protestant churches' Year of Evangelism in 1965 by 'sharing their faith and the gospel' with their neighbours. Direct evangelistic work, though rare, is part of the 'discursive repertoire' (Hilhorst, 2003, p. 51) available to MCCers at certain junctures.

A key reason for this possibility is the ambiguous policy of MCC vis-à-vis 'mission' work. While many MCCers, as noted above, see themselves as engaging in work that is distinct from evangelism, MCC has long disarticulated a clear organizational theology on these issues. It has done so because of widely differing theologies among diverse Mennonite constituents in North America. While MCC is not mandated by these churches to carry out church planting, to rule out the possibility of engaging in mission work would be to offend significant portions of MCC's support base inclined towards conservative or evangelical theologies. This ambiguity opens up considerable 'room for manoeuvre' (Bierschenk et al., 2002, p. 10; Hilhorst, 2003, p. 106; Mosse and Lewis, 2006, p. 17; Rottenburg, 2009, p. xx) for MCCers in their organizing and running of MCC's field programs, including the possibility of direct involvement in church planting work.

In order to understand the West Kalimantan evangelistic turn, it is imperative to pay attention to local 'brokers and translators' (Lewis and Mosse, 2006) who helped shape the field programme at that particular juncture. The successive Annual Reports discussed earlier illustrate the progressive construction of imaginative space in MCC Indonesia to support and engage in church planting work. Howard Miller, as the Country Representative during this time, played a pivotal role in re-formulating MCC's praxis in Indonesia to enable the new programmatic direction. MCC has a long history of promoting a 'field-driven' approach to planning, based on the assumption that the field-based staff are more aware of influential dynamics than distantly placed administrators in Canada or the United States. But Howard did not act alone. His reports were sent up the MCC hierarchy to the administrators in Akron, Pennsylvania, and their implicit approval of the new direction is apparent in the decision to recruit expatriate MCCers to participate in the work in Kalimantan. Such a move could not take place without North American consent. At other times in MCC, in Indonesia and elsewhere, openness to such possibilities has been closed off, but at this particular juncture other key actors within MCC appear to have been agreeable to Howard's intentions. Further, PIPKA and wider GKMI church leaders were also supportive of the work. In fact, MCC played a relatively minor role in the partnership, with a PIPKA staff member being appointed as team leader in Kalimantan and PIPKA staff taking the lead in strategizing and planning the operations.

What is needed, therefore, is an understanding of the working of development organizations, which reasserts the centrality of human agency in enacting programmes (Doolittle, 2006; Mosse, 2004). The view that development organizations are merely 'machines' (cf. Ferguson, 1994) or involve the operation of unquestionable ideological or discursive hegemony (Escobar, 1995; see also Hobart, 1993), and the idea that development is a 'monolithic enterprise, heavily controlled from the top, convinced of the superiority of its own wisdom and impervious to local knowledge, or indeed common-sense experience, a single gaze or voice which is all-powerful and beyond influence' are challenged by Grillo (1997, p. 20) as pure 'myth'. Individuals at key nodes within MCC saw church planting as a viable enterprise at that time and, mediating between local partners and wider webs of relationships, facilitated a transition in MCC's work.

This analysis of programmatic transition is specific to MCC, but wider implications about development processes can be drawn. As Hilhorst (2003, p. 4) has argued, rather than treating NGOs as singular, coherent, internally unified things, they should be thought of as 'open-ended processes' shaped by multiple, and sometimes competing, discourses. A crucial dimension in all NGO work is the translation into practice of broader ideas about doing Good Things (cf. Cornwall, 2007, p. 472) circulating within and beyond any particular NGO; a process that is inherently open to transformation. The relationship between concepts like 'mission' and 'development' is therefore always-already open to metamorphosis and should be seen as dynamic, fluid, contingent and constantly remade by the actors involved.

The question of how MCC came to plant churches in West Kalimantan is not adequately addressed solely with reference to internal organizational dynamics, as important as these are. The dissolving of the mission–development distinction also requires attention to the politics and authority structures that operated *around* and *on* MCC. MCC had 'room for manoeuvre' within a wider constellation of actors. Crucially, actors within the New Order Indonesian state were able and willing to facilitate the church planting work in the Kalimantan interior. While the role of the Indonesian State is largely absent from MCC documentation, I argue that attention to its interests are critical for understanding MCC's 'evangelistic turn'.

## Development in West Kalimantan

In 1965, General Suharto's coup d'état inaugurated the New Order and precipitated far-reaching political, social and economic change throughout the Indonesian archipelago. The new regime quickly went about eliminating its primary opposition, the Indonesian Communist Party (*Partai Komunis Indonesia*, PKI), which was blamed for an assassination attempt on senior military figures (Roosa, 2006). Communism was demonized in official public discourse and communists portrayed as vile threats. Estimates vary on the number of deaths resulting from the pogroms with Cribb (2001; see also 2002, pp. 557–9) suggesting that 'perhaps' the figure is between 200,000 and 800,000 casualties. The killings were carried out primarily by military and vigilante groups (Cribb, 2009). Massive detention of suspected communists and others opposed to the new regime also ensued.

The New Order also reworked the notion of religion. Connolly (2009, p. 182) argues that the state rejected 'a secularist separation of the state and religion' and instead became 'actively involved in religious affairs' to such an extent that it took 'control of the religious marketplace'. In 1966, Suharto's government reinforced an earlier declaration that all Indonesians should profess one of the five officially recognized *agama* [religions]: Islam, Hinduism, Buddhism, Roman Catholicism or Protestantism (Aritonang and Steenbrink 2008, p. 691). The intent of this emphasis on adopting official religions was to marginalize (supposedly) 'atheist' communists. The requirement of religious adherence left those who did not belong to one of the officially recognized *agama* in potentially perilous positions. Unsurprisingly, hundreds of thousands of alleged communists and awkwardly aligned groups sought refuge by adopting religious identities, particularly Christianity.

By the late 1970s, having cemented its hold on state power, the New Order tightened its control over religious affairs. Particularly important here were a series of decrees issued by the Minister of Religion to limit missionary activity (Mujiburrahman, 2006, pp. 81–91). From interviews with MCCers who worked in Indonesia at that time, it is clear that these policy changes had a significant impact on MCC. Up until the end of the 1970s, most expatriate MCC workers entered Indonesia on church-related visas, but from this time forwards this type of visa became virtually inaccessible. It was also at this time that MCC embarked on its 'evangelistic turn'. If religion in general, and religious propagation in particular, was being more tightly disciplined by the state in late 1970s, how then did MCC carry out evangelistic work in West Kalimantan at precisely this time?

Three issues are particularly important. First, as Mujiburrahman (2006, p. 90) argues, not all decrees were implemented rigidly or comprehensively. In the case of the laws on missionary activity, the practice of governmental discipline was sometimes more lax or even contrary to stated policy. Second, while the restrictions tightened 'evangelistic' activities, they did not attempt to restrain 'development' work. This is the familiar mission–development dichotomy played out again. Third, however, although evangelism to adherents of other official *agama* was restricted, the decrees made no mention of limiting proselytizing to the followers of 'native religions' or those who had 'no' religion (Mujiburrahman, 2006, p. 81). This crucial distinction meant that evangelism to most indigenous groups was not foreclosed. In fact, the New Order state took active steps to encourage and enable evangelistic work during the 1970s and 1980s to these latter groups. So while the Indonesian state drew a mission–development dichotomy in some instances, it was blurred and/or erased in others.

A focus on the Dayak and other 'interior' peoples helps ground these wider dynamics. In West Kalimantan, many Dayak communities found themselves in the unfortunate position of having no recognized *agama*. By the 1970s, Sukarno's *Ganyang Malaysia* ('Crush Malaysia Campaign') had morphed into Suharto's pogrom against communism. Many Chinese in West Kalimantan were suspected communist-sympathizers and state-sanctioned violence against them was rife. There was therefore intense pressure for non-affiliated groups to identify with a particular religion, which had standing in the new political environment. The New Order was intent in encouraging precisely such a move and, as a consequence, actively encouraged Christian evangelism such that the Indonesian 'army and the local government supported the spread of Christianity in the remote regions' (Aritonang and Steenbrink, 2008, p. 521).

Further depth is added to this picture by Aragon's (2000, pp. 275–7, 305) study of Salvation Army Christianity in the highlands of Central Sulawesi. According to Aragon, Suharto's New Order saw the *suku terasing* ('isolated', 'estranged' groups) or *terbelakang* ('backwards') interior peoples as problematic on account of their marginal incorporation into the Indonesian nation-state and its drive towards *pembangunan* (development). For these groups 'without religion' (*orang yang tidak ada agama*), the state initiated an aggressive campaign of 'human engineering' promoted through 'godly means' by making use of Indonesian churches and foreign missionaries. This strategy was deployed to such an extent that churches became 'proxies' for the Indonesian state such that 'the church . . . is the government of the interior highlands, or at least the most familiar branch of it'. Aragon (2000, p. 279) suggests that government officials 'recognize that foreign Christian missions are still one of the most promising and cost-effective methods to extract knowledge, cooperation, and products from remote interior areas' and therefore facilitated their access through the provision of visas and tacit permission. Such access was often tentative so as to ensure a certain ongoing vulnerability and dependence on state largesse. It could also be revoked when state goals were accomplished and the missionaries could be channelled to other areas of 'underdevelopment' (Aragon, 2000, p. 280). Christian mission to interior peoples was an important tool in the governance apparatus of the New Order, with conversion to Christianity perceived as involving a dual transformation. In joining a 'modern' religion, interior peoples were seen as also integrating into the Indonesian nation-state and coming to adhere to the New Order ideology of *Pancasila* (which Aragon (2000, p. 310) regards as the New Order's 'civil religion') and devotion to *pembangunan* (see also Connolly, 2009, p. 182).

Aragon's insights into evangelism in Sulawesi provide evidence of why the New Order state was willing to facilitate access for MCC's work in evangelism and agricultural development among Dayak communities in Kalimantan. As conspicuous American foreigners, the expatriate MCCers certainly required state approval for their presence and work. Here, therefore, is an instance of a further blurring of mission and development. It is possible to read MCC's evangelistic turn as one in which MCCers became 'missionaries of the state (cf. Hartch, 2006). The 'religious' mission involved in this evangelistic turn was therefore always-already intimately entwined with the political and economic dynamics. MCC's 'holistic' use of evangelism and agricultural development in West Kalimantan was enmeshed in wider dynamics of governance and nation formation. Aragon's (2000, p. 305) assessment of the case of Christian mission in Sulawesi is directly relevant to MCC's work in Kalimantan: '[r]eligious devotion and economic development have become quietly indexed to one another'.

Without having carried out field research in West Kalimantan, it is impossible for me to be anything more than speculative about the motivations of the Dayak converts. A part of the reasons for their conversion may have been, as Aragon (2000, p. 284) suggests for the Tobaku of Sulawesi, a strategy adopted by marginal groups who felt 'disadvantaged without an authorized religion'. Helliwell (pers. comm.), drawing on her anthropological research among Gerai Dayaks of West Kalimantan, concurs that Dayak conversion to Christianity was often profoundly pragmatic, emerging out of the necessity of complying to the demands by government agents to have an officially recognized religious adherence inscribed on their identity cards, as well as premised on a 'deep conceptual opposition' (Helliwell, 1991, p. 212) between Dayak and Malay Muslim identity, which ensured the attractiveness of Christianity vis-à-vis Islam. Connolly's (2009) recent account of Dayak conversion provides evidence of similar motivations among Dayaks of East Kalimantan. Connolly argues that conversion was undertaken within increasingly reified religious boundaries between Dayak and Malay Muslims and should be viewed as an attempt among Dayaks to differentiate themselves from Malay Muslims. Connolly (2009, p. 185) also suggests that access to education was particularly influential in conversion decisions as well as in the ability to 'lay claim to the power and prestige' of European and

American Christians. These motivations defy any sharp distinction between 'mission' and 'development'. Regardless, it seems apparent that members of these Dayak communities *wanted* PIPKA and MCC missionaries to come to their communities and invited them to carry out their work. If such a desire did not exist at least among some in the community, it is difficult to imagine the creation of various churches being a likely outcome, unless one makes the problematic assumption that the hegemonic forces of 'cultural imperialism' were so powerful as to devoid the Dayaks of any agency in the process (Dunch, 2002). Such arguments predominated in the not-too-distant past, but simplistic narratives of conversion as foreign imposition (of state or missionary power) fail to recognize that the Dayaks too surely understood conversion in their own ways and made use of conversion for their own purposes.

## Making Indonesian Mennonites

MCC's evangelistic turn in West Kalimantan took place due to a particular convergence of factors. Within MCC the in-country leadership sought to construct space in MCC's programmes to include church planting work. Particular MCCers who were amenable to embracing the 'holistic' model of activity deployed were recruited. Beyond MCC, the New Order state facilitated MCC's access in an attempt to incorporate 'interior' peoples into its project of nation-building and *pembangunan*, and the Dayak communities concerned also saw value in engaging with Christian missionaries and adopting the new faith. The approach adopted by each of these actors was a necessary prerequisite for MCC's evangelistic turn to take place. A clear mission–development distinction was repeatedly breached and dissolved and not just by MCC, with each actor having an interest in blurring the boundaries or simply failing to perceive any boundaries in the first place. But while the programme in West Kalimantan was an aberration to MCC's modus operandi in Indonesia, it was not the only blurring of mission and development in MCC's work in that country. MCC's long-standing involvement with the Indonesian Mennonite churches provides a more subtle, yet more pervasive, example of mission–development blurrings. MCC has been active in re-working Mennonite identities in Indonesia through affiliation-creating activities from the very earliest years of its presence in the country.

The first MCC workers to visit Indonesia arrived in 1947 and by early 1948, they had initiated a relief and medical programme in Sumatra (Dyck, 1980, pp. 91–104). Erb (1969, p. 164) believes, although his sources are uncertain, that MCC was 'the first foreign agency in Indonesia' after the Second World War. The Sumatra programme, involving the distribution of material aid and medical supplies, was brief. The impetus for MCC entering Indonesia was to provide support to the two Mennonite churches, both of which were based in the Muria region of Central Java. Gereja Injili di

Tanah Jawa (GITJ) was a predominantly Javanese denomination founded in the 1850s by Dutch Mennonite missionary Pieter Jansz (Hoekema, 1978, 2001). Gereja Kristen Muria Indonesia (GKMI) was formed in the 1920s by a Chinese convert, Tee Siem Tat, and became loosely affiliated with Dutch and European Mennonite missionaries (Yoder, 2006).[11] It was the Dutch Mennonites, crippled by the war in Europe and unable to immediately return to active work in Indonesia, who invited the North American MCC to work with the Indonesian Mennonite churches (Yoder, 2006, p. 200). At first, this was impossible due to the ongoing disruptions associated with the national revolution and the Dutch-led 'police actions', but by 1949, the situation had become settled enough for MCC to shift the focus of its operations to Central Java, which had been devastated by years of war and brutal military rule (Vickers, 2005, pp. 85–103). The primary raison d'être for MCC to enter Indonesia, therefore, was to work alongside the Indonesian Mennonite churches.

According to Orie O. Miller, MCC's executive secretary at the time, the types of assistance desired by these churches 'more properly fall into the area of possible Mission Board concern and service than MCC relief service' (Dyck, 1980, p. 94). Nevertheless, in the absence of North American mission board activity in Indonesia, which has remained limited and sporadic, MCC filled the vacuum and in doing so has often blurred the development-mission distinction. As a consequence, while MCC's partnerships with the Indonesian Mennonite churches have included the provision of relief supplies, funding and staffing medical and education programmes and financing agricultural development work (Yoder, 2006, pp. 340–4), a range of other activities were also supported.

These included helping sponsor the 'The Literature Project' in the late 1950s, which printed Indonesian-language translations of European and North American Mennonite literature on 'Mennonite history and principles (including war, peace and baptism); doctrinal and general problems; tracts' (Mennonite Central Committee Indonesia, 1958), facilitating teaching visits to Indonesia by North American Mennonite theologians and helping finance a Mennonite seminary in Pati, Central Java (Akademi Kristen Wiyata Wacana) in the 1960s as well as helping write its curriculum, and also providing opportunities for Indonesian Mennonites to attend North American Mennonite seminaries for theological training (Yoder, 2006, pp. 200–4). MCC Indonesia has been actively involved in building, maintaining and enacting relationships between North American and Indonesian Mennonite churches; programmes that have cumulatively had far-reaching effects on both GITJ and GKMI. While these are important, perhaps the most influential impact MCC has enabled is that there are *many* groups who see themselves linked to Mennonites today.[12]

The Japanese occupation of Indonesia (1942–5) initiated a period of dramatic change in the Indonesian Mennonite churches. Not only did the numbers significantly drop off, partially due to coercive pressure, but also the former Dutch missionary leaders were removed from positions of authority within GITJ, necessitating significant new-found autonomy. Though continuing to identify as Christian churches, their sense of *Mennonite* identity was weak (see for example, Shenk, 1988, p. 110; Yoder, 2006, p. 210). Further, immediately after the end of the Second World War, there emerged new widespread ecclesial currents, which moved GITJ and GKMI leaders in new directions. Particularly important here was a strong ecumenical movement, which paralleled the rise of Indonesian nationalism with its emphasis on creating new institutions and identities that would embody the spirit of national unity. This ecumenism was institutionalized with the creation of the Dewan Gereja-Gereja Indonesia (Indonesian Council of Churches, DGI) in 1950, which was the purpose of '*pembentukan Gereja Kristen yang Esa di Indonesia*' (the forming of the One Christian Church in Indonesia) (Aritonang and Steenbrink, 2008, p. 833; see also Titaley, 2008, p. 80). The goal of the DGI was to amalgamate all Protestant churches within a single ecclesial structure, and a number of churches merged as a consequence of this drive for national church unity. Both GKMI and GITJ were members of the DGI and were also influenced by this ecumenical fervor (Yoder, 2006, pp. 194–6).[13] In discussing one such Protestant merger in Java during this period, Aritonang and Steenbrink (2008, p. 687) note that GITJ and GKMI were 'a little more fortunate' because 'as early as 1949, 1950 the North American *Mennonite Central Committee* (MCC) was able to send some personnel, and in 1953 Dutch and German mission workers, too, were welcome again' (emphasis in original). Therefore, while there was significant pressure for the Indonesian Mennonite churches to integrate with other Protestant churches, the Mennonite churches were able to maintain their ongoing autonomy because of the arrival of MCC (and the return of European Mennonite missionaries). This was not explicit evangelism as such but the maintenance of Mennonite identity after World War Two at this time of precarious denominational affiliation was decisive. MCC's work with GITJ and GKMI significantly reduced the pressure to subsume this 'Mennonite' identity within wider Protestant ecclesial affiliations. Equally important, MCC has also played a key role in enabling a sense of belonging to an imagined global Mennonite community among the Indonesian churches.[14] Through facilitating flows of people, finances and information between 'Mennonites' in North America and Indonesia, MCC's work was crucial in the construction of this imagination.

But this analysis of maintaining Mennonites is still too limited to adequately conceptualize the blurrings of MCC's practice of mission–development. For even when MCC was *not* involved with Mennonite partners, churches or efforts at evangelism, its work can still be understood as 'mission'. For example, MCC's efforts in interfaith bridge building, particularly with Muslims in the wake of the 11 September 2001 disaster in New York and the widespread disparaging of Islam in the North American media (Watt, 2008; Ibrahim, 2010; Jackson, 2010), has been described by Epp Weaver (2007, p. 14) as a 'form of Christian witness and mission' despite explicitly acknowledging that it is 'not about adherents of different faiths relinquishing their truth claims'. Instead, Epp Weaver argues that in their interactions with persons of other faiths, Christians should cultivate a 'receptivity to hearing Jesus' voice' and therefore embody faithful Christian praxis. Discussing MCC's current interfaith work in Indonesia, Jantzi (2007, p. 29) discards the idea of making Mennonites as the real intention of MCC's work:

> Our real goal is faithfulness. We are called to follow Jesus, the Prince of Peace. We cannot strategize the outcomes of our relationships. But what we can control is our response to God's call in our lives and our openness to share that life in service with others. As MCC workers, we seek to bear witness to the reign of Christ in our work and relationships in Indonesia.

Such articulations of MCC's work deconstruct any attempt at clear separation of mission and development. Even the most mundane (or apparently profane) acts of bureaucratic administration, understood within these terms, can be interpreted as expressions of a missional impulse to be faithful.

## Conclusion

Scholars have long called for careful analysis of local understandings of development and modernity (Pigg, 1996, p. 163; Ferguson, 1999, pp. 84–5; Dove and Kammen, 2001; Bubandt, 2004). Analysis of vernacular approaches challenges preconceptions of 'development' as a monolithic and unchanging enterprise and re-focuses attention to the multiple and often contradictory ways development is enacted. The 'everyday practices' (Hilhorst, 2003, p. 24) of development are much more complex than abstracted theory has tended to suggest. This chapter has attempted to examine the vernacular practices of the mission–development nexus in the work of the Mennonite Central Committee. While MCCers frequently drew a mission–development separation in discussions with me, such distinctions frequently dissolved in practice. The case of the evangelistic turn where MCC carried out church-planting and evangelistic work in West Kalimantan was my initial entry point. By situating the work within a wider constellation of actors, it is clear that MCC was not the only actor to blur the boundaries of mission and development; just as MCC mixed evangelism and agricultural development, so too the New Order state made use of Christian missionaries for purposes of nation-forming and development. Though this evangelistic turn was an anomaly, the blurring of mission and development in MCC was not. MCC's work in Indonesia has always been intimately intertwined with the Indonesian Mennonite churches and was crucial in maintaining GKMI and GITJ as autonomous Mennonite-affiliated denominations under the very real possibility of their being subsumed within Protestant mergers. However, MCC's far-reaching impact in re-shaping Mennonite identities in North America is perhaps the most influential 'mission' the organization has undertaken. Attention to the re-working of religious identities 'at home' should also be included within the frame of analysis of any discussion of mission and development.

The dynamics at work within MCC identified in this chapter—the nature of MCC as a *process* rather than a 'thing', the dynamic and transformative realities associated with the *translation* of MCC's programmes into practice, the influential work of key brokers endowed with considerable *room for manoeuvre*—are regarded by Mosse and Lewis (2006) as being pervasive throughout the world of aid and development (and, it should be added, mission). Their prevalence calls for close attention not only to the ways in which the development-mission nexus is framed within policy documents, but also to how such framings are enacted into practice. It is appropriate, therefore, to conclude by returning to the example of CIDA raised in the introduction. While CIDA and other official development agencies have sought to articulate a clear mission–development separation in policy documents, far too little research has been carried out on the ways such distinctions work in practice. It seems fair enough to speculate that actual practices may be far more complex than the policies suggest.

# Notes

1 I thank the participants at the Deakin Religion and Development Roundtable for their helpful feedback on an earlier version of this paper and also Christine Helliwell, Patrick Guinness and Iris Lee for their helpful and constructive comments. I am especially grateful to the many staff at the Mennonite Central Committee (MCC) who welcomed and assisted my research.

2 Likewise, Berger (2003, p. 17) suggests religion is 'largely ignored', Selinger (2004) has contended that it constitutes a 'forgotten factor' and Bornstein (2003, p. 1) has argued that scholarly studies of development have largely 'excluded the topic of religion'. Reflecting these views, only a decade ago the newly formed World Faith Development Dialogue (2001, p. 2) stated its intention to '*start a debate* about the ways in which culture and spirituality can be taken into account in development processes' (my emphasis).

3 The use of scare quotes is meant to draw attention to the deeply problematic nature of the concept of religion and its current uses as analysed by Asad (1983, 1993) and Cavanaugh (2009).

4 The research took place between March 2007 and December 2008. In Indonesia, I was based in Central Java. I am grateful to the Indonesian Institute of the Social Sciences (LIPI) and its successor for handling foreign researchers, the State Ministry of Research and Technology (RISTEK), for sponsorship of my research in Indonesia. I also carried out research in Canada

and the United States for 3 months between June and August 2008. The fieldwork was made possible through grants from the Australian National University and the Religious Research Association's Constant H. Jacquet Award.

5 On the concept of the Mennonite 'peoplehood', used widely by North American Mennonites and scholars of Mennonite history and sociology (see, Loewen, 2008; Nolt, 1999; Urry, 2006, p. 6; Winland, 1992, 1993).

6 The origins and growth of MCC is an example of a 'hidden history' (Lewis, 2005, pp. 207–9) that is generally ignored in the mapping of the rise of the contemporary NGO movement.

7 This emphasis on the transformative impact of MCC on North American Mennonites is a recurrent theme in much Mennonite history and sociology. Kreider (1970, p. 245), for example, describes MCC as a 'generator of change' among North American Mennonites. Kraybill (1996, p. 23) argues that MCC has 'helped to restructure the meaning and essence of Mennonite identity'. Toews (1996, p. 213) notes that the impact of MCC was extremely far-reaching, touching virtually every Mennonite congregation in North America. According to Yoder et al. (2004, p. 56), 'few would deny the powerful socializing force MCC exerts in the Mennonite constituency'.

8 Discussions of 'mission' and 'development' often assume a cartographic dichotomy with an exclusive emphasis on overseas work as the only relevant field of action. Religious transformations 'back home' are often overlooked. Here mission is either ignored or seen as irrelevant. Yet, many Christian NGOs, such as MCC, make extensive use of religious ritual, sacred texts, religio-ethical norms and theological imperatives in explicit attempts to re-shape their donor constituents' religious identities.

9 All personal names of research participants in this chapter are pseudonyms.

10 *Yayasan Pekabaran Injil dan Pelayanan Kasih*, The Foundation for Service and Evangelism.

11 Another Indonesian Mennonite church, the charismatic Jemaat Kristen Indonesia (JKI), split off from GKMI in the late 1970s and was formally established as autonomous church denomination in 1985. Because MCC's relationship with this church has historically tended to be more restrained, I restrict myself to discussing only GKMI and GITJ.

12 None of the three Indonesian Mennonite Churches use the term 'Mennonite' or 'Anabaptist' in their titles. Nevertheless, all three are affiliated with Mennonite World Conference, the global umbrella body of Anabaptist church groups.

13 The drive towards amalgamation in the DGI was only officially relinquished at a 1984 conference during which the name was changed from DGI to Persekutuan Gereja-Gereja di Indonesia (Fellowship of Churches in Indonesia, PGI). Ecumenical ties were still important, but the goal of uniformity of structure or liturgy was abandoned (Aritonang and Steenbrink, 2008, p. 835; Titaley, 2008, p. 84).

14 This notion of 'imagined community' is drawn from Benedict Anderson's (1991, p. 4) seminal study on the role of imagination in the construction of the modern nation-state in which he argues that all communities not reliant on face-to-face encounters should be considered 'cultural artefacts'.

# References


Anderson, B. R. O. (1991), *Imagined communities: Reflections on the Origin and Spread of Nationalism*, London and New York: Verso.

Aragon, L.V. (2000), *Fields of the Lord: Animism, Christian Minorities, and State Development in Indonesia*, Honolulu: University of Hawai'i Press.

Aritonang, J. S. and Steenbrink, K. (2008), *A History of Christianity in Indonesia*, Leiden and Boston: BRILL.

Asad, T. (1983), 'Anthropological conceptions of religion: reflections on Geertz', *Man*, 18(2), 237–59.

—. (1993), *Genealogies of Religion: Discipline and Reasons of Power in Christianity and Islam*, Baltimore and London: The Johns Hopkins University Press.

—. (2003), *Formations of the Secular: Christianity, Islam, Modernity*, Stanford, CA: Stanford University Press.

Balchin, C. (2007), 'The f-word and the s-word—too much of one and not enough of the other', *Development in Practice*, 17(4), 532–8.

Belshaw, D., Calderisi, R. and Sugden, C. (2001), *Faith in Development: Partnership Between the World Bank and the Churches of Africa*, World Bank Publications.

Berger, J. (2003), 'Religious nongovernmental organizations: an exploratory analysis', *Voluntas*, 14(1), 15–39.

Bierschenk, T., Chauveau, J. and Olivier de Sardan, J. (2002), *Local Development Brokers in Africa: The Rise of a New Social Category*, Mainz, Germany: Institut für Ethnologie und Afrikastudien, Johannes Gutenberg-Universität.

Bornstein, E. (2002), 'Developing faith: theologies of economic development in Zimbabwe', *Journal of Religion in Africa*, 32(1), 4–31.

—. (2003), *The Spirit of Development: Protestant NGOs, Morality, and Economics in Zimbabwe*, New York: Routledge.

Bowie, F. (2006), *The Anthropology of Religion: An Introduction*, Oxford, UK: Blackwell.

Brubacher, R. (1991), 'A missiology for MCC', *Intercom*, 35(9), 8.

Bubandt, N. (2004), 'Genesis in Buli: christianity, blood, and vernacular modernity on an Indonesian island', *Ethnology*, 43(3), 249–70.

Bush, P. (1998), *Two Kingdoms, Two Loyalties: Mennonite Pacifism in Modern America*, Baltimore and London: The Johns Hopkins University Press.

Cavanaugh, W. T. (2009), *The Myth of Religious Violence: Secular Ideology and the Roots of Modern Conflict*, Oxford: Oxford University Press.

CIDA (1995), *Christian NGOs and CIDA: Guiding Principles, Understandings and Affirmations*, Ottawa: CIDA.

Clarke, G. (2006), 'Faith matters: faith-based organisations, civil society and international development', *Journal of International Development*, 18(6), 835–48.

Connolly, J. (2009), 'Christian conversion and ethnic identity in East Kalimantan', in DuBois, T. D. (ed.), *Casting Faiths: Imperialism and the Transformation of Religion in East and Southeast Asia*, London: Palgrave Macmillan, 175–89.

Cornwall, A. (2007), 'Buzzwords and fuzzwords: deconstructing development discourse', *Development in Practice*, 17(4), 471–84.

Cribb, R. (2001), 'How many deaths? Problems in the statistics of massacre in Indonesia (1965–1966) and East Timor (1975–1980)', in Wessel I. and Wimhöfer, G. (eds), *Violence in Indonesia*, Hamburg: Abera, 82–98.

—. (2002), 'Unresolved problems in the Indonesian killings of 1965–1966', *Asian Survey*, 42(4), 550–63.

—. (2009), 'The Indonesian massacres', in Totten, S. and Parsons, W. S. (eds), *Century of Genocide: Critical Essays and Eyewitness Accounts*, Routledge: New York, 193–217.

Deneulin, S. and Bano, M. (2009), *Religion in Development: Rewriting the Secular Script*, New York: Zed Books.

Deneulin, S. and Rakodi, C. (2011), 'Revisiting religion: development studies thirty years on', *World Development*, 39(1), 45–54.

Doolittle, A. A. (2006), 'Resources, ideologies, and nationalism: the politics of development in Malaysia', in Lewis, D. and Mosse, D. (eds), *Development Brokers and Translators: The Ethnography of Aid and Agencies*. Bloomfield, CT: Kumarian Press, 51–74.

Dove, M. R. and Kammen, D. M. (2001), 'Vernacular models of development: an analysis of Indonesia under the 'new order'', *World Development*, 29(4), 619–39.

Driedger, L. and Kraybill, D. B. (1994), *Mennonite Peacemaking: From Quietism to Activism*, Scottdale, PA and Waterloo, ON: Herald Press.

Dunch, R. (2002), 'Beyond cultural imperialism: cultural theory, christian missions, and global modernity', *History and Theory*, 41, 301–25.

Dyck, C. J. (ed.) (1980), *Responding to Worldwide Needs*, Scottdale, PA: Herald Press.

Dyck, P. and Dyck, E. (1991), *Up from the Rubble*, Scottdale, PA: Herald Press.

Epp Weaver, A. (2007), 'Introduction: meeting Jesus in the borderlands', in Dula, P. and Epp Weaver, A. (eds), *Borders and Bridges: Mennonite Witness in a Religiously Diverse World*. Telford, PA: Cascadia, 11–14.

Erb, P. (1969), *Orie O. Miller: The Story of a Man and an Era*, Scottdale, PA: Herald Press.

Escobar, A. (1995), *Encountering Development: The Making and Unmaking of the Third World*, Princeton, NJ: Princeton University Press.

Ferguson, J. (1994), *The Anti-Politics Machine: "Development", Depoliticization, and Bureaucratic Power in Lesotho*, Minneapolis; London: University of Minnesota Press.

—. (1999), *Expectations of Modernity: Myths and Meanings of Urban Life on the Zambian Copperbelt*, Berkeley: University of California Press.

Firoz, N. and Matthews, W. E. (2003), 'President George W. Bush and his faith-based initiative: creative solution or political minefield?', *International Journal of Nonprofit and Voluntary Sector Marketing*, 8(1), 43–58.

Glick, H. L. (1985), *Spiritsong: Mennonite Central Committees' 25 years in Bolivia*, Akron, PA: Mennonite Central Committee.

Grillo, R. D. (1997), 'Discourses of development: the view from anthropology', in Stirrat, R. L. and Grillo, R. D. (eds), *Discourses of Development: Anthropological Perspectives*. Oxford and New York: Berg, 1–33.

Hartch, T. (2006), *Missionaries of the State: The Summer Institute of Linguistics, State Formation, and Indigenous Mexico, 1935–1985*, Tuscaloosa, AL: University of Alabama Press.

Hauck, V., Mandie-Filer, A. and Bolger, J. (2005), *Ringing the Church Bell: The Role of Churches in Governance and Public Performance in Papua New Guinea*, Maastricht, The Netherlands: European Centre for Development Policy Management.

Hauck, V. A. (2010), 'The role of churches in creating social capital and improving governance in Papua New Guinea: lessons for working in fragile situations', *Public Administration and Development*, 30(1), 49–65.

Helliwell, C. (1991), 'Evolution and ethnicity: a note on rice cultivation practices in Borneo', *Bulletin of the Indo-Pacific Prehistory Association*, 10, 209–17.

Henkel, H. and Stirrat, R. (2001), 'Participation as spiritual duty; empowerment as secular subjection', in Cooke, B. and Kothari, U. (eds), *Participation: The New Tyranny*, London: Zed Books, 168–84.

Hilhorst, D. (2003), *The Real World of NGOs: Discourses, Diversity and Development*, London and New York: Zed Books.

Hobart, M. (1993), 'Introduction: the growth of ignorance?' in *An Anthropological Critique of Development: The Growth of Ignorance*, London and New York: Routledge, 1–30.

Hoekema, A. (1978), 'Pieter Jansz (1820–1904) first Mennonite missionary to Java', *The Mennonite Quarterly Review*, 52, 58–76.

—. (2001), *Dutch Mennonite Mission in Indonesia: Historical Essays*, Elkhart, IN: Institute of Mennonite Studies.

Hovland, I. (2008), 'Who's afraid of religion? tensions between 'mission' and 'development' in the Norwegian mission society', in *Development, Civil Society and Faith-Based Organizations: Bridging the Sacred and the Secular*. Houndmills, Hampshire: Palgrave Macmillan, 171–86.

Ibrahim, D. (2010), 'The framing of Islam on network news following the September 11th attacks', *International Communication Gazette*, 72(1), 111–25.

Jackson, L. (2010), 'Images of Islam in US media and their educational implications', *Educational Studies*, 46(1), 3–24.

Jantzi, J. Z. (2007), 'Indonesia: living in the mystery', in Dula, P. and Epp Weaver, A. (eds), *Borders and Bridges: Mennonite Witness in a Religiously Diverse World*, Telford, PA: Cascadia, 17–30.

Kraybill, D. B. (1996), 'From enclave to engagement: MCC and the transformation of Mennonite identity', in Kreider, R. S. and Mathies, R. J. R. (eds), *Unity Amidst Diversity: Mennonite Central Committee at 75*. Akron, PA: Mennonite Central Committee.

Kreider, R. (1970), 'The impact of MCC service on American Mennonites', *The Mennonite Quarterly Review*, 44(3), 245–61.

Kroessin, M. R. and Mohamed, A. S. (2008), 'Saudi Arabian NGOs in Somalia: 'Wahabi' Da'wah or Humanitarian Aid?' in Clarke, G. and Jennings, M. (eds), *Development, Civil Society and Faith-Based Organizations: Bridging the Sacred and the Secular*, Hampshire: Palgrave Macmillan, 187–213.

Lewis, D. (2005), 'Individuals, organisations and public action: trajectories of the non-governmental in development studies' in Kothari, U. (ed.). *A Radical History of Development Studies*, London: Zed Books, 200–22.

Lewis, D. and Mosse, D. (2006), *Development Brokers and Translators: The Ethnography of Aid and Agencies*, Bloomfield, CT: Kumarian Press.

Loewen, R. (2008), 'The poetics of peoplehood: ethnicity and religion among Canada's Mennonites', in Bramadat, P. and Seljak, D. (eds), *Christianity and Ethnicity in Canada*, Toronto: University of Toronto Press, 330–64.

Manji, F. and O'Coill, C. (2002), 'The missionary position: NGOs and development in Africa', *International Affairs*, 78(3), 567–83.

Marr, L. (2003), *The Transforming Power of a Century: Mennonite Central Committee and Its Evolution in Ontario*, Kitchener, ON: Pandora Press.

Marshall, K. (2001), 'Development and religion: a different lens on development debates', *Peabody Journal of Education*, 76(3 and 4), 339–75.

Marshall, K. and Keough, L. (2004), *Mind, Heart, and Soul: In the Fight Against Poverty*, Washington, DC: The World Bank.

Mennonite Central Committee (1985), *MCC in Indonesia – A Program Overview 1947–1985*, Jakarta: Mennonite Central Committee.

Mennonite Central Committee Indonesia (1958), *Annual Report and Program Plans – MCC Indonesia*, Pati, Central Java: Unpublished document.

—. (1975), *Annual Report and Program Plans – MCC Indonesia*, Pati, Central Java: Mennonite Central Committee.

—. (1976), *Annual Report and Program Plans – MCC Indonesia*, Pati, Central Java: Mennonite Central Committee.

—. (1977), *Annual Report and Program Plans – MCC Indonesia*, Pati, Central Java: Mennonite Central Committee.

Milbank, J. (2006), *Theology and Social Theory: Beyond Secular Reason* (2nd ed), Malden, MA: Wiley-Blackwell.

Miller, J. S. (2000), 'A history of the Mennonite Conciliation Service, International Conciliation Service, and Christian Peacemaker Teams' in Sampson, C. and Lederach, J. P. (eds), *From the Ground Up: Mennonite Contributions to International Peacebuilding*, Oxford and New York: Oxford University Press, USA, 3–29.

Morrison, D. R. (1998), *Aid and Ebb Tide: A History of CIDA and Canadian Development Assistance*, Waterloo, ON: Wilfrid Laurier University Press.

Mosse, D. (2004), Is good policy unimplementable? reflections on the ethnography of aid policy and practice, *Development and Change*, 35(4), 639–71.

Mosse, D. and Lewis, D. (2006), 'Theoretical approaches to brokerage and translation in development', in Lewis, D. and Mosse, D. (eds), *Development Brokers and Translators: The Ethnography of Aid and Agencies*, Bloomfield, CT: Kumarian Press, 1–26.

Mujiburrahman (2006), *Feeling Threatened: Muslim-Christian Relations in Indonesia's New Order*, Amsterdam: Amsterdam University Press.

Nolt, S. (1999), A 'two-kingdom' people in a world of multiple identities: religion, ethnicity and American Mennonites', *The Mennonite Quarterly Review*, 73(3), 485–502.

Pandian, A. (2008), 'Devoted to development', *Anthropological Theory*, 8(2), 159–79.

Parfitt, T. (2009), 'Countdown to ecstasy: development as eschatology', *Third World Quarterly*, 30(4), 635–48.

Pigg, S. L. (1996), 'The credible and the credulous: the question of 'villagers' beliefs' in Nepal', *Cultural Anthropology*, 11(2), 160–201.

Rakodi, C. (2007), *Understanding the Roles of Religions in Development: The Approach of the RaD Programme*, Birmingham: International Development Department, School of Public Policy, University of Birmingham.

Rist, G. (2009), *The History of Development: from Western Origins to Global Faith* (3rd ed), New Delhi: Academic Foundation.

Roosa, J. (2006), *Pretext for Mass Murder: The September 30th Movement and Suharto's Coup D'état in Indonesia*, Madison, Wisconsin: University of Wisconsin Press.

Rottenburg, R. (2009), *Far-Fetched Facts: A Parable of Development Aid*, Cambridge, MA: MIT Press.

Salemink, O. (2004), 'Development cooperation as quasi-religious conversion', in O. Salemink, O.; Harskamp, A. V. and Giri, A. K. (eds), *The Development of Religion/The Religion of Development*. Delft: Eburon, 121–30.

Selinger, L. (2004), 'The forgotten factor: the uneasy relationship between religion and development', *Social Compass*, 51(4), 523–43.

Shenk, S. (1988), *Mission in Asia*, Goshen College, Indiana: Pinchpenny Press.

Taylor, C. (2007), *A Secular Age*, Cambridge, MA: Harvard University Press.

Titaley, J. A. (2008), 'From abandonment to blessing: the theological presence of christianity in Indonesia', in Kim, S. C. H. (ed.), *Christian Theology in Asia*. Cambridge: Cambridge University Press, 71–88.

Toews, P. (1996), *Mennonites in American Society, 1930–1970: Modernity and the Persistence of Religious Community*, Scottdale, PA: Herald Press.

UNFPA, (2007), *Engaging Faith-Based Organizations in HIV Prevention: A Training Manual for Programme Managers*, New York: United Nations Population Fund.

Unruh, J. D. (1952), *In the Name of Christ: A History of the Mennonite Central Committee*, Scottdale, PA: Herald Press.

Urry, J. (2006), *Mennonites, Politics, and Peoplehood: Europe – Russia – Canada: 1925 to 1980*, Winnipeg, Manitoba: University of Manitoba Press.

Ver Beek, K. A. (2000), 'Spirituality: a development taboo', *Development in Practice*, 10, (1), 31–43.

Vickers, A. (2005), *A History of Modern Indonesia*, Cambridge: Cambridge University Press.

Watt, D. (2008), 'Challenging Islamophobia through visual media studies: inquiring into a photograph of muslim women on the cover of Canada's national news magazine', *SIMILE: Studies In Media & Information Literacy Education*, 8(2), 1–14.

Winland, D. (1992), 'Native scholarship: the enigma of self-definition among Jewish and Mennonite scholars', *Journal of Historical Sociology*, 5(4), 431–61.

Winland, D. N. (1993), 'The quest for Mennonite peoplehood: ethno-religious identity and the dilemma of definitions', *Canadian Review of Sociology and Anthropology*, 30(1), 110–38.

World Faiths Development Dialogue (2001), *Cultures, Spirituality and Development*, Oxford: World Faiths Development Dialogue (WFDD).

Yoder, L. M. (2006), *The Muria Story: A History of the Chinese Mennonite Churches of Indonesia*, Kitchner, ON: Pandora Press.

Yoder, R. A., Redekop, C. W. and Jantzi, V. E. (2004), *Development to a Different Drummer: Anabaptist/Mennonite Experiences and Perspectives*, Intercourse, PA: Good Books.

# 10

# UnitingWorld: Partnership for Effective Involvement in Mission Including Development

Kerry Enright and Vicki-Ann Ware

## Introduction

Until recent years, development studies have predominantly rejected the role of religion and religious organizations in the lives of people in developing countries (Clarke, 2007, p. 77). This has largely been a consequence of a prevailing 'theory of secularisation', which has permeated many social sciences. Such a theory suggests that as societies modernize, religion will gradually lose its relevance (Clarke, 2007, p. 77). Thus in terms of development, if religion is linked with being unmodern, it should be discouraged in modernizing contexts. This theory has impacted donor agencies in their funding practices and policies: many require that any religious activities be clearly separated out from development programmes before they approve funding.

Yet, in the case of Christian agencies, inspired by the call to participate in the mission of God in which witness is integral, there is not a neat dividing line between what is popularly thought of as mission and development. In fact, the missionary agencies of the denominations that formed the Uniting Church naturally entwined development, political action and evangelistic witness from their beginnings. In light of this, some argue that missionary agencies were the forerunners of the modern-day NGO (for example, see Clarke, 2006, p. 843).

Recent academic interest in the intersection of development and faith-based[1] organizations (FBOs) points to a growing discussion around the role of church, missionary and faith-based agencies in aid and development, and the relationship between these activities with more overt proselytization. It is becoming increasingly clear that the profile of religious organizations in developing countries is growing rather than reducing (Berger, 2003, p. 16; 2009, p. 69).

On the one hand, some suggest that these organizations and their activities inappropriately use development to influence people to change their religious loyalties. On the other, some note the increased involvement of church-based agencies in humanitarian and development work and are concerned with reductionist tendencies, asking whether they are but 'Oxfam with Hymns'.[2]

Amid these legitimate concerns, there is continuing evidence of the positive contribution of many religious organizations in providing services and contributing more broadly to the development of nations and the well-being of people, including where governments lack either the will or the capacity to provide for their people. In the striking example of Uganda, for instance, FBOs now provide 50 per cent of all education and health services (Marshall, 2001, p. 357). FBOs have also been central players in international campaigns against poverty and injustice, such as *Jubilee 2000* and *Make Poverty History* (Clarke, 2007, p. 85).

While more is being written about the positive impact of FBOs in the development sphere, there is also a desire to ensure that development and proselytization activities are kept strictly separated. The new *ACFID Code of Conduct*,[3] which is due to take effect in 2012, stipulates that:

> Funds and other resources designated for the purpose of aid and development will be used only for those purposes and will not be used to promote a particular religious adherence or to support a political party, or to promote a candidate or organisation affiliated to a particular party.

Signatories to this Code of Conduct are obligated to clearly separate aid and development activities from non-aid and development goals and actions, such as proselytization. Proselytization is defined by ACFID as 'activities undertaken with the intention of converting individuals or groups from one faith and/or denominational affiliation to another'.[4] Such separation is required in policies, fund-raising and programme activities, as well as in public communication such as annual reports. Separation is also required for partner and implementing organizations and must be documented (Australian Council for International Development, 2010).

Church-based agencies that are ACFID members, including UnitingWorld, have supported this principle of separation, on the basis that mixing relief and development with 'the intention of converting individuals or groups' is both bad evangelism and bad development.

Christian agencies such as UnitingWorld believe that the motivation of unconditional love inherent in how it approaches development is compromised when it is mixed with a motivation to convert people with whom development occurs. Any sense that acts of compassion are self-serving or self-promoting, for the sake of the church, of winning influence or of gaining conversions would appear to compromise the Christian valuing of good works. As Jesus teaches, good works are for their own sake, reflecting God's love for humankind.

It is likewise bad evangelism in that communicating the good news of Jesus Christ is compromised when it is accompanied with material inducement. The Uniting Church and others seek to critique vestiges of colonialism within their own operations where commerce and Christianity might become entwined. In the sensitized environment within which churches operate, stories of people being pressured 'to civilise' with Western values are regarded as alarming. In this respect, with the analysis Christian scholarship brings, churches are conscientized to exercise care in how Christianity is presented (Sanneh, 2008, p. 217nn).

At the same time, there is a need to widen the understanding of proselytism so that it is not restricted to what secularist approaches dislike. Church-based and faith-based agencies are not the only organizations tempted to engage in converting activities. Activities of many kinds can seek to convert, deter or entice people from their faith. Every agency brings to its work a set of beliefs, world views and values, including those of a secular nature, and inevitably, by the way in which they go about their activities, they communicate those. So the requirement to separate out some actions relating to beliefs from development activities has much wider relevance and needs to be debated beyond the context of FBOs.

Nonetheless, the mandate given to Christians is broad and encompassing. Prophets eschewing corruption, Hebrew poets picturing creation in balance, wisdom influencing the marketplace, Mary singing of God's societal revolution, Jesus casting out demons and returning people to right mind, Paul's outline of the right ordering of life affirmed by resurrection and many other stories and people, in light of Christ, all inform and inspire what Christians believe people are called to.

Church mission agencies are called to give expression to this wealth of insight and experience, and would deny their constitutions if they neglected major elements of it. Their mandate is nothing less than God's concern for the whole of creation and the whole of humankind within that. They also recognize that they are only part of the church's broad enterprise, and that they are called on to embody the good news within their particular discipline. They can therefore accept what a consensus of development expertise recommends for good development with the attendant limits on action.

In that context, however, the limit is not on mission as distinct from development. This chapter argues that, both theologically and practically, development is a form of mission and therefore dividing 'mission' and 'development' is artificial and confuses frames of reference. A theological understanding of mission clearly incorporates upholding rights especially of people most excluded and vulnerable, the core task of development. It also requires that Christians witness to what they have learned and believe. In this chapter, we use case studies from the work of UnitingWorld (one Australian-based church mission agency) in the Pacific region to show how they are partnering with a range of church agencies and others to engage in both development and witness.

This chapter first examines the theology that informs mission and development, how this is interpreted by UnitingWorld, and then describes several examples of how these principles are applied practically.

## A Protestant Theology of Mission

Christian understandings of *mission* have evolved considerably over the last 50 years. Language that previously emphasized *mission* as a dimension of organizational and human activity has been replaced by language emphasizing *mission* as a divine activity. *Mission* tended to describe dimensions of church life beyond the maintenance or self-preservation of the church as an institution (Flett, 2010, p. 6). It was not uncommon for agencies to be referred to as *mission agencies* or for church bodies to be involved in *international missions* or to send *mission groups* overseas (Bosch, 1991, p. 391; Flett, 2010, p. 123nn).

An ecumenical conference in Willingen in 1952 marked a shift in understanding to put more emphasis on the divine origin of *mission* eventually encapsulated in the concept *missio dei*, the mission of God (Bosch, 1991, p. 389nn; Flett, 2010, p. 123nn). It went alongside a refreshed understanding of God's Trinitarian nature referring to how God sent the Son into the world in the power of the Spirit.[5]

Fundamental to the shift was the idea of God's comprehensive concern for the well-being of the world and God's active engagement with creation. Mission is seen as central to God's own being. Flett (2010, p. 288) explains this idea as follows:

> The Father's begetting the Son is a deliberate act, not a second step alongside who God is in and for himself, but the determination of his own life. This act belongs to God's life from and to all eternity, for it is the nature of his perfect splendor that he is this living God.

Such an approach draws on a Trinitarian understanding of God by which God's being through eternity is expressed in the sending of the Son and the

Spirit, embodying 'the reaching towards' that the word *mission* describes. This reaching out in the relationship of Father, Son and Holy Spirit is inherent to God's being rather than a second step of action by God. In this understanding, *mission* is how God is.

Another reflection of the shift concerned how the role of the church was described within the mission of God. Whereas previous language had tended to put the church at the centre of God's concern, now the church was increasingly seen as an instrument of God's concern for the whole of creation. Bosch (1991, p. 491) suggests that 'To say that the church is essentially missionary does not mean that mission is church-centered . . . the church's missionary movement is only one form of the outward-oriented nature of the love of God'. The building up of the church was a step towards *shalom*, the complete peace, well-being and harmony of all that exists.

This shift was important in valuing yet relativizing the role of the church in God's mission. The church had a particular calling within the mission of God, to participate in that mission and to seek to embody what the fulfilment of God's mission would look like. Again, Bosch (1991, p. 391) suggests that

> mission is God's turning to the world in respect of creation, care, redemption and consummation. It takes place in ordinary human history, not exclusively in and through the church. God's own mission is larger than the mission of the church.

It was increasingly affirmed that God uses a variety of means to bring creation's completion and the outcome of God's mission was not a perfect church but a completed world. God worked through the church among other agencies, and sometimes despite the church. The church, then, fulfils its purpose only when it participates in the mission of God. Furthermore, if mission is comprehensive, encapsulating all that brings wholeness and reconciliation, justice and peace, then development is a dimension of mission (Bosch, 1991, p. 391).

## A Uniting Church Theology of Mission

These broader conversations and shifts are reflected in a paper approved by the governing body of the Uniting Church in 2010 to show how it understands the nature of mission today. The emphasis on God's priority in mission is evident from the opening words, 'God is the author of mission, Jesus Christ embodies the content of mission, the Spirit is the enabler of mission, the church is an agent of mission, and the world is the arena of mission' (Walker, 2010, introduction).

Archbishop Rowan Williams in noting the role of the church in relation to that mission is quoted as saying: '*It is* not the church of God that has a mission but the mission of God that has a church' (Walker, 2010, p. 1).

The paper emphasizes the encompassing nature of mission:

> Mission is not simply an extra activity to the life of the church to be added to faithful worship and compassionate service for example. God the Creator has a purpose for creation and engages with creation to move it towards its intended end. The whole church and not only parts of it are called to participate with God in this all encompassing mission process. It involves nothing less than the reconciliation and renewal of people and the whole creation. Because of this all inclusive nature of mission it is not possible to define mission in any formula (emphasis ours). It also means that the different aspects of mission are necessarily interrelated. In dealing with separate categories in what follows for the sake of clear discussion, it is not implied that they are discrete in reality (Walker, 2010, p. 1).

For the church, the shape of God's mission is discerned in Jesus Christ:

> Jesus Christ as the image of the invisible God gives clear form to God's mission. The nature of God's reconciling and renewing mission is seen in Jesus' words and actions. Near the commencement of his public ministry Jesus went to his home town of Nazareth where he made use of a passage from the prophet Isaiah to describe his mission (Lk. 4:16-20). It involved being anointed by the Spirit to bring good news to the poor, release to the captives, sight to the blind, freedom for the oppressed and to proclaim the year of the Lord's favour (Walker, 2010, p. 2).

It is noteworthy that the ministry of Jesus is portrayed in Luke's gospel as strongly developmental, 'good news to the poor', 'sight to the blind', 'freedom for the oppressed'. The intention of God is that all humankind participates in that mission, and so the church is called to invite people into that movement of human development.

At the same time, Christian theology takes seriously the challenging dimensions of human existence, not pretending that all is easily resolved or that development is a smooth incremental progress:

> Human societies develop patterns of living that can become so entrenched that they develop their own spirit, with power over people and society. Walter Wink calls them 'the powers that be'. Positive patterns can foster justice, reconciliation and peace. Negative ones can lead to oppression, division and enmity. God blesses those powers that enhance life and opposes powers that diminish or destroy it (Walker, 2010, p. 3).

It is noteworthy that in its statement about mission, the Uniting Church uses a language that strongly resonates with the development agenda. The mission of God invites people to make choices. Ways of living can enhance or destroy and the church is called to identify choices:

> This new creation, or realm, or commonwealth of God contrasts with the empires of this world. 'Empire names the destructive and unhealthy dynamics of the world. Empire is self interested approaches to life that take more from the earth than it was created to give, that arrogate power to themselves which should be God's alone, and undermine the cherishing of people and nature. People are invited to disbelieve and turn from the empire's ways and become citizens of the kingdom of God, thus subverting imperial systems. Not 'Caesar' but Jesus alone is recognised as Lord' (Walker, 2010, p. 4).

People participate in the mission of God by a variety of means:

> Mission encompasses a range of activities. These include such elements as the church being with and for others, mediating salvation, evangelism, concern for justice and peace and the environment, common witness including witness to people of other living faiths, liberation, and action in hope (Walker, 2010, p. 6).

These concepts are not new to the Uniting Church. The international dimension of God's mission has also been emphasized in the Uniting Church since its inception in 1977:

> The scope of God's mission is the whole of creation, so world mission is necessarily fundamental to mission. All churches should have not only local and regional mission but also world mission as a vital component of their corporate life. The Basis of Union affirms 'that Christians in Australia are called to bear witness to a unity of faith and life in Christ which transcends cultural and economic, national and racial boundaries, and to this end the Uniting Church commits itself to seek special relationships with churches in Asia and the Pacific' (Walker, 2010, p. 7).

The statement explicitly addresses the issue of evangelism, contrasting it with proselytism:

> One important aspect of mission is evangelism in which the church invites people to consider Jesus and his message of the reign of God and provides opportunities to respond and become consciously part of God's people and mission in the world . . . The Basis of Union says the churches coming into union 'hear anew the commission of the Risen Lord to make disciples of all nations' (Basis of Union para.1). Evangelism involves witnessing in the power of the Spirit to the good news of Jesus Christ in word and deed. It recognises that the grace and truth of Jesus Christ is greater than any particular person's presentation. It invites people to discover for themselves the truth of Jesus and the message of the reign of God he proclaimed.

Evangelism contrasts with proselytism which is the attempt by people to impose on others their faith perspective. In responsible evangelism there is sensitivity and respect for the other. Nevertheless, the gospel is also subversive and challenges other positions including our own preconceived ideas. The ground for the meeting is the opening of both partners in the conversation to God's reality and purposes . . . Witness to people of other living faiths and persuasions means also being willing to learn from them including discovering more of the truth disclosed in Jesus Christ in the encounter (Walker, 2010, p. 7).

Another dimension of the church's activity in the mission of God is prophetic witness:

> Prophetic witness calls for this reconciliation to become a reality in and through the church and in the world. God's desire is for justice and righteousness to be practiced, for fair and honest dealings in public life to be carried out, for the rights of those with no power to be respected, for compassion for the poor and needy to be shown, for care for the environment. There is no real peace without justice. Wherever there is brokenness, violence, racism and injustice the people of God are called to be involved in peacemaking and work for justice (Mt. 5:9-10) (Walker, 2010, p. 7).

The Uniting Church's theology of mission highlights the encompassing nature of mission and the call on all humankind, not just Christians, to participate in God's movement for justice, peace and the well-being of creation embodied in Jesus Christ. In this understanding, evangelism seeks to enlist people to the cause and the Christ who is actively engaged with the world in achieving these ends. Evangelism is not some predatory mechanism or sales-talk to persuade people to a distinct religious experience (Uniiting Church in Australia, 2009).

Evangelism and development are therefore closely related, because they each, in personal and corporate dimensions of life, contribute to the struggle for justice and dignity. As the former general secretary of the World Council of Churches, Emilio Castro (1985, p. 101) puts it: 'No Christian solidarity with the poor can exist which does not point to the totality of the kingdom promises, including the invitation to personal faith and witness'.

In this understanding, evangelism is clearly different from the more secular concept of proselytization.

As the international partnerships agency of the Uniting Church, UnitingWorld adheres to the above theology. This theology provides the primary principles upon which UnitingWorld plans and delivers a range of programmes and activities. It also demonstrates how integrated the concepts of mission and development are for this agency, which makes separating them out, an artificial exercise. The agency interprets and manifests these integrated principles within the particular realm and limits of development.

## UnitingWorld's Concept of Rights-Based Development

UnitingWorld seeking to apply a rights-based approach to its relief and development activities because it believes the mission of God is concerned with the upholding of human dignity both in its personal and communal expressions. UnitingWorld is therefore a signatory to the *ACFID Code of Conduct* referred to earlier, which states that signatory organizations' aid and development activity is 'informed by and implemented with an understanding of the human rights dimensions of the activity' (2010, p. 7).

In particular, signatory organizations must ensure that they are committed to internationally recognized human rights principles both within the organization and by conducting activities consistent with these precepts. Human rights, as described by ACFID include 'civil and political, economic, social and cultural rights' (2010, p. 9).

In taking up this theme, UnitingWorld seeks to discern the mission of God by reflecting on the Bible and the history of Christian reflection. In 2001, the Eleventh Assembly of the Uniting Church adopted a statement about Human Rights. Paragraphs 12-14 of the statement affirm the church's support for human rights as set out by the United Nations and recognize that these rights are 'indivisible, universal and inalienable'. These rights include civil and political, economic, social and cultural rights.

The statement also affirms the declaration made at the Eighth World Council of Churches (1998), which commits to promoting and defending human rights in a way that is mindful and respectful of 'people's religion, cultures and traditions', the rights of communities *and* individuals, and equal rights for men and women, old and young.

Finally, the Eleventh Assembly commits itself to promote human rights in its work. This includes increasing awareness and understanding of human rights 'through our education, justice and mission programs' as well as standing in solidarity with partner organizations 'advocat[ing] and work[ing] for human rights in their countries'.

A Christian perspective on development arises from a view about how society is rightly ordered where everyone enjoys economic, social and spiritual well-being (Wolterstorff, 2008, p. 311). Reflection is needed to determine the shape of those rights in particular contexts. They at least include what is needed for people to live adequately. Such an approach implies that development arises from more than charity and compassion. It has to do with more than attending to people's needs and providing welfare. It seeks to address systems and structures, principalities and powers and the societal mechanisms that determine people's social location. Such an approach reflects the theology of mission outlined in the previous section.

UnitingWorld affirms that people are not poor because of their own lack of ability or choice. People are poor because there are people with power who benefit from existing systems of disparity and cannot or will not see that the system needs to change. UnitingWorld is committed to responding to need compassionately, and at the same time acts on the basis that there are human rights, and that systems need addressing to ensure that rights are upheld.

A human rights-based approach to development perceives the development process to depend upon the relationship between rights-holders and duty-bearers in an exercise of power and law. Through this perspective, poverty becomes the inability to exercise rights and duties. Thus, the emphasis is largely on discrimination, exclusion and disempowerment as the foundational causes of poverty. There are four key elements that amount to a human rights-based approach:

1 Promoting *accountability* and *transparency* among duty-bearers, including Non-Government Organizations themselves.
2 Fostering *empowerment* and *capacity development* of rights-holders to hold duty-bearers to account.
3 Working in *partnership* with rights-holders and, when relevant, with duty-bearers and other rights-focused alliances.
4 Ensuring meaningful *participation* of rights-holders.

These are core principles for how UnitingWorld operates arising from the Uniting Church's theology of mission.

## Integrated Development and Mission: The Key Concept of Partnership

As stated in the previous section, one of the four key elements to a human rights-based approach to development is working in partnership with local organizations in project countries. The Uniting Church has a strong commitment to international partnerships, an emphasis noted in its foundational Basis of Union referred to above (1977). The Assembly agency charged with the responsibility for ensuring that those relationships are lived out is UnitingWorld.

This agency is a recent manifestation of a long history of partnership stretching back to the constituting denominations of the Uniting Church—the Presbyterian, Congregational and Methodist Churches. These churches had a long history of overseas engagement, for example, in the case of the Methodist Church with Fiji since 1844, in the case of the Presbyterian Church with Korea since 1889 and in the case of the Congregational Union through association with the London Missionary Society since the early 1800s.

Partnerships have endured and spread so the Uniting Church now has 36 formal partners mainly in the Pacific and Asia, with some in Africa, as well as many other ecumenical partners and other informal partnerships.

The Uniting Church is also a member of the World Council of Churches, the Christian Conference of Asia and works closely with the Pacific Conference of Churches.

UnitingWorld has four dimensions to the way it expresses partnership:

- The *Church Solidarity* programme enables the church to support partners in their non-development activities including Christian education and ministry.
- The *Experience* programme enables Uniting Church people to serve with partners, about 60 people per year.
- The *Relief and Development Unit* has its own governance structure and operates as a unit within UnitingWorld.
- Within the Relief and Development Unit, *Young Ambassadors for Peace* is a *Peace-making* programme that has established eight centres in the Pacific and Asia.

The Uniting Church works through in-country partners and does not seek to establish itself in any location beyond Australia. It thus seeks to enhance the mission and ministry of its 36 partners.

The Relief and Development Unit in its most recent strategic plan, describes its mission as 'connecting church communities and people worldwide to partner in God's mission through relief and development'. In particular, it sees this mission being worked out through its vision:

- We see transformed communities where peace and justice reign and poverty is alleviated, reflecting our hope and life in Jesus Christ.
- Partners see trusted friends for the long run who are committed to understanding and serving them; and Australian church communities with global radars, educated and rejuvenated through meaningful engagement.

UnitingWorld is putting equal emphasis on the relationship with Australian church communities as with overseas partners. This grows out of the conviction that we are part of, and potentially influential in, the systems that benefit some and disadvantage others. The rights-based approach aligns with an increasing emphasis on Australians developing more responsible lifestyles and more assertive advocacy for what is good.

Engagement with partners and their circumstances raises fundamental questions about worldwide economic, social and political actions. Events such as the Global Financial Crisis emphasize our connectedness as prime mortgages in USA and consequential bank bailouts lead to millions of people dying before their time. Environmentally, climate change highlights the impact of Australian lifestyles on countries with partner churches such as Kiribati and Tuvalu. In those countries, the Congregational churches are highlighting our need to advocate in Australia for adequate mitigation to parallel their required adaptation. The two major issues being addressed by the Pacific Conference of Churches are climate change and trade justice.

These partnerships help generate the theological reflection and consequent action of the Uniting Church in Australia. At its triennial Twelfth Assembly in 2009, the Uniting Church adopted a statement titled *An Economy of Life: Re-imagining Human Progress for a Flourishing World*. This paper calls Uniting Church members to re-examine their lives to inhabit the world in a more sustainable and just way, allowing all people to have reasonable opportunity for just and productive lives. It also calls on the Australian Government to develop economic systems and structures that deal fairly with other nations, to lead planning and provision of more sustainable and just communities at home and to move away from a focus on continual economic growth, which perpetuates the disadvantage of other nations (Uniting Church in Australia National Assembly, 2009, pp. 10–11).

This statement sits alongside a submission to the Department of Foreign Affairs and Trade regarding trade justice, which arose from the priority given to that issue by the Pacific Conference of Churches, as well as the experience of how Australia and New Zealand are negotiating with Pacific nations as part of PacerPLUS—the *Pacific Area Closer Economic Relations Agreement* (UnitingWorld, 2009).[6] The submission calls on the Australian Government to negotiate with Pacific nations at their pace, in genuine consultative processes, in ways that encourage holistic development of all citizens and communities of these nations and in a culturally sensitive manner (UnitingWorld, 2009, p. 8).

UnitingWorld sees, therefore, that to address the dimensions of development, both global action and reflection that involve the whole lives of God's people are required. Development is not a discrete exercise of giving overseas, but one of addressing dimensions of how humankind lives as exemplified in the rights-based approach to development. For the Uniting Church, this requires continually revisiting sources of revelation and wisdom in the scriptures and tradition of theological reflection in the church.

In this context, evangelism takes on fresh purpose. Evangelism as announcing good news involves challenging and empowering people to see the signs of what is life-giving and healthy, empowering and heartening, just and fair. Evangelism involves personally enlisting people to challenge the systems that prevent people experiencing the good news announced in Jesus Christ, the broad dimensions of which are outlined earlier in this chapter. In this respect, although theologically somewhat reductionist, there is a similarity with other agencies that are also seeking to enlist people to what they see as life-giving world views, whether they are the secular Oxfam or the church-based Caritas. People are being invited to live justly, and for Christians that justice is embodied in the figure of Jesus Christ. This involves deep conviction and whole of life, not some discrete religious practice.

In enticing Australians to respond to the invitation to live responsibly, UnitingWorld has been helped by a range of social trends highlighting personal responsibility and connection and by the recent history of international engagement. Responsibility for international engagement has shifted from missionaries and church officials to more local actors. The history is that in the Uniting Church and its predecessors, missionaries were engaged in establishing and developing churches throughout the Pacific and Asia. Over time, indigenous leadership was trained and encouraged and missionaries stepped back to provide assistance rather than major leadership.

A common story in Pacific churches, for example, is that in the 1950s and 1960s, Australian missionaries were presidents, moderators or general secretaries and were quite quickly replaced by local leaders. Missionaries almost entirely withdrew within a few decades. In their place, partnerships became increasingly managed by national church offices and communication became more centralized. This had the effect of distancing the engagement from local Australian church communities—who had often provided a strong support base for missionaries. To ensure that there was no continuing colonialism, funding shifted to bulk grant, a straight gift of funds that were spent according to the priorities of the overseas church.

More recently, this pattern has also changed as the need for the Australian church to learn from overseas churches has been increasingly affirmed. Immigration has made the Uniting Church more multicultural with diaspora communities wanting to link back to their countries of origin, supported by the wider church community. Instead of partnerships being from 'head office' to 'head office', generally involving a diminishing number of paid staff, they are being increasingly embedded in the various councils and communities of the church, particularly in congregations. Australian grassroots church connections are growing again.

It becomes clear, then, that UnitingWorld and the communities of the Uniting Church are called on to participate in the integrated mission of God of which development is one dimension. It is very difficult to untangle the various dimensions of that participation. It is a misnomer to see mission and development as parallel activities because the rich breadth of the church's understanding of mission is needed in order to ensure that development has its full effect. This understanding requires the broad practice of mission in order to address the societal structures and dynamics and the personal and communal failings that prevent people enjoying the fullness of life for which the church lives.

## Case Studies: How UnitingWorld Applies These Concepts in Practice

What has been said in relation to the Australian context is also true for partner churches. Partner churches seek to participate in the broad mission of God in ways they find difficult to untangle and in ways that are inappropriate for people who have much more integrated views of societies and people. Many of these societies have not been so affected by the Enlightenment's separation of political, spiritual, economic and social dimensions of existence. This is particularly evident in Pacific nations where churches are so embedded in cultural and political dynamics that it is difficult to satisfy Australian secularist desires to separate them off. For example, the classic division of church and state, influential in much of the approach to development, is not so easily maintained or appropriate in Pacific nations.

The entwined nature of church and state in the Pacific is reflected in the actions of the Interim Government of Fiji, which took power in the coup of 2006, to limit the influence of the Methodist Church. Despite these attempts, it is recognized that any significant change in Fiji, even to achieve the vision outlined by the Interim Government, must in some way involve the Methodist Church. Seventy five per cent of indigenous Fijians belong to that church. Even if the church withdraws from partisan political involvement, its size and central place within the lives of most Fijians and its desire to be faithful to the understanding of mission outlined earlier mean that it must inevitably reflect and comment on what is important in the lives of Fijian people.

This section presents four case studies to illustrate how UnitingWorld approaches mission and development in a holistic and integrated way, based upon its theology of mission and its understanding of and commitment to rights-based development.

## Case Study One: Vanuatu

A further example of how UnitingWorld works with partner churches in a holistic understanding of development, reflecting its theology of mission, is in its partnership with the Presbyterian Church of Vanuatu. When UnitingWorld staff recently visited Vanuatu to see various development and educational projects, the church there saw it as a natural step also to arrange a meeting with the prime minister of Vanuatu. Given the breadth of concern implicit in the church's theology of mission, discussion ranged across diplomatic, political, social and economic issues. UnitingWorld staff joined in advocating with its Vanuatu partner for attention to land registration issues including the loss of access by local people to traditional fishing grounds and the commodification of resources once regarded as communally owned and managed. Could the engagement be classified as development or evangelism, or prophetic witness or advocacy, or a mixture of each?

The delineation is harder to sustain as the discussion proceeded on the basis of shared assumptions, values and faith because the then prime minister was an elder and lay preacher in the church. Indeed within Vanuatu, church and culture are so entwined that the church's role of an elder is a recognized position within local communities, often more influential than the role of other leaders. The first Vanuatu cabinet contained many ministers and priests; the prime minister was an Anglican priest and the deputy prime minister a Presbyterian minister. In this context, development is seen as a process that engages every dimension of human existence including the so-called spiritual that approaches influenced by the Enlightenment can undervalue.

## Case Study Two: Papua New Guinea

An exciting example of the value of retaining an integrated approach in development, reflecting the breath of church's theology of mission, is in Papua New Guinea (PNG). Increasing recognition by AusAID and other actors of how central the church is in the cultures, politics and economies of Pacific peoples is exemplified in an innovative model of collaborative action for development, the Papua New Guinea Church Partnership Program (CPP). In this fully AusAID-funded programme, Australian churches partner with their PNG equivalents to achieve agreed development outcomes. The weight of governance and leadership rests with the PNG partners while the Australian partners ensure that they exercise their full accountability to AusAID.[7]

This programme involves collaboration between AusAID and seven Christian denominations, with support and guidance provided by the PNG Government. On the programme website, AusAID states that it recognizes that churches are an integral part of daily life for the people of PNG, providing essential health and education services in remote areas.[8] As part of the partnership, these seven denominations share their long-standing experiences working in PNG in planning, resources and human capital. The programme ' . . . aim[s] to strengthen church leadership in society, improve the quality and reach of basic services, and improve churches' institutional capacity for development. CPP supports churches to promote accountable governance, peace building and community participation in decision-making and local governance'.

The Uniting Church in Australia partners with the United Church of PNG for development. Over the past 4 years, as a result of the programme, the United Church Development Unit has been established and has grown from nothing to having over 30 employees. Their major activities include peace building, community awareness-raising and education.

The *Young Ambassadors for Peace* programme conducts peace-building workshops in the Southern Highlands and Bougainville, which have resulted in peace agreements between rival clans. The Women's, Men's and Youth Fellowships have put together a programme of *Creativity Movement*, which uses drama, song and poetry to raise awareness of community concerns such as domestic violence, drug abuse and alcoholism.

Scholarships are offered to teachers in the Southern Highlands and countrywide in-service training is provided for United Church Headmasters to improve the governance of schools. A *Personal Viability* programme acts as 'a grass roots university', teaching people how to make the most of local land and resources such as timber, fish and minerals. This is being expanded to assist people find employment and establish small businesses. HIV/AIDs education is underway and the church is looking for ways of helping the community develop small businesses to make a creative response to the PNG Liquefied Natural Gas project.

Some of the concrete outcomes of this programme thus far include:

- Seventeen graduates of a teacher training programme in 2008 returned to their villages to commence teaching.
- Forty women have received livelihood training as well as assistance to establish a small business.
- Two voluntary HIV/AIDS testing and counselling centres have been established and two peace workshops have been held.[9]

The Church Partnership Program reflects increasing recognition of the world views of partners where different dimensions of life are not as delineated and valued less as commonly occurs in Western countries. The Church Partnership Program reflects a positive valuing of the cultures of partners. In that culture, for example, the personal viability programme combines personal spiritual strength with hard-nosed economic analysis to empower people to take more active responsibility to act towards a more just system.

## Case Study Three: India

An example of how the church's integrated theology of mission influences its approach to development is in its partnership with the Diocese of Amritsar in North India. Amritsar is the location of the Golden Temple, a central institution for the Sikh faith. UnitingWorld supports the Diocese's development programmes including the provision of clean water and sanitation, health services and education about human rights. The approach taken reflects the church's theology of engagement with people of other faiths in which value is put on collaborative action and respectful engagement. The Diocese seeks to have positive relationships with people of other faiths in that area, even when people in the diverse faiths are provoked by fanatics from other areas.

Diocesan schools in Amritsar have been burnt down by extremists. Despite provocation, religious leaders look for ways of building positive relationships. When one is holding a religious pilgrimage through the city, they make sure they advise the others. People of Sikh and Hindu faith are employed at senior levels in the Diocese and lead Christian devotions.

This capacity to be religious in a sympathetic and respectful way, while holding to the characteristics that are cherished in one's own faith, reflects the theology of mission of the Uniting Church. Indeed, development is a means of bringing Sikhs, Christians and others together to achieve positive outcomes. Religious sensibility thus becomes a rich resource for development and for more than the addressing of identified needs by the building of strong communities.

An approach that minimized the place of religion in such contexts would make little sense and would limit the positive outcomes that arise from people's religious convictions and the resulting impulse to work collaboratively. It would make it easier for Christians and other extremists to damage the well-being of communities in a way very counter to how the Uniting Church understands people of different faiths need to relate to each other. In such contexts, the discouragement of faith involvement would obstruct development.

## Case Study Four: The Uniting Church Response to PacerPLUS

The church's response to the PacerPLUS negotiations (explained above) is another example of how the Uniting Church seeks to address broader issues raised by development within a church partnership context.

PacerPLUS involves Australia and New Zealand negotiating closer economic relationships with Pacific nations. The positions taken by the Australian and New Zealand Governments is that Pacific nations need to undergo the kind of economic changes that Australia and New Zealand underwent in the mid-1980s. These involved such steps as the reduction of tariffs and subsidies, the privatization of what had been government services, the floating of the dollar and a strong emphasis on growth and competition.

The Uniting Church has argued that in the promotion of trade and the negotiation of trade deals, respect needs to be paid to the cultural and spiritual resources of Pacific nations that form the basic societal grounding on which economy is built. The danger is that the dynamic of colonialism, to which the church has become increasingly sensitized, is replayed this time by governments, as influential neighbours like Australia and New Zealand seek to persuade Pacific nations to adopt practices at odds with their accepted world views. Sensitivity becomes especially important where there is a power and resource imbalance as in these negotiations.

In several ways, the kind of ideology driving Australia's approach to PacerPLUS is counter to that of Pacific cultures and religions, which aim to respect the limits of creation, affirm the value of community and mutual care and value people as children of God rather than primarily as consumers in a growing economy.

For the church, there is nothing inevitable about this dynamic, because the upholding and proclaiming of core human values as embodied in Jesus Christ, however sparse the success, remains a central calling. The church believes, within its own lights, that what it is seeking to uphold is of value to all humankind and to creation itself and that, in the fullness of time, that way will prevail. It looks on activities as seemingly secular as trade negotiations in a more holistic way than simply a transaction among nations.

Such a view underpinned by a theology of mission that recognizes the significance of principalities and powers and the need for thoughtful reflection and discernment, and the struggle that is involved in upholding central values, led the church to become involved in advocacy. In affirming that the mission of God occurs through other bodies where the sought outcome reflects how the church understands the completion of creation, UnitingWorld collaborated with organizations such as trade unions, an advocacy collective, non-church agencies and concerned individuals to raise concerns and educate the wider public about the implications of PacerPLUS.

These case studies demonstrate the way in which UnitingWorld is partnering with church agencies, governments and other organizations with the prayer that in so doing it participates, with them, in the mission of God. It seeks to maintain the capacity to discern that mission, which is why it puts so much emphasis on having a robust theology of mission and a holistic understanding of development. In so doing, and in order that development may lead to the most positive outcomes, it seeks to resist the division of concepts that belong together, like mission and development, that inevitably lead to reductionism of one or the other, or that fails to sufficiently acknowledge important dimensions of human existence such as those highlighted by the church and other religious bodies.

## Conclusion

It is often a challenge for people to come to terms with the religious dimension of life because religious people, believing that much is at stake, seem to be both peculiar in their reference points and aggressive in their communicating. The discussion of the place of religion in development and other dimensions of life can be strangely awkward because it appears to question and indeed challenge the lack of capacity of many Australians to deal with it straightforwardly. However, in order to be healthy, religion needs conversation partners, including the input of competent and confident anthropologists, sociologists and development commentators as it reflects on whether it is providing helpful input into communities.

Conversation is often discouraged because of prevailing narratives that result in the undervaluing of church and mission engagement. An example of that is highlighted by Lamin Sanneh in his book, *Translating the Message*. Sanneh, who is a professor of World Christianity at Yale Divinity School, seeks to counter the view that mission and Christianity always undermine culture (Sanneh, 1989). While noting the scandalous impact of unhealthy collusion between commerce and Christianity in the form of colonialism, he also notes that in his homeland of Gambia in which he grew up as a Muslim, the translation of the Bible into the vernacular had an ennobling impact on local cultures.

Sanneh sought to trace the correlation between the translation of the Bible in Africa and the development of independence movements there. If people felt they had an inherent dignity, enhanced by hearing what they perceived as divine scripture in their own language and using their local cultural concepts, they carried that dignity into other realms of life, including the political realm.

The kind of perspective Sanneh represents needs to contribute to the conversations that occur about the relationship of religion and development and whether in fact churches and other bodies are helpful.

Similarly, we need to be thoughtful in questioning the dimensions of religion that do not appear to assist development. The level of population growth continues to be a major impediment to development in Melanesian countries. The Uniting Church believes the responsible practice of contraception is helpful. In this respect, it supports women's movements, reproductive health networks and others as important conversation partners in questioning the churches, rather than seeing such groups as undermining church teaching.

The same approach applies to a range of issues such as the leadership of women, the inclusion of children, respect for other faiths and an overemphasis on personal salvation. It operates under an ecumenical rubric by which all churches belong to one body, are more connected than separate and are mutually accountable. We have much to learn from our partners just as they seek to learn from us.

In such circumstances, like-minded development agencies need to find ways of collaborating with church agencies so that the rich resources of biblical and theological reflection can enhance what secular agencies seek to do. Again, some knowledge of the religious spectrum is required for people to know who and how to approach churches. Not all churches and not all 'gospels' are helpful, and it is entirely appropriate for bodies to be discriminating in their choice.

In the development realm, churches are becoming more engaged, and through such agencies as ACFID, secular NGOs are developing greater knowledge of the realm of religion. In this respect, it is appropriate that as participants in the development realm, churches are questioned even when they may seek to play the trump card of divine revelation. Churches in turn need to find ways of engaging that require more thought than simple assertion, and people with secular world views need in turn to subject those to reciprocal questioning.

In some circles, the word 'spirituality' has a softer sound and is therefore more acceptable than the word 'religion'. To make something *sound* more acceptable does not make it so. Fascism can be regarded as embodying spirituality and yet it is difficult to imagine an approach more antithetical to positive development outcomes. It is religious *thinking* and *practice* that need engaging, one way or another.

Religion is increasingly recognized as an inherent dimension of culture. The view that education and economic development inevitably secularize has been discredited by scholarly attention (for example, see Berkley Centre, 2010; Clarke, 2007, p. 78; Haynes, 2009; Oluwafunmilayo, 2006). Theories of secularization that arose in the 1960s, shaped by the mood of the age, have been replaced by recognition that humankind is significantly religious.

Government bodies such as AusAID and the Department of Foreign Affairs and Trade will need to find mechanisms of treading amid the eggshells of religious rhetoric and thinking with increasing confidence and ability both within Australia and with partners beyond Australia. In this respect, Australia has much to learn from other cultures.

The examples in this chapter show how UnitingWorld is working with a range of partners in various parts of the Asia-Pacific region to uphold and enhance the dignity of people and the sustainable development of societies. In this context, practices such as evangelism, often easily caricatured and dismissed, can be seen more positively within an encompassing theology of mission and a broad approach to development. This chapter agrees that proselytization should be discouraged and that motives for development need questioning. At the same time, it argues that to distinguish mission from development is a misnomer and a pairing of concepts as equals that are not equals. Development is, rather, an important dimension of mission that needs to be informed by a robust theology of mission.

## Notes

1 Although some writing sees church agencies as faith-based organizations, they are a distinct group because their catholicity suggests that churches are inherently internationally entwined and are called to reflect the fullness of Christian mission in ways not always true of local faith-based organizations.

2 World Council of Churches 2010, <www.oikoumene.org/fileadmin/files/wcc-main/2010pdfs/Religion_and_development_seminarNov2010.pdf>.

3 ACFID stands for Australian Council for International Development. It is the Australian peak body for aid and development organizations (see www.acfid.asn.au).

4 Proselytization is generally perceived as being equivalent to what Christians term evangelism. We would argue that the terms are substantially different in motives, methodology and power relations.

5 Flett questions the extent to which Trinitarian theology was as influential as had been claimed.

6 PacerPLUS is an ongoing regional trade and economic agreement between Australia and Pacific Island Forum leaders, which was launched in August 2009. The PacerPLUS website states that 'Australia's primary motivation in supporting PACER Plus is to help the Forum Island Countries promote their own economic growth. The negotiation of a new regional trade and economic agreement provides the long term opportunity to create jobs, enhance

private sector growth, raise standards of living, and boost economic growth in Forum Island Countries. PACER Plus negotiations will include elements of trade capacity building and trade development assistance designed to strengthen Forum Island Countries' ability to trade. Australia is conscious of the negotiating capacity constraints faced by Forum Island Countries and has committed to providing Forum Island Countries with appropriate capacity building and support' (www.dfat.gov.au/fta/pacer/index.html).

7 Source: <www.ausaid.gov.au/country/png/partnerships.cfm>.

8 Source: <www.ausaid.gov.au/country/png/civil."fm>.

9 Source: <www.unitingworld.org.au/wp-content/uploads/2009/05/PNG-Church-Partnership-Project-She"t.pdf>.

# References


Australian Council for International Development (2010), *ACFID Code of Conduct* (Revised edition to take effect 1 January 2012).

Berger, J. (2003), 'Religious nongovernmental organizations: an exploratory analysis', *Voluntas: International Journal of Voluntary and Nonprofit Organizations*, 14(1).

Berger, P. (2009), 'Faith and development', *Society*, 46(1), 69–75.

Berkley Centre (2010), 'Mozambique: religious peacebuilders broker end to civil war', *Berkley Centre Case Study Series*.

Bosch, D. (1991), *Transforming Mission: Paradigm Shifts in Theology of Mission*, Maryknoll, NY: Orbis Books.

Castro, E. (1985), *Sent Free: Mission and Unity in the Perspective of the Kingdom*, Grand Rapids, MI: Eerdmans.

Clarke, G. (2006), 'Faith matters: faith-based organizations, civil society and international development', *Journal of International Development*, 18(6), 835–48.

—. (2007), 'Agents of transformation? donors, faith-based organizations and international development', *Third World Quarterly*, 28(1), 77–96.

Flett, J. G. (2010), *The Witness of God:The Trinity, Missio Dei, Karl Barth and the Nature of Christian Community*, Grand Rapids, MI: Eerdmanns.

Haynes, J. (2009), 'Conflict, conflict resolution and peace-building: the role of religion in Mozambique, Nigeria and Cambodia', *Commonwealth & Comparative Politics*, 47(1), 52–75.

Marshall, K. (2001), 'Development and religion: a different lens on development debates', *Peabody Journal of Education*, 76(3/4), 339–75.

Oluwafunmilayo, J.P.-M. (2006), 'Faith, gender and development agendas in Nigeria: conflicts, challenges, and opportunities', *Gender & Development*, 14(3), 409–21.

Sanneh, L. (1989), *Translating the Message: The Missionary Impact on Culture*, New York: Orbis Books.

—. (2008), *Disciples of All Nations: Pillars of World Christianity*, New York: Oxford University Press.

Uniting Church in Australia (1977), *Basis of Union*. Uniting Church in Australia.

—. (2009), 'Doc.bytes: discussion starters offered by the national working group on doctrine', *Worksheet 7: Evangelism*. Uniting Church in Australia.

Uniting Church In Australia National Assembly (2009), *An Economy of Life: Re-Imagining Human Progress for a Flourishing World*, Uniting Church in Australia.

UnitingWorld (2009), *Trade Justice*, Sydney: UnitingWorld.

Walker, C. (2010), *Towards a Theology Relating to Mission*, Assembly of the Uniting Church in Australia.

Wolterstorff, N. (2008), *Justice: Rights and Wrongs*, Princeton: Princeton University Press.

# 11

# Mission and the Wane of the Secular

Gerhard Hoffstaedter and Matthew Clarke

## Introduction

Throughout this book, the intersection of mission and development has been primarily considered from the standpoint of the mission organization or missionary. Given the dominance of the secular over the sectarian within development discourse, this bias was purposely sought but is also entirely appropriate. Certainly, much of recent development theory has been premised on modernization theory to the exclusion of considerations of religion and religious activities. This is unsurprising, given modernization's inherent enlightenment claims for reason and its expected withering away of religion as reason comes to dispel the irrational and superstitious. Yet, religious belief and religious participation are rising. Religious belief remains a common human characteristic with 80 per cent of the world's population professing religious faith, including 2.1 billion Christians, 1.3 billion Muslims, 950 million Hindus, 400 million Buddhists and 13 million Jews. Moreover, the sacred texts of each of the world's major religions exhort believers on how to live a righteous life, including responding to poverty and assisting those with less (Clarke et al., 2011).

As many chapters in this book have argued, religion and more so religiosity and the drive of faith to go out and become engaged in development work broadly defined have not withered at all; if anything, these forces are on the rise. For their part government development organizations, bilateral and multilateral agencies, NGOs and academia have all 'rediscovered' religion and its role in development over the last two decades with a range of interactions, platforms and deliberations to better deal with, understand and engage with religion, faith groups and faith-based organizations, including missionary organizations.

As has become evident throughout this book, a central and historically important aspect of religion's role in development has been the role of mission and missionary organizations. As noted in Chapter 1, Western colonialism and Christian missionary organizations often had similar frameworks of subjugation (Beidelman, 1982) in that both required the 'native' to be subjected. Beidelman argues that Christian missionaries required a wholesale subjugation and reordering of the entire world view, whereas traders and colonial administrators often only changed the aspects of people's lives, such as the administration of public or work life. Religious mission extended into the psychic and ideational realms. The so-called civilizing mission of empire and religious groups was to make 'them' like 'us'. Many imperial administrations curtailed proselytizing for fear of backlashes from local populations leaving the religious mission to pursue evangelizing among the non-believers, that is, those untouched by organized religion—pagans, heathens or animists in often far flung and interior locales.

While there is a clear history of the impact of missions on indigenous culture and tradition, especially in light of renewed pushes of Pentecostalism and the deculturation of religion at present (Roy, 2010), it is important to note that it was and is not always a one-way street. Local customs, ideas and cosmological views also impact faith and religious practice. There are notable examples of missionaries looking intently at local cultures and beliefs in order to find points of commonality rather than difference. Missionaries such as Ricci in China and Nobilli in India during the early seventeenth century are examples of this counter-colonial relationship (Luzbetak, 1988).

The missionary as cultural changer is a common trope, which requires discussion. Some missionaries were prototypical anthropologists who embedded themselves in 'the other' and studied the customs, language, rites and more in order to better understand the people they had come to work with. These reports, papers and books formed the basis of much 'armchair anthropology' in the eighteenth and nineteenth centuries. Missionaries, however, were interested in who the people they lived with were with a motive of changing their customs, rites, language and so on. Yet, this motive was neither always effected, nor acted upon.

Indeed, it can be argued that this history has been forgotten with 'development' forgoing this history in favour of a much briefer history that dates only back to post-World War Two with the Marshall Plan and Truman's Inauguration Speech. As a result of this historical rebirth, religion and mission are downplayed by not just secular aid agencies but also many religious organizations themselves who present 'development' as their core (and often sole) business. As the contemporary case studies presented in this book show, many religious development organizations struggle in reconciling God's work with good works, but there is increasing maturity to claim that both complement each other. To draw a line between the two is not only difficult, but arguably impossible.

## Overcoming Secular Suspicion of Mission and Religion

It is precisely this 'complementarity' in which most misunderstanding and mistrust between secular development and religious and missionary organizations lie. A secular world view still predominates the international aid and development community (Wallis, 2005). There also exists in the wider aid community what Carter has termed, in the context of American social policy, a 'culture of disbelief' (Carter, 1993). This means religion has been trivialized and thus ignored, or worse, taken over by the political Right—a matter that Wallis seeks remedy for. He argues that 'Only a new moral, spiritual, and even religious sensibility, in relation to the problems of global poverty will enable us to reach that critical tipping point', at which point a minority opinion will become mainstream and poverty will be addressed adequately (Wallis, 2005, p. 271). While these debates are US-focused, they remain forceful as reminders that the debate must now include religious sentiment and religious groups in order to move forwards. Faith is a force that people like Wallis want to utilize for the broader development agenda in a domestic arena. This has many precursors, as faith has been a potent force in rallying support for the Jubilee 2000 coalition, itself based on Biblical inspiration. The Micah challenge and Make Poverty History are further examples of the mobilizing power at the command of religious organizations.

Clarke (2007) argues that religious organizations involved in development work have become 'agents of transformation, by shedding their traditional focus on charity and by galvanising their moral authority to demand better governance' (Clarke, 2007, p. 90). This view is supported by Tripp's (1999) argument that faith values enhance their capacity to deal with the spiritual and emotional issues that surround development. For example, the large international aid agency World Vision developed its gender policy framework by using examples from the Bible to support a gender equality stance. This faith framework provides a stronger emotional support mechanism for women suffering fistula in Africa, for example, that might have otherwise not been possible from technical assistance alone.

It is important though to acknowledge real limitations to such moral drivers in aid. In particular, Flanigan (2010) highlights the disadvantages these religious aid agencies face in providing aid in situations of religious conflict, even if they have made every effort to demonstrate that their development work is independent of or apart from their religious identity. Flanigan argues that these organizations are less likely to provide aid to individuals of other religions and there is a significant risk of evangelical coercion where there are uneven power dynamics in communities. As globalization increases, religion plays a stronger role in mobilizing transnational networks. De Cordier (2009) argues that, for example, the concept of the Muslim *Ummah* was hugely important for mobilizing transnational donations to UK Muslim aid agencies during the Bosnian and Palestinian conflicts. McGregor builds on this argument by contending that secular transnational networks need to 'acknowledge, incorporate, and involve religious spaces and institutions rather than continue to promote a culture of secularism' (McGregor, 2010, p. 730). This relationship is increasingly two-way. Religious organizations working in this sector have harnessed international rights-based frameworks such as the Millennium Development Goals in recent times as a basis for action. World Vision's 2006 research into the aid gaps in South-East Asia, for example, demonstrated their commitment to working within this particular framework (World Vision Australia, 2006, p. 2).

These moves by World Vision International (as opposed to World Vision Australia) to use human rights language in combination with what Bornstein calls 'lifestyle evangelism'—a missionizing through praxis approach—have also been subject to criticism (Bornstein, 2005). Mission is often equated with conversion, but that underplays the complex intentions that are embodied in the missionary work of religious organizations and individuals who are called to mission. Bradbury in this book demonstrates that at least in the Micah network there is agreement that proselytizing vulnerable and dependent communities is wrong and not to be their modus operandi. However, faith-based organizations more than other development agencies are susceptible to any suggestions of evangelism or misconduct in a given situation. Thus, they must be more vigilant in their actions and how those actions may be perceived by others.

In simple terms, mission can be seen to be the drive to do something that will change the world, if not of others', then one's own. This change is to affect behaviour, culture, habitus and indeed the entire cosmology of others. Yet, this definition is akin to that of development aid in general. After all, secular aid agencies such as *Médecins Sans Frontières* display 'religoid' trappings in their praxis, organization and foundation history (Benthall, 2008). Thus, the theology of development is not much different from the religiously motivated one. Development is the belief in a model of and for change with predictable and knowable outcomes. Mission, similarly, is the belief in a grand plan that conveys a knowable truth and certainty. Both systems of belief depend on their 'missionaries' to change the world and make it into something more akin to their own (Hoffstaedter and Roche, forthcoming). Mission is a theological practice, that is, mission is integral to the theological precepts of many religions. Thus, a division between the two cannot be made in practice, even if in theory the two can be cordoned off in separate spheres for a specific project proposal or even the duration of a project. Such a division is always spurious as it depends upon an imagined division where in practice only a whole entity exists. For how can one separate one's beliefs and world view from one's actions? One can try to rationalize that one's actions are not directed or influenced by one's world view at all times and rely on one's agency and will to supersede any such mediating influences.

The role of religion in development and in particular the role of missionary activities must be represented in a full and holistic picture of mission with all its aspects of providing vital health, educational, political and social services as well as the detrimental effects of their activities on people and their belief and social systems. As Watson argues in his chapter, this must be done on a case-by-case basis, for either generalization does neither justice.

## Reconciliation and Authentic Engagement

We must research the holistic approach of the Christian mission beyond the secular-religious divide that seeks to manifest Jesus and God as standing side by side with the poor, the downtrodden and the oppressed. This sets up and maintains the duality between the lived reality of most poor, downtrodden and oppressed and the utopian God's kingdom. Mission is one of many bridges to integrate the two. How far this is possible in the face of today's food, human and environmental crises is to be seen.

The mission–development split is a theoretical one, much like the religion–development one, yet often not in practice. For most people working in development, their faith and belief are inherently embedded in why and how they practice development. The fact that the Canadian International Development Agency (CIDA) has engaged (Christian) NGOs and drafted a document that acknowledges spirituality as a key driver in development is crucial (CIDA, 1995). Similarly, the Australian Agency for International Development (AusAID) funds a *Church Partnerships Program* that explicitly seeks to help 'PNG churches promote good governance by strengthening their role in policy discussions, service delivery and peace and reconciliation activities' (AusAID, 2007). In this regard, AusAID is seeking religious organizations to influence development outcomes. While both donors continue to prohibit funding for building church infrastructure and proselytizing, their recognition of the 'spiritual' dimension is novel and important for the work of faith-based development organizations.

The question of how development can further 'take advantage' of religious values held by individuals and communities is therefore important. As Goulet (1980) noted 30 years ago, religious beliefs

> 'harbour within them a latent dynamism which, when properly respected, can serve as the springboard for modes of development which are more humane than those drawn from outside paradigms. When development builds from indigenous values it extracts lower social costs and imposes

> less human suffering and cultural destruction then when it copies outside models. This is so because indigenously-rooted values are the matrix whence people derive meaning in their lives, a sense of identity and cultural integrity, and the experience of continuity with their environment and their past even in the midst of change' (Goulet, 1980, p. 485).

It is important though that engagement with religion is authentic and not simply seen as an opportunity to 'clothe' mainstream interventions in religious garb (Clarke et al., 2011).

The Archbishop of Canterbury, Rowan Williams, calls for a better understanding of religion by secular NGOs and argues that it 'requires a deepening fluency in the language of religious discourse, to understand the intention and nuance behind religiously inspired definitions of mission and human development' (Williams, 2009). A religious literacy is required in which both secular NGOs and religious organizations can understand the world view of the communities in which they are working. Such an improved literacy does not equate to acceptance that religion is the holy grail that will deliver better development outcomes for those who are most marginalized and at risk in our societies. Nor does religious literacy require an acceptance of religious 'truths'. Rather, it is possible to undertake a 'value-free exploration of religious meaning and institutions' (Flood, 1999, p. 19). This requires an agnostic approach to the 'truth of religious beliefs' (Tomalin, 2007, p. 4) that 'take(s) all expressions of religion at face value and attempt(s) to capture subjects' accounts of their views and experiences as faithfully as possible' (Rakodi, 2007, p. 30). In this manner, a case exists for a realistic appreciation of the centrality religion has in certain communities and for some individuals. Failure to be cognizant of this constrains efforts to properly engage with communities. Religion has an inherent dynamism that informs both people's perception around the concept of development and also their response to circumstances of poverty or deprivation. In this regard, religion is both a lens by which to understand the world and a catalyst that changes the world. To state it again, this literacy is not interested in claims of 'authenticity' of religious belief or tenets of faith in the religious sense, but rather, it is interested in developing an authentic understanding of religion by development scholars, practitioners and policy-makers that may aid those actors in achieving more effective development outcomes.

# Conclusion

Faith-based organizations and the mission ingrained in their praxis have both positive and negative effects, as some of the histories of missions and their impact have shown in this book. More research is clearly required to further probe and investigate many of the issues raised in this volume. This book has predominantly focused on established Churches and their missionary activities in development contexts. New religious movements (NRM) are on the rise and have focused their activities in areas that are also major development arenas: South America, Africa and Central and Southeast Asia. There, these NRMs are making inroads in converting Catholics, Muslims and members of local traditions.

What remains to be explored is the non-Christian missionary encounter. This raises two issues: first, is the Christian mission a phenomenon separate from other missionary movements? Secondly, do non-Christian missionary encounters engender different responses from the development community?

Another issue is whether the missionary encounter engenders a space outside of the dominant paradigms of the development encounter. The predominantly instrumental and managerial encounters have established paradigms for development (Fforde, 2009). Can or does missionary encounter attempt to change this system or is it itself a driver of the neo-liberal instrumentalization? (Pelkmans, 2009).

As pointed out in a preceding chapter, mission goes beyond both the liberal reduction to social action and the evangelical response of focusing on making converts (Grant and Hughes, 2009). As the wane of the secular becomes the dominant trope, the state, researchers and the development community in general must re-engage the religious. If this occurs, the perceived chasm between God's work and good works will greatly diminish and more accurately reflect the reality experienced by many fulfilling their vocation.

# References

AusAID (2007), *Partnerships in Aid Delivery*, retrieved 11 May 2011, <www.ausaid.gov.au/country/png/partnerships.cfm>.

Beidelman, T. O. (1982), *Colonial Evangelism: A Socio-Historical Study of an East African Mission at the Grassroots*, Bloomington: Indiana University Press.

Benthall, J. (2008), *Returning to Religion: Why a Secular Age is Haunted by Faith*, London: I. B. Tauris.

Bornstein, E. (2005), *The Spirit of Development : Protestant NGOs, Morality and Economics in Zimbabwe*, Stanford: Stanford University Press.

Carter, S. L. (1993), *The Culture of Disbelief: How American Law and Politics Trivialize Religious Devotion*, New York, NY: BasicBooks.

CIDA (1995), *Christian NGOs and CIDA: Guiding Principles, Understandings and Affirmations*, retrieved 20 March 2011, <www.ccrda.org/.../CIDA-NGO_Paper_-_Guiding_Principles,_Understandings_&_Affirmations.doc>.

Clarke, G. (2007), 'Agents of transformation? donors, faith-based organisations and international development', *Third World Quarterly*, 28(1), 77–96.

Clarke, M., Charnley, S. and Lumbers, J. (2011), 'Churches, mosques, and condoms: understanding successful HIV and AIDS interventions by faith-based organisations', *Development in Practice*, 21(1), 3–17.

De Cordier, B. (2009), 'Faith-based aid, globalisation and the humanitarian frontline: an analysis of Western-based Muslim aid organisations', *Disasters,* 33(4), 608–28.

Fforde, A. (2009), *Coping with Facts: A Skeptic's Guide to the Problem of Development,* Bloomfield: Kumarian Press.

Flanigan, S. (2010), *For the Love of God: NGOs and Religious Identity in a Violent World,* Sterling: Kumarian Press.

Flood, G. (1999), *Beyond Phenomenology: Rethinking the Study of Religion,* London: Cassell.

Goulet, D. (1980), 'Development experts: the one-eyed giants', *World Development,* 8(7–8), 481–9.

Grant, J. A. and Hughes, D. A. (eds) (2009), *Transforming the World: The Gospel and Social Responsibility,* Nottingham: Apollos.

Hoffstaedter, G. and Roche, C. (forthcoming) 'All the world's a stage': structure, agency and accountability in international aid', *Journal of the Asia Pacific Economy.*

Luzbetak, L. (1988), *The Church and Cultures,* New York: Orbis Books.

McGregor, A. (2010), 'Geographies of religion and development: rebuilding sacred spaces in Aceh, Indonesia, after the tsunami', *Environment and Planning A.* 42, 729–46.

Pelkmans, M. (2009), 'The "Transparency" of Christian Proselytizing in Kyrgyzstan', *Anthropological Quarterly*, 82(2), 423–45.

Rakodi, C. (2007), 'Understanding the role of religions in development', *Religions and Development Research Program, Working Paper 9*, Birmingham: University of Birmingham.

Roy, O. (2010), *Holy Ignorance: When Religion and Culture Part Ways,* New York: Columbia University Press.

Tomalin, E. (2007), 'Religious studies and development: a literature review', *Religions and Development Research Program, Working Paper 6*, Birmingham: University of Birmingham.

Tripp, L. (1999), 'Gender and development from a Christian perspective: experience from World Vision', *Gender and Development,* 7(1), 62–86.

Wallis, J. (2005), *God's Politics: Why the Right Gets It Wrong and the Left Doesn't Get It,* San Francisco: HarperSanFrancisco.

Williams, R. (2009), *New Perspectives on Faith and Development*, retrieved 20 November 2010, <www.archbishopofcanterbury.org/2606>.

World Vision Australia (2006), *How Are the Neighbours? The Millennium Development Goals & Our Region.* Melbourne: World Vision Australia.

# INDEX